Getting into

Oxford &
Cambridge

2018 Entry

Lucy Bates

20th edition

Getting into guides

Getting into Art & Design Courses, 10th edition
Getting into Business & Economics Courses, 12th edition
Getting into Dental School, 10th edition
Getting into Engineering Courses, 4th edition
Getting into Law, 11th edition
Getting into Medical School: 2018 Entry, 22nd edition
Getting into Pharmacy and Pharmacology Courses, 1st edition
Getting into Physiotherapy Courses, 8th edition
Getting into Psychology Courses, 11th edition
Getting into Veterinary School, 11th edition
How to Complete Your UCAS Application: 2018 Entry, 29th edition

Getting into Oxford & Cambridge: 2018 Entry

This 20th edition published in 2017 by Trotman Education, an imprint of Crimson Publishing Ltd, 19–21c Charles Street, Bath BA1 1HX

© Crimson Publishing Ltd 2017

Author: Lucy Bates

17th–18th edns: Seán P. Buckley
15th–16th edns: Jenny Blaiklock
13th–14th edns: Katy Blatt
7th–10th & 12th edns: Sarah Alakija
11th edn: Natalie Lancer

British Library Cataloguing in Publication Data
A catalogue record for this book is available from the British Library

ISBN: 978 1 911067 44 3

Typeset by IDSUK (Dataconnection) Ltd
Printed and bound in Malta by Gutenberg Press Ltd

Contents

Contents

About the author

Lucy Bates secured an offer from Queens' College Cambridge before reading Theology at King's College London. After some months as an independent scholar at the University of California, she completed her MPhil in Early Modern History at Clare College, Cambridge. Subsequently, she was awarded her PhD from Durham University as a member of St Chad's College. She has been helping students with university applications for over ten years and is currently Assistant Principal at MPW Cambridge.

Lucy is married with a son, James, and a Labrador called Penny. She spends much of her free time throwing tennis balls for them both.

Acknowledgements

I am very grateful to the generous Oxbridge students who donated their personal statements and case studies. Thanks are also due to my colleagues who provided helpful suggestions and my students who keep me inspired. I am also indebted to my husband for all his support during the production of this book.

I dedicate this book to all those who inspire my own love of learning and curiosity, especially my grandmother whose work at the Cambridge University Library was a constant source of fascination.

Foreword

I was the first member of my family to attend university. Neither of my parents completed A levels and while my grandmother had worked as a primary school teacher and then in the manuscripts department of the Cambridge University Library she did not have the opportunity to apply. Nonetheless, from a very young age books and learning were central to my life and happiness. I had no doubt that I would go to university, though it was not until much later that I decided to spend quite so long there.

A school project at the age of eight first introduced me to Cambridge and its collegiate system. Initially awestruck, as the years went by and I progressed to senior school in Cambridge I decided that Oxford must be the better choice. A fresh start in a new city. It was time to move away from home. Naively, I came to this conclusion without even visiting Oxford. When finally persuaded to do so by my personal tutor, 'just in case it's not for you', I had a huge shock. I really didn't like it. In fact, I returned to my tutor proclaiming that 'I hated Oxford', which was rather unfair since I had only been there for a day! I still cannot answer the question as to why I had such a strong reaction aged 17. Indeed I returned to Oxford several times whilst conducting PhD research and thoroughly enjoyed my time in the Bodleian and several college archives. Looking back, I suspect the larger size of the city combined with a feeling of loneliness (this was my first university visit completely unaccompanied) frightened me, but it is also true that I prefer the 'vibe' of Cambridge to Oxford. Both are fantastic universities, but something about Cambridge makes me feel more confident and at home. The 'vibe' is something I always impress upon my students that they must investigate for any university they are seriously considering applying to. An undergraduate degree is a huge commitment and it is incredibly important that you are happy in your environment. This is not something you can glean from websites or online tours. Just as you would not buy a house without viewing it first, it is imperative that you visit your top few choices of university. Ideally this should be on a rainy and cold winter's afternoon because if you like it then, you will like it all year round. Thanks to a fantastic personal tutor, I had now switched from Cambridge to Oxford and back again. Now the application process began.

As highlighted above, I was lucky to attend a school that had a very supportive pastoral system. My personal tutor and several of my teachers helped me to prepare my UCAS application. In those days this was completed by hand and I remember doing several versions of the final copy because I was so nervous I made spelling mistakes or smudges –

something students today are spared. However, the best preparation my school gave me was a mock interview. To date, this is hands-down the worst interview I have ever had in my life. This remains a huge source of comfort to me – no job interview or appraisal will ever be as bad. Into that interview went a very confident and cocky girl convinced of her own intellect and ability. My aim had been to secure high praise from the two mock interviewers (two of my teachers that I liked and admired) and further assurance that I would secure an offer. After ten minutes, my sole aim was to get out of the room without crying and humiliating myself even further. I made countless mistakes. Panicked, I opened my mouth without thinking. Not only did I try to support arguments and views that I did not hold with any conviction, but I doggedly kept sticking to these views, digging bigger and bigger holes, as the flaws were pointed out to me. I came across as arrogant and stupid (and I knew it). I was trying to be someone else, someone I thought Cambridge would want, and it showed. I learnt a huge amount from that experience, much of which I share in the pages that follow. I am convinced that had it not been for that mock interview not only would I not have secured an offer from Cambridge but I probably would have failed to secure many jobs too.

My actual interviews at Cambridge were tough but a considerable improvement. I remember leaving the last one thinking that I was happy with my performance overall and if I didn't get an offer that was ok. I couldn't have done any more. Certainly, I was relieved that the application process was over. The wait for an answer was agonising but here again I learnt a valuable lesson: don't listen to gossip. The rumour going around my school at the time was that a fat letter from Cambridge indicated an offer, while a thin one was a rejection. I came home one evening to a thin letter. Tears sprung up in my eyes as I thought about all the effort that had gone into the application. I told my father that I hadn't got an offer. He pointed out that I hadn't actually opened the letter. I told him it didn't matter; it was a thin letter and I knew that was a rejection. He said something about a cup of tea. Then I gathered myself and thought that there might be some useful feedback for other university interviews inside so I opened the letter. It was very short, but it was definitely an offer.

Between receiving my offer at Christmas and completing my exams in the summer I came to a significant realisation. Cambridge as an undergraduate was not for me. I achieved my very best when I was competing for top of the class but I needed the security of knowing that with an average amount of effort I would still be near the top. The praise of my teachers mattered hugely to me, I wanted an environment where they saw me as 'special'. At Cambridge I knew that I would not be at the top. I would, at best, be average. This would have made me miserable aged 18. I went to KCL and finished as a prize-winner with the highest marks in the year as well as my first-class degree. I was nurtured by one lecturer in particular, David Crankshaw, who surprised me by suggesting graduate work in my second year. Having struggled with the transition to university in the first term despite my strong A level results, I was amazed that the idea had a huge amount of appeal. I decided to take a year away from studying after my undergraduate degree (partly to avoid graduate university applications during my finals) and travelled to California but instead of going to the beach I kept being drawn to the library. I charmed a professor there into teaching me Medieval Latin Palaeography (the study of handwriting) and delved into digital copies of Early Modern manuscripts. With the help of David Crankshaw I made an application for the MPhil in Early Modern History at Cambridge and secured a place at Clare College. This time I was ready. I had a very encouraging and supportive supervisor, Elizabeth Evenden, and at 22 I was less concerned about being top and more interested in simply learning as much as I could. I loved my time at Cambridge and the research skills I honed during the MPhil made me determined to continue and complete a PhD.

My journey to, and through, Cambridge is not typical but it serves to show that there is a lot to be gained simply from applying to Oxbridge. Had I not received the offer as an undergraduate, I still would have learnt some valuable lessons. Had I not realised that Cambridge was not the right place for me aged 18 I would have been miserable at university and definitely would not have done graduate work. I may even have dropped out of university altogether. Equally, without the skills and support I gained from my time at Cambridge, I would not have succeeded in completing my PhD. I am a firm believer in only applying to Oxbridge because you want to – not because your parents or teachers want you to. Equally, you should only apply if you know you could handle rejection as that is the most likely outcome. Ultimately, ask yourself what you will regret more in five years' time: having applied and been rejected or not having applied and wondering if you could have got in?

There is no such thing as a typical Oxbridge student. There are students from every single type of background you can think of. It is true that there are some students there who come from very wealthy backgrounds and attended very famous public schools. However, you will also find some students from very poor backgrounds who went to state schools in special measures. There are international students from all over the world. There are very confident students and there are also students who spend several weeks wondering if they got in by mistake (they didn't). What these students all do have in common is a passion for their subject and learning in general. All are curious people who always want to know more and know why. They love to find the limits of their knowledge and try to push them further. If you have a curious nature and a love of learning you will make friends at Oxbridge.

I will always look back at my time at Cambridge with fondness. I made some fantastic friends and was privileged to experience many things that only a few people ever have the opportunity to do. Those of you who are successful in your applications to Oxford and Cambridge – and I hope many of you reading this are – will have the thrill of walking in the footstep of giants as you pass through colleges, faculties and libraries. Oxford and Cambridge are both very special places to study.

The extra-curricular opportunities at Oxford and Cambridge are enormous. The trouble is not finding societies that you are interested in but in ensuring that you leave enough time for your studies. I thoroughly enjoyed the historical societies, seminars and workshops as well as Clare's wine society. Formal hall is a fantastic way to unwind with your friends and a very cost-effective way of enjoying a great meal and getting dressed-up. Themed formals are a great source of amusement – it is perfectly normal to walk past several students dressed as zombies, characters from Harry Potter or Father Christmas and his elves on their way to formal. Taking advantage of the array of exhibitions and one-off talks can be a very welcome distraction, and I found it often had the effect of helping me to see a problem in my own work, in a new way, by adapting methodologies from other disciplines.

The end of the academic year is marked by May Balls, which despite their name take place in June. These are a wonderful mix of tradition, with black tie, ball gowns and lots of dancing, combined with activities such as fairground rides and games. There are fireworks towards the end of the evening and the survivors' photograph. Why is it an achievement to have survived? Well the evening starts around 7 or 8pm and continues until 6am. Partying for that long requires the kind of concentration and determination Oxbridge graduates develop during their degrees.

Lucy Bates

Introduction

The title of this book says it all. Its purpose is to tell you everything you need to know to help you get into Oxford or Cambridge. It will also try to give you a flavour of what it's like to study there. My hope is that this book will help to demystify the whole application process and encourage you to apply if you feel you've got what it takes to get in.

You may already know quite a lot about the Oxbridge system and simply need a checklist of things you should do to ensure your best entry. This book certainly aims to be as comprehensive as possible and will cover all stages of the admissions procedure in detail.

Or, you may know nothing at all about how to get in. Many potential applicants can be put off applying on the basis that Oxford or Cambridge somehow isn't right for them and that the odds of getting in are weighted towards students who have knowledge of a mythical 'old boys' network'. You would be wrong if you believe this. It is simply not true that Oxbridge operates in favour of those students who can somehow play the system. I have spoken to many admissions tutors in researching this book, and I can guarantee that your application will be judged, more than ever before, on your potential to succeed and your willingness to work hard. The school you went to, how much money you have and how many of your ancestors went to Oxford or Cambridge count for nothing; getting in is about your academic potential alone.

You also shouldn't be dissuaded because you're worried that you're not a geeky Oxbridge type or that you're somehow not posh enough to hold your own there. Perhaps with all the publicity about the government wanting to encourage applications from state school pupils, you're worried that your application will be prejudiced because you go to an independent school. You shouldn't be concerned about this either. Both universities are keen to encourage applications from academically talented students whatever their background. If you're passionate about your subject and have the ability to excel at university, you're almost certainly a strong candidate for admission.

The aim of this book is to take you through the application process step by step: from making sure you're studying the right A levels, or equivalent qualifications, in the first instance to giving you tips to help you sail through your interview.

Chapter 1, What studying at Oxbridge is really like, explores why Oxford and Cambridge are so special and how they differ from other universities, giving the reader some idea of what it's like to study there. It also aims to demystify the selection process by outlining Oxbridge's equal opportunities policy. It explains the policy for disabled students; students with children; students from ethnic minorities; lesbian, gay and bisexual students; and educationally disadvantaged students or students who have had a disrupted education.

Chapter 2, Money matters, explains the financial aspects of studying at Oxbridge. Many students are put off by the idea that studying at Oxbridge is more expensive than at other universities. This chapter explains that this is not the case, and gives a breakdown of costs incurred over a year. The chapter also introduces the bursary schemes and music scholarships at the universities, and includes a case study of the spending habits of a new student at Cambridge.

Chapter 3, Entry requirements, discusses things you should consider well before the UCAS application. The chapter includes a section on choosing your A level subjects and the concept of 'facilitating' A levels. It also discusses the importance of high grades and the alternatives to UK A levels that are accepted by Oxford and Cambridge (including the Baccalaureate and Scottish Highers).

Chapter 4, Early stages of preparation, discusses the importance of choosing the right subject for you. Your choice of subject is more important than any other decision you will have to make during this process; more important than your choice of university and college. This chapter looks at the workload placed on students and the need to be prepared for this by reading widely and in depth. Also included in this section is a reading list that will give you a few ideas.

Chapter 5, Choosing your university and college, considers the best way to choose a university and college. It mentions the differences between Oxford and Cambridge, highlighting the importance of choosing the university that offers the subject that most suits you. Although this chapter refers to the Norrington and Tompkins tables as points of reference (see pages 212 and 245), it advises against a tactical approach to college choice. Instead, it offers alternative methods for picking your future home. This chapter also explains the option of the 'open application'.

Chapter 6, Experience to support your UCAS application, discusses the importance of 'super-curricular' experience in the application process. Super-curricular experience comprises the types of activities students have engaged in outside of their school curriculum that are directly relevant to their chosen course and will strengthen their personal statements. The option of a 'gap year' is considered, and how this 'time out' can be advantageous in some circumstances but disadvantageous in others. It looks at the importance of work experience, particularly if you wish to study a vocational subject at university, and how essential it is to be aware of events in your area, current affairs and news stories that are relevant to your chosen subject.

Chapter 7, The UCAS application and the personal statement, gives advice on how to make your UCAS application shine, as well as example personal statements with analysis. After you have completed your personal statement, Cambridge (but not Oxford) automatically sends a Supplementary Application Questionnaire (SAQ), and this chapter also gives advice on how to fill in this form. Many subjects require you to send in examples of written work and this section explains why written work is required, for which subjects essay submissions are usual and how best to satisfy the universities' requirements.

Chapter 8, Succeeding in written tests, discusses the exams that are taken in addition to A levels for some subjects. These are taken either in advance of interviews or during the interview week in order to help interviewers decide on the best applicants. This chapter explains why these tests are necessary; gives lists of the subjects requiring additional testing at Oxford and details of the Cambridge admissions tests that were introduced in September 2016. It also provides example questions, dates for testing and useful website links; and provides reading lists so that you can find out more for yourself.

Chapter 9, Surviving the interview, explains the interview process. General information about interview practice is given, as well as a breakdown of what interviewers are looking for. In addition, there is information about different interview styles and how to deal with them; a comprehensive list of interview questions for a range of subjects; and interview stories from previous applicants. Finally, there is a word of advice about presentation skills and an explanation of the pooling system.

Chapter 10, Non-standard applications, discusses the application procedure for mature students and international students and gives information on specific issues relating to these categories.

Chapter 11, Getting the letter, looks at the final stages of the process: receiving an offer or coping with rejection; stress; and how you can make this experience a success, whether or not you obtain a place at Oxbridge.

In the **appendices** you will find a useful timeline of the application process and a **glossary** of important terms.

College profiles provides a profile on each college at Oxford and Cambridge, with information on a range of areas, including courses offered, accommodation and catering provision, facilities, financial aid and interesting facts specific to each college. Here you will also find the Norrington and Tompkins tables, and maps of both Oxford and Cambridge with the locations of the colleges marked.

Throughout the book, the examples that quote university entrance requirements often use A level and AS grades both for the reformed and legacy specifications.

A levels in England are in a transition period, with new specifications being phased in for first teaching between September 2015 and September 2017 to replace the 'legacy' modular specifications. 'legacy' specifications refer to old-style A level qualifications composed of AS and A2 units; AS and A2 scores had equal weighting towards the overall A level mark. Under the reforms, the new, 'reformed' A levels are linear rather than modular, and the AS and A level have been decoupled, which means that the new AS is now a separate qualification and no longer counts towards the A level. Not every school is offering the decoupled AS under the new system.

Some subjects moved to the reformed specifications in September 2015, for the first A level examinations in June 2017, while a second group of subjects was introduced for first teaching in September 2016 and will have their first examinations in June 2018. Some subjects (including mathematics) are still following the 'legacy' (modular) specification, with the reformed A level coming into effect for first teaching in September 2017. For more information on what will be available for examination in which year of the course up until summer 2019, visit www.gov.uk/government/publications/get-the-facts-gcse-and-a-level-reform.

Note that the A level reforms are different in each country of the UK: www.ucas.com/sites/default/files/ucas-guide-to-qualification-reform.pdf. The changes discussed above apply to A levels for students sitting the qualifications through the English examination boards, but there are also separate educational reforms taking place in Wales and Northern Ireland (as listed on the UCAS website).

The advice throughout is applicable to students studying Scottish Highers, the International Baccalaureate, Pre-University (Pre-U) and other qualifications. The UCAS website (www.ucas.com) lists entrance requirements for all of the major examination systems in its 'Course Search' section. If you are unsure about what you need to achieve, individual universities will be happy to give you advice; contact details are given on all of their websites.

1 | What studying at Oxford and Cambridge is really like

If you are considering an application to Oxford or Cambridge, you are probably keen to understand what makes these two universities such special places to study and why places are so fiercely fought over. This chapter will explain what sets Oxford and Cambridge apart from other universities and examines the advantages and disadvantages of studying there.

Previous editions of this guide have talked about eminent and famous Oxford and Cambridge alumni, such as British prime ministers, international leaders, Nobel prize winners and so on. Clearly, there are excellent, aspirational places of study, known the world over. However, so much else can and does go on at these universities. For the sports fans reading this book, I shall give one example of an Oxford student who managed to combine his academic pursuits with his sporting prowess, with not a little success. Cuthbert Ottaway was a student at Brasenose College, Oxford, reading Classics when he became the first captain of England in the first-ever official international soccer fixture, against Scotland in 1872. Incidentally, he also captained the Oxford University Cricket Club against Cambridge while he was a student. This serves as one example to show that the determined, motivated and well-rounded undergraduates that universities such as Oxford and Cambridge value can balance their studies with other activities.

What is important is that Oxford and Cambridge are at the forefront of academic excellence. It is also important to note that both Oxford and Cambridge produce rates of graduate employment that are among the highest in the UK.

Why study at Oxford or Cambridge?

Oxford and Cambridge are always top of the university league tables

In 2016 the *Guardian* ran a survey that ranked UK universities according to teaching excellence (see www.theguardian.com/education/

ng-interactive/2016/may/23/university-league-tables-2017). Cambridge topped the league table, with Oxford holding on to second place. The tables rank universities according to the following measures:

- how satisfied their final-year students are
- how much they spend per student
- the student–staff ratio
- the career prospects of their graduates
- a value-added score and what grades pupils have to achieve to stand a chance of being offered a place.

The tutorial system

Unlike at most universities, teaching at Oxford and Cambridge is built around the tutorial system. Tutorials (or supervisions as they are called at Cambridge) involve a meeting with your tutor, alone or with one or two other students, and generally last about an hour. Often, one of you will read your essay or written work aloud and this will act as a catalyst for discussion of the work that has been done independently during the week.

What makes an Oxbridge education so special is that you will have personal access to some of the world's experts in your chosen subject. Your tutor may be the person who actually 'wrote the book' on the subject you're studying, so being able to discuss topics with them in depth every week is an invaluable experience.

Case study: James, Cambridge

For me, one of most useful aspects of studying at Cambridge is the supervision system. In some ways, supervisions are a bit like interviews. If part of you actually enjoyed the interview, then Cambridge is for you. Supervisions are designed to see what you know already, test how much depth you have already acquired and then push you a bit further. Most supervisions are in a very small group: two or three students. This can be helpful if the supervisor asks a particularly difficult question, but I found in my first term it also made me more self-conscious about 'having a go' than if I had been on my own. Now I always try to tackle these questions, partly to push myself, but also, to be honest, because the 'tumbleweed' moments are really awkward.

Supervisions are where you get really detailed feedback on your essays, both written and verbal. Occasionally, you are asked to read sections aloud, which can be pretty embarrassing. However, this made me read my essays out loud to myself before I submit them, which is a good way to spot inconsistencies or an awkward point in your essay's structure. I must admit a slight fear of the supervision also pushes you to strive for the best possible essay; no one wants to have the weakest essay of the group. When I speak to my friends at other universities about the learning they do outside of lectures I am grateful for the amount of attention paid to my progression. My lectures and independent work give me excellent foundations on each topic, but I learn so much from my supervisions – I'm not sure how other students manage without them.

Case study: Kapish, Oxford

Reading PPE (Philosophy, Politics and Economics) at Oxford was one of the most challenging and rewarding experiences of my life. The degree requires a momentous commitment towards academic study, both in terms of intensity and the quantity of work involved. The degree itself, and Oxford generally, provides you with an inimitable set of skills and an outlook on life that are not only enduring, but also highly sought after. For me, the rewards were a radically sharpened analytical ability, acquiring resourceful working patterns, and new, higher goals.

One of the prime benefits of the degree is acquiring the ability to think critically about any issue, from a complex mathematical problem to a controversial policy issue. No assumption is unquestioned. Indeed, by the end of the degree it becomes second nature to analyse everything from 'the ground up', the Cartesian way. The result of this is that you end up coming up with ideas and solutions that are often highly effective but extremely simple. This skill is honed repetitively during weekly hour-long tutorials with a leading academic in the relevant field of study and another student taking the same paper. The tutorials are the 'engine room' of an Oxford education as it is during tutorials that the students learn how to put forward their own viewpoint, defend their analysis and, indeed, quash their peers' arguments.

The tutorials (and examinations) require the extensive study of several works in a relatively short space of time, from classic and modern texts to the latest journal articles, across all the modules in the degree. Indeed, the term-time work entails writing at least two 2,000-word essays on a weekly basis, which are the focus of the tutorials. This routine forces you to become significantly more productive and efficient with your time, training you to become a skilled hunter of the necessary information and ideas from the dense volumes of text. This capacity to multitask and work industriously is universally applicable and allows you to do more – be it work or extra-curricular activities – in less time.

An important feature of Oxford is that you are surrounded by some of the best minds in the world – be they your tutors or your peers – who constantly inspire you with new ideas, their person-alities and, indeed, their lifestyle choices. People around you often seem unafraid to try new things, to challenge themselves and to pack more extra-curricular activities into an already limited schedule. This not only means that you are pushed by 'soft' peer pressure to take on more challenges, it also means that you dis-cover facets and skills in your personality you thought you never had. For me, this meant participating in debating and student polit-ical organisations, standing for elections and taking up golf. But more pertinently, this constant need to challenge yourself also takes a more profound form when you start setting yourself much higher goals than before.

This triad of heightened analytical ability, focused industry and superior goals forms a formidable combination, for which I have my Oxford education to thank. A perhaps more tangible result of attaining these skills is your increased worth in the labour market after graduation. Suffice it to say that my degree has allowed me to explore various career opportunities that would not have been available without it.

Case study: Catherine, Cambridge

My first visit to my faculty library was like stepping into the best bookshop in the world. I could not believe all the works available to me – those I knew about but more significantly those I did not. Having the world-class Fitzwilliam museum practically next door to the department is a wonderful academic escape after a tough lec-ture. Similarly, Kettles Yard and Hamilton Kerr are both exciting places to visit. As a university student, it is thrilling to go to Kettles Yard and be allowed to borrow a piece of art in the same way you would a library book. The archives available to students are so inspiring. Having such amazing resources and such knowledge-able specialists on your doorstep means that you cannot help but want to learn more. Ultimately, the Cambridge environment with its historic buildings and supportive community of scholars affects you in ways you cannot possibly imagine. I love it!

Case study: Toby, Cambridge

Life at Cambridge is very, very busy. The work isn't huge by itself but it is when you are fitting in hobbies, sports and socialising on top. Natural sciences has perhaps the highest workload of the courses at Cambridge so it doesn't represent Cambridge life in general. Most people have less contact time – particularly those studying arts/humanities. I have two lectures a day Monday to Saturday (I'm pretty sure only computer sciences and natural sciences have Saturday lectures), alternating with two or four practicals a week – practicals can last anywhere from one and a quarter hours to six hours – and four one-hour supervisions weekly which each set three to four hours of homework. So my best day involves lectures from 11am to 1pm, and my worst day combines lectures from 9am to 11am, then a practical from 11am to 5pm, and then some homework after. I have a Sunday supervision so no days are completely free! However, there is still time for extra-curricular activities. Despite doing natural sciences I want to be a musician and so I still have time to practise on average an hour per day, go to the gym and do sport five or six times per week and socialise every day (either chilling at the bar or going out).

The course content is mostly really interesting, but of course there are some bits that are more dull, and having a maths lecture at 9am following a night out can be a bit of a struggle! But it is so cool to be taught by people who really are leading experts, and supervisions allow you to ask loads of random questions and help with understanding (lectures go through material so, so fast – I'm not quite sure how I'm going to be able to learn everything come exam time). Plus most of the discoveries I'm learning about were made at the university!

If you are worrying about Cambridge being full of 'nerds', that isn't true and I've found the vast majority of people to be completely normal and a lot of fun. In addition, people gravitate to those who they have things in common with anyway. However, if you want to spend university doing the odd bit of work but care more about partying, then Cambridge isn't for you; but if you enjoy your subject, then definitely go for it; I couldn't recommend it enough. I really wouldn't have my life any other way!

Please note that while juggling work and other commitments is the case for some students, it is not typical. Indeed, some colleges do not allow students to undertake paid employment.

The colleges

Oxford and Cambridge colleges are an integral part of both universities. They are independent, self-governing communities of academics, students and staff. The relatively small number of students at each college means that you receive plenty of personal academic and pastoral support.

The collegiate system is a key strength of both institutions, giving students and academics the benefits of belonging both to a large, internationally renowned institution and to a smaller, interdisciplinary, academic college community. Colleges and halls enable leading academics and students across subjects and year groups, and from different cultures and countries, to come together and share ideas. Membership of an Oxbridge college, as well as a department or faculty, can add a whole new dimension to your university experience.

Your college can provide you with the perfect forum to discuss your work in seminars, over meals in the dining hall or in your room late into the evening. It will help you to make friends quickly, and give you the opportunity to try a wide range of social and sporting activities.

All colleges invest heavily in facilities for library and IT provision, accommodation and pastoral care, and offer sports and social events. Undergraduate students benefit from the junior common room or junior combination room (JCR) in their college – both a physical space and an organisation, it provides social events, advice and a link to the undergraduate community.

The standard of accommodation and food offered by some colleges is generally superior to that offered by most UK universities. Certain colleges have Michelin-starred chefs overseeing their kitchens, and wine cellars that equal those of some of the best clubs in the world. Unlike most universities, many colleges can accommodate you for the whole of your time at university, saving you the trouble and expense of finding your own accommodation.

The best libraries and research facilities

Oxford and Cambridge are consistently placed among the highest-ranked universities for their research performance and have been shown to outperform UK competitors in the scale and quality of their research across a wide range of subject areas.

The two universities also far outstrip other universities in terms of income from endowments and other private sources because of their age and their ability to attract funds from alumni and other donors.

Oxbridge students have access to the Bodleian (Oxford) and the Cambridge University Library copyright libraries, which hold a copy of every book, pamphlet, journal and magazine ever published in the UK. They are also non-lending, so students can always access the texts they need quickly, no matter how obscure. There are also hundreds of other libraries in Oxford and Cambridge, including at least one for each faculty and college.

The people you'll meet

Contrary to popular belief, people who study at Oxford and Cambridge come from very diverse backgrounds and have many different interests and personalities. There really is no such thing as an 'Oxbridge type'. If you enjoy art, music, sport, acting, drinking, clubbing or just about any sort of activity imaginable, there will be many like-minded souls waiting to share your interests. Students come from private schools, state schools and from overseas. It's up to you to decide whether you want to spend your time punting along the river, attending May balls, writing for the university magazines, speaking at the Students' Union, drinking in the JCR or doing none of these things. Your Oxbridge experience is one only you can create; forget the clichés.

It is true, however, that Oxford and Cambridge attract the highest-performing undergraduate students, so you will be keeping company with some of the brightest people in the country and from abroad. Indeed you may find yourself moving from the top of the tree to the bottom and this can require a period of adjustment. Not everyone you meet will become your friend or be your type but you are sure to find their company stimulating and intellectually satisfying.

Case study: Tom, Oxford

I had always done well at school, but didn't really have the confidence to consider applying to Oxford or Cambridge, partly because I didn't know anyone who had gone there before. In fact, I didn't know many people who had been to university at all. However, when I got my AS grades, which were all As, my head teacher suggested it might be worth trying, especially as I already had a strong track record at GCSE.

I had already undertaken some work experience in a legal firm and had been visiting law courts on a regular basis. Once I had made the decision to apply to read law at Oxford, I began to read more widely around the subject, keeping up to date with legal developments through articles in newspapers, magazines and journals, as well as watching items related to law on the television news. I also made my visits to law courts more systematic and kept notes of what I had observed and learned.

I was conscious not to over-prepare for the interview, but I was also proactive in getting some interview practice from family or friends. Although they did not have direct experience of law at university, it was really useful for them to ask me questions about what I had learned in my research and why I wanted to study law. My school also put on a couple of practice interview sessions. All of this made me more confident about the real interview. I knew I would feel prepared, but would still be natural.

Case study: Keith, Cambridge

The facilities at Cambridge are amazing. There are facilities both in your own college but you can also join university-wide societies. I enjoy doing drama productions and being involved in the university paper. Over the past couple of years I have gained particularly fond memories of the social community of my college – I know I have made friends for life. In terms of teaching, there is an incredibly high standard. My lecturers are extremely dedicated and the other students are very engaging to debate ideas with. Mixing with people in college who study other subjects at an equally high level means that without realising it you are constantly exposed to interdisciplinary thinking.

I am a keen musician and am part of CUMS (Cambridge University Musical Society). CUMS gives you real opportunities to nurture your choral or orchestral talents to the highest level and take part in concerts not only in Cambridge and around the UK but even internationally. Similarly, given the small size of the city, it is amazing how many top international musicians play in Cambridge venues. I have found that my musical education has broadened a great deal too with exposure to so many talented individuals with so many different musical tastes and backgrounds.

The location

Both Oxford and Cambridge are undeniably beautiful places to live and each has its own very special character.

Cambridge is much smaller than Oxford and has a market-town feel about it. The university buildings are set much closer together, with a few exceptions such as Girton. Oxford feels more like a university set inside a city; colleges and faculty buildings are spaced out over a wider area and you will probably need a bike to get around easily.

Both universities have many beautiful buildings and each has its own architectural integrity. The colleges are stunning, whether you're into ancient architecture or modern chrome and glass.

Employers are impressed by an Oxbridge degree

While having a First Class degree will improve your employment prospects more than anything else, employers are always impressed by an Oxbridge degree. The tutorial system will have taught you many useful skills: how to formulate and articulate a logical point of view, how to work independently, how to assimilate large amounts of information and how to prepare for tight deadlines. Oxbridge graduates have the confidence, intellect and skills that employers are looking for.

It can also be easier to get an internship while you're studying at Oxbridge because the university terms are shorter and can be fitted around relevant work experience, and, if travel is your thing, you'll have long vacations in which to explore the world.

Case study: Alexander, Oxford

Now that I have been working for a few years, I have come to know the value of my Oxford degree. While no degree will guarantee you a job, it certainly opens doors to interviews. The last few months of my degree were extremely intense with revision for finals and completing multiple job applications, which all required bespoke covering letters and approaches. While many were not ultimately successful, almost all my applications resulted in me securing an interview. I am sure that my experience in tutorials and my Oxford interview really helped me to perform well in job interviews and the careers advice I received at Oxford was excellent.

In fact, my very first position I secured directly as a result of my Oxford degree. I was told informally six months after gaining the role that it had come down to me and another chap but that my Oxford degree had clinched it because the employer knew that I would be used to high pressure working environments and would be efficient and able to think on my feet with clients. I have since moved on and am now teaching. In the education sector my degree is definitely a 'brand' that impresses students, parents and future employers. I also try to incorporate many of the tips for revision and different ways of explaining new concepts that I learnt in tutorials. I look forward to inspiring future Oxbridge candidates in the years to come.

Are there any disadvantages?

The eight-week terms make your studying time very intensive and you will have to work hard outside term time too. Some students find the atmosphere highly pressured; you will constantly be called upon to meet deadlines and assimilate large amounts of information in a very short time. You will also have to balance your extra-curricular activities alongside your demanding academic schedule.

Neither of the universities allows undergraduate students to take on part-time work (which should be taken into consideration when you're planning your finances), although there may be limited opportunities for paid employment within the college, for example in the libraries or JCR.

Some people will tell you that Oxford and Cambridge are not good places to go if you want to play masses of sport or be in a band or basically do anything other than study. It is certainly difficult to strike the right balance but many fine sportsmen and women, musicians, actors, artists and novelists have managed to do just that. Nonetheless, it must be said that the atmosphere is shifting at both universities and it is now harder to devote lots of time to extra-curricular activities than it once was.

Will it be suitable for me?

Just because Cambridge and Oxford are two of the leading universities in the world, this does not mean that you should be daunted by their reputations. Their sole criterion for accepting new undergraduates is academic excellence. This is assessed through academic qualifications, during interviews and through special written tests prior to or during the interview stage. If you have good academic qualifications and are passionate about learning, you are eligible and they will welcome your application.

Equally, being eligible does not make Cambridge and Oxford a good choice for you if you are not prepared to consistently put your studies first. Their university terms are very short and intense compared to other institutions and you will find yourself working harder than your peers elsewhere. If this is not for you, you should consider other options.

Students with disabilities and special educational needs (SEN)

Students with disabilities and SEN students are welcome at both universities and are in no way disadvantaged in their application. Disabilities must be declared on the UCAS form in order for the university and college to pool their resources and you must contact the admissions office at university and college level to discuss your individual needs.

For students with physical disabilities and impaired movement, living in older colleges can be tricky. Because Oxford and Cambridge are so old, much of the architecture is 'listed', making it illegal to make changes to the buildings in any way. This means that it is sometimes impossible to install lifts. The same is true of some faculties, for example the architecture faculty at Cambridge. There are, however, many faculties with new buildings that do not pose such problems, and several colleges in both universities have recently been renovated. You will need to consult your chosen college to advise you on whether it is able to accommodate your needs.

Students with Specific Learning Difficulties (SpLDs), such as dyslexia and dyspraxia, are given the opportunity to write using a computer and extra time during exams; they should feel in no way anxious about applying. Those with visual or hearing impairments are also welcome to apply.

Each college should have a member of staff responsible for disabled students. You should ring the admissions tutor at your chosen college, who will put you in touch with the disability staff member to discuss its resources and your needs. Students can also apply for the Disabled Students Allowance (DSA). Cambridge offers advice on this at www. disability.admin.cam.ac.uk/students/financial-support/disabled-students-allowance, while information about the DSA at Oxford can be found at www.ox.ac.uk/students/welfare/disability/funding. For more information in general, look at the Cambridge Disability Resource Centre at www.disability.admin.cam.ac.uk, or the Oxford University Disability Advisory Service at www.ox.ac.uk/students/welfare/disability.

Students with children

Both Oxford and Cambridge welcome applications from prospective students who have children. Several colleges provide accommodation for couples and families and some colleges have their own nurseries. They each also have a university-wide nursery. You should ring the admissions office at your chosen college for more information.

Although the Access to Learning Fund has been scrapped, there is a Parents' Learning Allowance; more information about this can be found at the following link: www.gov.uk/parents-learning-allowance/overview.

UK students at both universities can ask to be considered for a university and college hardship fund (www.gov.uk/extra-money-pay-university/university-and-college-hardship-funds). Students should contact the student services department at their university to see if they are eligible. Students with children, especially single parents, could qualify, as students with children are one of the priority groups for support. More information is available at the following websites:

- Cambridge: www.childcare.admin.cam.ac.uk/supportwithchildcare costs
- Oxford: www.admin.ox.ac.uk/childcare/feesandfunding.

The 'Cambridge Guide for Student Parents' is written yearly by the Cambridge University Students' Union (CUSU) and is available online at www.studentadvice.cam.ac.uk/welfare/childcare. Some colleges are also members of the Central Childcare Bursary Scheme, which currently offers means-tested grants to overseas and EU students to help with the costs of childcare. This is not a loan and does not need to be repaid. Application forms are available from college offices, the childcare information adviser and CUSU. Applications can be made at any time during the academic year.

The University of Oxford provides similar support, heavily subsidising the cost of local nursery care, as well as funding holiday play schemes. See www.admin.ox.ac.uk/childcare for further details. Oxford University Student Union (OUSU) provides useful information on childcare, funding and other necessities for students who are also parents (www.ousu.org/advice/life-welfare/student-parents).

Students from ethnic minorities

It must be said that the number of students from ethnic minorities at Oxbridge is low. This has generated a large amount of bad press for both universities, perhaps undeservedly. Statistics show that the percentage of minority applicants accepted out of those who apply is very similar to the percentage of white Western applicants who are successful. This suggests that the cause of under-representation of ethnic minorities is primarily due to the lack of applications from these groups rather than a bias against them, and both universities have outreach policies that aim to attract students from under-represented groups.

The University of Cambridge states in its Equal Opportunity Policy and Codes of Practice that it is committed to supporting under-represented groups and takes a hands-on, inclusive approach to equality. Applicants, students or staff members who belong to a protected group (defined under the 2010 Equality Act as sex, gender reassignment or civil partnership, pregnancy or maternity, disability, sexual orientation, age, religion or belief) will not be treated less sympathetically than another.

The full policy is available to view on www.equality.admin.cam.ac.uk/ equality-and-diversity-cambridge/equal-opportunities.

The University of Oxford takes an equally proactive approach to equality; in its Race Equality Policy, Oxford states that admissions decisions will be judged on the individual merits of candidates alone, and stresses its commitment to establishing an environment that respects the rights and dignity of all its members and creating a culture that advocates equality, diversity and values. The full document is available to view at www.admin.ox.ac.uk/eop/policy/equality-policy.

Lesbian, gay, bisexual and transsexual (LGBT) students

Oxford and Cambridge are inclusive universities. Not only is there a central LGBT society at each university but each college also has its own LGBT representative. There are plenty of events to help you feel comfortable. For further information have a look at these websites:

- Cambridge: LGBT information from CUSU: www.lgbt.cusu.cam. ac.uk
- Oxford: LGBTQ Society at Oxford University Student Union (OULGBTQ): www.oulgbtsoc.org.uk.

Educationally disadvantaged students or students who have had a disrupted education

Oxford and Cambridge are committed to helping applicants who have in some way been disadvantaged by a poor school education or by significant disruption to their educational career, which may have resulted in candidates getting lower grades at A level than they might otherwise have achieved.

The Extenuating Circumstances Form (www.undergraduate.study. cam.ac.uk/applying/decisions/extenuating-circumstances-form) enables teachers to provide detailed background information about Cambridge applicants so they can be assessed fairly. The admissions tutors will also have access to publicly available data on school performance that can help them place a student's educational achievement in context.

Cambridge advises that a school or college should submit the Extenuating Circumstances Form by the 15 October deadline if a student:

- has had a medical condition that has significantly affected their educational progress, particularly since the age of 14
- has major caring responsibilities, has suffered a recent bereavement or has a close family member with a serious illness
- has experienced significant disruption to their education provision at school or college.

There are four main categories of genuine Extenuating Circumstances Form applicants:

- applicants whose family or school backgrounds have no experience of Cambridge's application procedure
- those who, due to circumstances outside their control, such as family problems, disability, illness or difficulties at school, have been negatively affected
- those applicants who have experienced circumstances beyond their control that have had an adverse impact on their education
- students who have spent time in care.

Extenuating Circumstances Forms can be obtained from any college admissions office, from the University's admissions office or from the university website (shown above).

Oxford suggests that teachers include details of any special circumstances or other supporting information on the UCAS form in their reference. As with Cambridge, Oxford makes use of publicly available information for applicants who may have been subject to educational or socio-economic difficulties. Oxford advises that if an applicant shows evidence of the academic prowess required for Oxford, it is likely that they will be given consideration for interview alongside those shortlisted in the normal way. Aspects of contextual data that will be considered by Oxford admissions staff include:

- how the applicant's school or college performs at GCSE, A level or equivalent
- students who have spent longer than three months in care.

Both universities are keen to identify bright students whatever their background. If applicants can show the necessary academic aptitude, they will probably be considered for interview and seen in addition to students identified through the standard UCAS process.

2 | Money matters

This chapter will try to give you an idea of what it costs to study at Oxford or Cambridge. There is a commonly held misconception that an Oxbridge education is more expensive than other universities; however, this is not the case.

Both universities are keen to ensure that no talented student should be barred from studying with them because of the cost, and they are aware that the financial backgrounds of their applicants are varied. There are generous bursary schemes available if you are facing financial difficulty – most colleges want to take the best students regardless of income and don't want money worries distracting you from your degree.

Accommodation in both cities is expensive compared with that in other regional universities, but many colleges provide accommodation for their students for all three or four years of their courses. Oxford suggests budgeting between £5,627 and £8,006 per year for college accommodation; this would be for term time only (www.ox.ac.uk/students/fees-funding/living-costs). These figures are an example of 2016-17, as of 6 January, 2017. Please note that the figures may be refreshed online at any time, and make sure to check the university's website (www.ox.ac.uk) for the latest up-to-date information. Private accommodation varies, but it will be higher (www.oxfordstudentpad.co.uk/accommodation and www.admin.ox.ac.uk/accommodation/private).

Suggested costs at Cambridge, are available on the website at www.undergraduate.study.cam.ac.uk/finance/living-costs.

For information on accommodation prices for individual colleges, it is best to consult the relevant websites using the following link: www.undergraduate.study.cam.ac.uk/colleges/college-contacts. On top of this is of course the cost of meals, additional course costs (dependent upon course) and transport.

If cost is a consideration, you should ensure that the college you choose offers accommodation for the whole of your course, as 'living in' is generally cheaper than 'living out'.

Living expenses are generally in line with other universities in the south of England.

The cost of studying at Oxford or Cambridge

When you are studying at any university in the UK, you will have to take into account two main types of cost: your tuition fees and your living costs. Government loans are available for all students towards both types of cost and you should contact your local student finance office to see what is on offer. You do not need to pay either for your tuition fees or for your basic term-time living costs up front. It is worth visiting the relevant funding website for your country for more details:

England: www.gov.uk/student-finance

Wales: www.studentfinancewales.co.uk

Scotland: www.saas.gov.uk

Northern Ireland: www.studentfinanceni.co.uk

Tuition fees

With the UK voting to leave the EU it is unclear, at the time of writing, how long the exit process will take or how it will affect fees and funding in higher education. As such, the fees for all applicants (which includes Home/EU students) who are considering entry to university in 2018 (whether deferred or not) are still under review. The information set out in this book is based upon information currently available but it is recommended that students making an application check fee information for their respective courses at the time of applying.

The University of Cambridge confirmed that the fee for undergraduate EU students who are current students, offer holders and those applying for 2017 entry would be at the current Home/EU rate (for undergraduates, this may be up to the maximum fee caps, as set by the UK government) and they will continue to pay the Home/EU rate for the duration of their course, rather than the higher international fee rate. Tuition fees may, however, increase year on year. Beyond 2017 entry, the fees for all applicants (including Home/EU students) are still subject to confirmation.

As with many other UK universities the usual annual cost of tuition fees at Oxford and Cambridge from September 2017 for EU and UK undergraduates is £9,250. It should be borne in mind that students at Oxford and Cambridge benefit from far more teaching time and individual attention than the average student at other UK universities. In Oxford, tuition fees are reduced for students from some low-income families (see Table 1).

For overseas students the cost of tuition fees is higher. At Oxford, the annual cost ranges between £15,755 and £23,190, and this cost is further increased for clinical medicine. At Cambridge, the annual fees will depend upon the course being studied and range from £16,608 for the humanities, through to £25,275 for engineering and science degrees, to £40,200 for medicine and veterinary science. Further information can be found on www.gov.uk/student-finance/new-fulltime-students, www.ox.ac.uk/admissions/undergraduate/fees-and-funding/tuition-fees and www.undergraduate.study.cam.ac.uk/finance/tuition-fees.

Table 1 Oxford bursary*

Household income	Annual Oxford bursary
£16,000 or less	£3,700
£16,001–£20,000	£2,700
£20,001–£22,500	£2,500
£22,501–£25,000	£2,200
£25,001–£27,500	£1,700
£27,501–£30,000	£1,400
£30,001–£32,500	£1,100
£32,501–£35,000	£1,000
£35,001–£37,500	£800
£37,501–£40,000	£600
£40,001–£42,875	£200
£42,876+	£0

Source: http://www.ox.ac.uk/admissions/undergraduate/fees-and-funding/oxford-support
The above is an example of figures for 2017–18, as of 6 November 2016. Please note that the figures may be refreshed online at any time, and make sure to check the university's website (www.ox.ac.uk) for the latest up-to-date information.

Living costs

Maintenance grants have been scrapped in England for courses starting from September 2016 onwards. Instead, all money available to students for living expenses will be provided as a maintenance loan, to be paid back once students start earning £21,000 or more. Table 2 (below) shows the figures for what a student in England might receive, however figures for students from different parts of the UK will vary slightly. For further details please refer to the UCAS website, www.ucas.com.

Table 2 Maintenance loan for living costs from September 2017

Full-time student	Loan for courses from September 2017
Living at home	Up to £7,097
Living away from home, outside London	Up to £8,430
Living away from home, in London	Up to £11,002
You spend a year of a UK course studying abroad	Up to £9,654

Source: www.gov.uk/student-finance/new-fulltime-students

Table 3 Estimated living costs at the University of Oxford*

	Per month		Total for nine months	
	Lower range	Upper range	Lower range	Upper range
Food	£250	£350	£2,250	£3,150
Accommodation (including utilities)	£538	£619	£4,844	£5,569
Personal items	£115	£255	£1,035	£2,295
Social activities	£40	£119	£358	£1073
Study costs	£38	£83	£338	£743
Other	£22	£45	£196	£407
Total	£1,002	£1,471	£9,021	£13,237

Source: www.ox.ac.uk/admissions/undergraduate/fees-and-funding/living-costs

*The above is an example of figures for 2017–18, as of 06 November 2016. Please note that the figures may be refreshed online at any time, and make sure to check the university's website (www.ox.ac.uk) for the latest up-to-date information.

Table 3 (above) provides an estimation of your living costs at the University of Oxford.

Cambridge living costs are available to view on the website (www. undergraduate.study.cam.ac.uk/finance/living-costs), where you will find breakdown costs for accommodation, college meals, course costs and transport, food, learning costs and personal expenses.

As with Oxford, there are government loans available to all UK students to cover living costs.

Financial support for UK students at Cambridge

Cambridge offers an additional scheme to students, the Cambridge Bursary Scheme. The Cambridge Bursary Scheme provides bursaries for UK/EU students each year. The scheme is for students whose household incomes are below a certain threshold. Any student who meets the eligibility criteria may be awarded a bursary. For 2016/17 entry, students whose household incomes were below £42,620 per annum were offered up to £3,500 per year. In the case of some mature students, bursaries of up to £5,600 were granted. Bursaries of up to £3,500 were available on a sliding scale to students with a household income of £42,620 per annum or less.

The Cambridge European Bursary Scheme provides support for students whose household incomes are lower than a stated threshold. In 2016/17, this threshold was set at £42,620. The most that students were able to receive under this scheme was £3,500, provided they could demonstrate that their household income was equivalent to

£25,000 per annum or less. For students with household incomes of between £25,001 and £42,620, bursaries were awarded on a sliding scale. Please note that these figures are an example from 2016–17 as of 6 January 2017 and are subject to change; make sure to check the website for the most up-to-date information on these two bursaries at www.admin.cam.ac.uk/univ/cambridgebursary and www.admin.cam.ac.uk/univ/cambridgebursary/eu.

Practicalities

At both universities, you may prefer to prepare your own food rather than eat in hall all the time. Most colleges have adequate kitchen facilities and you can buy fresh food from the local markets and super-markets quite cheaply. You will also need to budget a small amount each week to do your laundry. Most colleges have a laundry room with washing machines and tumble dryers and these cost approximately £3. Of course, this would all depend on your lifestyle.

Transport

You won't need to spend money getting around the university as both are easily navigable by bike or on foot.

If it is raining, some students prefer to take the bus to their lectures at a cost of about £1.50 per ride. However, most students cycle every-where. This is by far the fastest and the cheapest way to travel. If you don't have a bike already you can pick one up from one of the many second-hand bike shops in both cities for as little as £35 (although if you want a better ride you will obviously have to pay more). Additional costs to consider when investing in a bike include: the helmet at approximately £25; locking systems to prevent theft (very important) at about £20–£25; and servicing charges. There are many bike mechanics across both cities who will fix your bike for a fee. However, college porters usu-ally have free bike repair kits and there are normally bike reps (students whom you can call on for help with mending and servicing your wheels for absolutely no charge) at each college.

Study materials

Most books that you'll need are available in college and university librar-ies, so your expenses should be limited to the usual items of stationery that you had at school. Unless you're specifically instructed to buy books by your faculty, it's probably best to wait until you arrive before spending lots of money unnecessarily.

You will probably want to purchase a laptop, if you don't already own one.

Scientists may need to purchase lab coats and mathematicians may need to buy calculators. Again, you will be told by the college if you need any specific study materials for your course.

Case study: Kim, Oxford

It can be difficult to manage your finances at any university and in life in general, but I have tried to work out a basic budget that helps me to make my money last longer. I tend to write down how much I spend or am likely to spend on clothes, food, books and socialising at the start of each term. I then assess how closely I have kept to my budget at the end of each term. Sometimes it is not as close as it could have been!

I sell my books at the end of the academic year, so this allows me to recoup some of my costs. However, I try not to spend too much on books in the first place. I do this by making as much use of the college and faculty libraries, as well as the Bodleian Library, as possible. I tend to find everything I need there, especially if I do not leave everything until the last minute. My family are also very good at asking me about my required reading, so that I often get some of the books I need for birthday and Christmas presents.

I go to the college bar when socialising, as not only are most of my friends based in college so it is convenient but because it is cheaper than the pubs in Oxford. If a big night out is being planned, I usually set a little extra money aside for that. I do not spend much on travel when I am in Oxford, as I can quite easily walk to most places I need to go to.

I am lucky enough to get a regular part-time job during my vacations and since the terms are only eight weeks long I do manage to save a little bit during this time, which I can then use during term time.

Case study: One parent's view on the cost of studying at Cambridge

My daughter Alice certainly overspent in her first term as many students do when they first move away from home. This was more to do with inexperience in terms of budgeting than any necessary costs. After she started to keep a note of how much she was spending, particularly in coffee shops and restaurants, she was more aware and thus more careful with her student loan money.

Now she describes herself as fairly average in terms of spending. She still treats herself occasionally but takes most of her meals at college and chooses formal hall for a special night out rather than more expensive restaurants. She and a friend have also taken to scouting charity shops as well as popular chains for clothes and share outfits between them as they are a similar build. This definitely reduced her outgoings.

One area which has never been a problem is books. While some of my friends with children at other universities occasionally get panicked phone calls from their children in desperate need of £50–£100 for a textbook this has not happened to me. Alice can always find a copy of the books she needs in her college, her faculty or the university library.

Scholarships, college awards and prizes

Oxford and Cambridge are two of the most well-endowed universities in the UK and provide generous support to students at both university and collegiate level throughout their studies. Similarly, there are academic scholarships and prizes available to students once they have commenced studying, which are often awarded at the end of the first year. Sources of funding may be available from your college and you should consult individual college websites for full details. These can include:

- prizes for academic and other achievements
- grants for study-related books and equipment
- travel grants
- grants and loans to help with unforeseen financial difficulties.

There are a number of university-wide academic scholarships available at Oxford and Cambridge.

These include:

- Moritz-Heyman Scholarship (www.ox.ac.uk/admissions/undergraduate/fees_funding/oxford_support/moritz-heyman-scholarship)
- Oxford Centre for Islamic Studies Scholarship (www.ox.ac.uk/admissions/undergraduate/fees-and-funding/oxford-support/oxford-centre-islamic-studies-scholarship)
- Palgrave Brown UK Scholarship (www.ox.ac.uk/admissions/undergraduate/fees-and-funding/oxford-support/palgrave-brown-scholarship-non-uk)
- Lloyds Scholars Bursary (www.ox.ac.uk/admissions/undergraduate/fees-and-funding/oxford-support/lloyds-scholars-programme).

Individual colleges may also offer scholarships and bursaries generously provided by former students. Cambridge advises that individual colleges may have specific awards and grants, which are listed on the college websites (www.undergraduate.study.cam.ac.uk/finance/financial-support/cambridge-financial-support/college-awards-and-grants).

Music awards and scholarships

Both universities are well known for the excellence and diversity of their music-making. One of the ways they maintain their high standards of musicianship is by offering music awards to students. Music award-holders are among the hardest-working students in the universities, as they have to juggle extensive musical commitments with their academic studies. The experience they gain is huge, though, and the opportunity to sing with, play in orchestras with or conduct some of the best young musicians in the country is unique. Many award-holders go on to careers in music.

If you're a talented musician, it is worth considering applying for a scholarship. The way you apply is different from the normal route and needs careful explanation. At both universities you can apply for organ, choral or instrumental scholarships and there are some special awards for répétiteurs and chamber music.

Most colleges have open days where you can find out more about the awards and you are strongly advised to attend them to better understand the application process. You will also have the opportunity of meeting current music award-holders and visiting the colleges to see their facilities for music-making.

Auditions generally take place in September. An offer of a choral, organ or instrumental scholarship does not guarantee you a place at a college as you will still need to go through the normal admissions procedure and achieve the necessary grades.

Some colleges will not allow students studying certain subjects to be music scholars because the academic demands of their courses are too great. It is worth checking this information with the college before making a scholarship application.

Anyone wishing to apply for a music award needs to read the relevant university and college websites very carefully for full details of the awards and the application process. For more information visit:

- Cambridge: www.undergraduate.study.cam.ac.uk/finance/music-awards
- Oxford: www.ox.ac.uk/admissions/undergraduate/applying-to-oxford/choral-and-organ-awards.

Choral awards

In all, 13 colleges at Oxford and more than 20 colleges at Cambridge offer choral awards, covering the whole range of voices: sopranos, contraltos, countertenors, tenors, baritones and basses. The basic duty of choral scholars is to sing at chapel services, but their involvement in college and university music goes further than this, extending to solo work, chamber groups and choruses. These and several of the mixed-voice choirs undertake concerts, tours and recordings, with some of these activities falling within the vacation periods. A number of colleges offer singing lessons as part of the award.

Case study: Jack, Cambridge

Being a choral scholar is one of the best experiences that Oxbridge has to offer. It's enormously enriching musically, is masses of fun and has some amazing perks. There are also choirs for all levels of commitment and ability: John's and King's do around seven services per week, Trinity do three, while some smaller colleges only do one. Shop around to find a choir that suits you!

I'm a choral scholar at Trinity, and it has been the best part of my time at Cambridge. We sing three services and rehearse for around five hours per week. It seems a lot, but one of the best things about being a choral scholar is … well, the other choral scholars! We're all pretty firm friends, and this makes rehearsals fly by – there are also regular pub trips, film nights, etc. It's a fantastic group to be part of socially, and I'm sure all Oxbridge choirs are the same.

This is without mentioning the rest of the perks of the job: free Feasts (five-course dinners) six or seven times a year, money off our college bill each term, free singing lessons with internationally renowned teachers, lots of drinks parties hosted by our amazing Chaplains and Directors of Music, all-expenses-paid tours abroad … (Canada last year and the USA and Australia in the next couple of years – guaranteed to be among the most fun weeks of your entire life).

If you're interested in singing and interested in being a choral scholar, then the best thing to do is to get in touch with some of the Directors of Music at Oxford or Cambridge and arrange an informal meeting. They'll be able to give you advice as to which college might be best for you, what life as a choral scholar is like, and how to balance work–life commitments while at Oxbridge. Their email addresses will be on their college's website, and they are always happy to field any queries. It's worth mentioning also that you don't have to have been a chorister/sung your whole life;

the majority of choral scholars haven't, and some of Cambridge's best singers only began singing in the sixth form at school. Neither should you feel hidebound to apply to your own college's choir – many people sing at colleges other than their own.

For me, singing in Trinity Choir has been a real privilege. We get to work with some amazing musicians and at a really high standard while having enormous amounts of fun. Whether you are interested in singing seven services a week or one, it's a decision that you won't regret.

Organ awards

Organ scholarships are offered by 22 Oxford and 23 Cambridge colleges. The organ scholar is responsible for supporting the director of music and in some cases running the chapel music where there is no music tutor involved, and also for playing a leading part in the college's musical life in general. The experience is invaluable for musicians interested in directing and organising musical activities across a wide spectrum. Colleges normally assist in the cost of organ lessons. Interviews for prospective organ scholars take place at the same time as the auditions and tests before the main interview period in December.

Répétiteur scholarships

The répétiteur scholarship is open to pianists in Oxford who are interested in coaching singers. It is offered jointly by St Catherine's College, Oxford and New Chamber Opera. This offers the possibility of extensive experience as a répétiteur in the musical theatre (www.newchamberopera.co.uk/about/repetiteur_scholarship).

Instrumental awards

At Oxford, many colleges offer instrumental awards for which you can audition once you have begun your studies; for a list of colleges and requirements, visit www.ox.ac.uk/admissions/undergraduate/applying-to-oxford/choral-and-organ-awards/other-ways-get-involved?wssl=1

At Cambridge, the Instrumental Awards Scheme is open to the following instrumentalists: violin; viola; cello; flute; oboe; clarinet; bassoon; French horn; and piano.

The award runs for one academic year and offers the opportunity for students to hone their chamber music performance skills. As well as receiving a small sum, successful applicants benefit from masterclasses, subsidised music lessons, recital opportunities and professional tuition for their ensemble. For more details on requirements and how to apply, visit: www.undergraduate.study.cam.ac.uk/finance/music-awards/instrumental-awards.

3 | Entry requirements

By now you may have decided that you'd like to apply to Oxford or Cambridge. How do you know if you're a suitable candidate and if you have a realistic chance of getting in?

It goes without saying that entry is very competitive and we've all read stories in the newspapers about students with perfect grades failing to get a place and others with lesser grades somehow being successful. It's important to understand the facts and forget the fiction.

The University of Oxford makes conditional offers for students studying A levels ranging between A*A*A and AAA depending on the course (or 38–40 points in the International Baccalaureate including core points, or AAAAB/AAAAA in Scottish Highers, supplemented by at least two Advanced Highers) depending on the subject. For humanities at Oxford the offers are generally AAA, for sciences A*AA and for mathematics A*A*A (with A* in mathematics and further mathematics if taken). It has to be said that students who gain a place generally have A*A*A for the whole range of courses. Specific A level (or equivalent) subjects may be required to apply for some subjects, especially in the sciences, and some subjects require applicants to sit a written test or submit written work. (www.ox. ac.uk/admissions/under graduate/courses/entrance-requirements).

Cambridge colleges will require A*AA–A*A*A in three A level subjects (or equivalent), although they have the discretion to make non-standard offers where appropriate as part of their holistic assessment of candidates. The typical conditional A level offer for arts subjects (except economics), as well as for psychological and behavioural sciences and veterinary mediciine, for 2018 entry will be A*AA, while the typical offer for the other sciences and economics will be A*A*A. Offers for certain applicants may be dependent on them achieving A* in a specific subject or subjects. Applicants may also be asked to submit written work, depending on the subject, and most applicants are required to take a written admission assessment, either pre-interview or at interview (www. undergraduate.study.cam.ac.uk/applying/admissions-assessments). More details can be found in Chapter 8.

Both universities interview the majority of undergraduate applicants. For some courses, for example those with fewer applicants, more than 80% of applicants are shortlisted for interview. However, for more competitive courses as few as 30% of applicants may proceed to the interview stage (www.undergraduate.study.cam.ac.uk/applying/interviews).

So, here are some important questions to consider before you apply.

Are you studying the right subjects?

The A level subject choices you make in Year 11 (or equivalent) can have a significant impact on the course options available to you at university.

The Russell Group, which represents the 24 leading UK universities (including Oxford and Cambridge), has produced a detailed guide to post-16 subject choices, *Informed Choices*. First published in 2011 and revised annually, this report should now be obligatory reading for every A level candidate (http://russellgroup.ac.uk/for-students/school-and-college-in-the-uk/subject-choices-at-school-and-college).

Informed Choices, produced in collaboration with the Institute of Career Guidance, is aimed at all students considering A level and equivalent options. It includes advice on the best subject combinations for a wide range of university courses as well as advice on the best choices if you don't know what you want to study after school and need to keep your options open.

Informed Choices lists the so-called 'facilitating' subjects. These are the ones that the Russell Group judges to be the most effective for gaining a place at university. They are:

* mathematics and further mathematics
* English (literature)
* geography
* history
* biology
* chemistry
* physics
* languages (classical and modern).

The guide states that even where these choices are not specified as required subjects, universities may still have a preference for them.

It warns: 'If you decide not to choose some of the facilitating subjects at advanced level, many degrees at competitive universities will not be open to you.' It suggests that 'soft' subjects such as critical thinking, citizenship studies and general studies would best be considered as extra subjects and should not be considered as part of any core offering.

When the Oxford and Cambridge admissions tutors assess candidates, they consider not only the individual A level (or equivalent) subjects taken but also the combination of subjects. Generally they prefer applicants to have taken certain subjects or combinations of subjects that they feel will help their studies once they arrive at their universities. Recommended subjects required by Oxford and Cambridge are in accordance with the *Informed Choices* list.

Many Oxford and Cambridge courses require prior knowledge of certain subjects. If you have already decided on a course that you would like to study at university, it's recommended that you review the information given on the Oxford and Cambridge websites (www.undergraduate. study.cam.ac.uk/courses and www.ox.ac.uk/admissions/undergraduate/ courses-listing) before you finalise your A level subject choices, to check that they will be appropriate for an Oxbridge application. The Cambridge website specifies that there are some A levels that are useful for specific courses, some that are desirable, some that are highly desirable and some that are essential and similar information can be found on the Oxford website.

Some students choose to take two arts and two science subjects in the lower sixth when they begin their A levels because they believe it will keep their options open. While such a subject combination does provide a suitable preparation for many arts and social science courses at university, you should be aware that it can make you a less competitive applicant for broad-based science courses.

Some A level subjects are considered either essential or useful for a number of courses at Oxbridge, therefore choosing one or more of these will help keep your options open.

Please note, in the following information referring to GCSE qualifications, in England, the specifications are being reformed such that students will no longer be awarded letter grades but will be given grades 1–9 (with 9 being the highest awarded). While the vast majority of students using this guide will be awarded letter grades (number grades are not coming into effect until the 2017 exam season) there may be some exceptional circumstances where this affects you (e.g. GCSEs followed by one year of A levels). In such cases any requirements of GCSE grades should be checked with the university you are applying to.

Arts and social science courses

If you are undecided about which arts or social sciences course you'd like to study at university, then English literature, history, languages and mathematics are good 'facilitating' subjects: choosing one or more of these will provide a good foundation for your subject combination.

Other good choices to combine with these subjects include: an additional language, ancient history, classical civilisation, economics, further mathematics, geography, philosophy, religious studies and sciences (biology, chemistry or physics).

Other possible subject choices might be archaeology, English language, environmental science, government and politics, history of art, law, music, psychology or sociology.

Science courses

If you are interested in studying a science course at university but you are not sure which one, you are advised to take at least two, and ideally three, of biology, chemistry, mathematics and physics. Some pairings of these subjects are more natural than others. The most natural pairs are biology and chemistry, chemistry and physics, and mathematics and physics.

In practice, the vast majority of applicants for science courses at Oxbridge take at least three of these subjects. Another useful combination is mathematics, further mathematics and physics. Many students take four of biology, chemistry, mathematics, further mathematics and physics.

If you are planning to study biological or medical sciences you should take chemistry; for physical sciences or engineering you should take mathematics and physics and, ideally, further mathematics.

Other possible subject choices, for instance computing, design and technology, electronics or psychology, may be useful preparation for some science courses but as always it is advisable to check for any more information about the course at the time of applying.

Medicine

If you are considering applying for medicine at **Oxford**, you will need to achieve A*AA in three A levels (which does not include critical thinking or general studies) taken in one sitting. The minimum requirements are a grade A in both chemistry and grade A in at least one of biology, physics or mathematics.

Scottish students must have AA (including chemistry) in their Advanced Highers plus AAAAA in their Highers, which must include biology or mathematics or physics. International Baccalaureate (IB) students need a minimum total score of 39 or 40 including core points depending on the course with 7, 6, 6 at Higher level. Candidates must take chemistry and a second science (biology or physics) and/or mathematics to Higher level (www.ox.ac.uk/study/medicine). If you have any concerns about what subjects are suitable, you can email Oxford at admissions@medschool.ox.ac.uk.

If biology, physics or mathematics have not been taken to A level (or equivalent), applicants must show that they have received a basic education in those subjects (achieving at least a grade C at GCSE, Standard Grade (Credit) or Intermediate 2, or equivalent). The GCSE Double Award Combined Sciences is also acceptable. (www.ox.ac.uk/admissions/undergraduate/courses_listing/medicine).

All candidates have to take the BMAT as part of their application (see Chapter 8 for more on this).

The **Cambridge Medicine Faculty** lists its requirements as follows: students will need a grade C or above in GCSE (or equivalent) Double Award Science and mathematics and you can substitute two single awards in GCSE biology and physics for Double Award Science. Students in England applying with reformed GCSE qualifications should contact the Cambridge undergraduate admissions office to check their requirements. At A level you need to aim for A*A*A grades in chemistry and two of biology/human biology, physics and mathematics. Most applicants for medicine at Cambridge have at least three science or mathematics A levels and some colleges require this or ask for particular A level subject(s). You will need to see individual college websites for details (www.undergraduate.study.cam.ac.uk/colleges/college-contacts). If you apply with only two science or mathematics subjects at A level, your likelihood of success will be reduced.

The GCSE and A level subject requirements also apply to the IB. Individual Middle Years Programme subject results validated by the IB at grade 4 or above will satisfy the GCSE requirements. Standard level subjects are approximately equivalent to lower sixth exams, and Higher level subjects are broadly comparable with full A levels. Your final IB score should be 40–41 points, with 7, 7, 6 at Higher level.

As with Oxford, all medical applicants have to take the BMAT test.

You can find full details at www.undergraduate/study.cam.ac.uk/courses/medicine.

Case study: Alex, Cambridge

The thing with medicine at Cambridge is that when you apply you aren't just applying to Cambridge but you are applying to a specific college, with its own rules and expectations. Although this can be said about all subjects at Cambridge and Oxford, it is especially true for medicine. For example, different colleges often have different BMAT score requirements, with different colleges placing different emphasis on different sections of the test. It is useful to make sure you are aware of these different expectations before you decide which college to apply for.

It is also important to keep in mind when writing your personal statement that the course offered at Oxbridge is quite different to that offered at other medical schools. It is helpful to mention your more scientific interests, given the strength of the scientific section of the course at Oxford and Cambridge. However there is no need to go overboard as the admissions tutors do understand that Oxbridge is just one option for which you are applying.

When preparing for your interview don't worry about the little things, like what to wear, as these should all be covered in your interview invitation (if not, then a suit for medical interviews is always a good bet, although I did not follow this very sound advice and still got in). The formats of the interviews themselves are another aspect of the application that varies between colleges. My college gave me two interviews, one which was a standard medical interview containing some unusual data analysis questions and the other followed the format that a biological NatSci applicant may expect from his/her interview. This goes to highlight the importance placed by Oxbridge on the scientific side of studying medicine, something that applicants need to make sure they are happy with before applying. It is worth mentioning that I wasn't asked any question specific to extracurricular reading I had done, but some of the topics covered in such reading helped me in my approach to answering questions at interview.

Although I found my interview challenging and the process as a whole demanding, I thoroughly enjoyed the experience. At the end of the day, like any other university, both Cambridge and Oxford are looking for applicants who do have a similar passion and interest in medicine.

Other A level subjects

There are other subjects not mentioned above, such as general studies and critical thinking, but Oxford and Cambridge will usually only consider these as a fourth A level subject.

Do you have the right qualifications?

There are no set 'grade requirements' for applying to Oxbridge but that doesn't mean that you don't have to be an excellent student to gain a place. Oxford and Cambridge are considered Britain's 'elite' universities; in the words of one Cambridge admissions tutor: 'We are the best university in the world and we want the best undergraduates in the world.'

There is an interactive graph generator into which prospective students can enter the name of the college to which they wish to apply and the course in order to see specific statistics on applications and acceptance rates on the Cambridge website: www.undergraduate.study.cam.ac.uk/apply/statistics. The figures for Oxford can be found on: www.ox.ac.uk/about/facts-and-figures/admissions-statistics.

You will need consistently high grades, a glowing reference from your current school or college, and to be able to demonstrate commitment to your chosen course in your personal statement and interview. Each year, thousands of students apply for a place at both universities; for instance, approximately 19,400 undergraduate applications were made to Oxford for 2016 entry for around 3,200 places, and over 16,750 applied to Cambridge, with the success rate standing at 20.6%. However, this should not put you off trying if you fulfil the universities' basic requirements. Remember, someone has to get in and not everyone who applies is a genius. To state the obvious: if you don't apply, you won't get in!

Set out below is information given by the Oxford and Cambridge websites regarding their requirements for an offer of a place.

Cambridge requirements in detail

Although the website mainly talks in terms of GCSEs and A levels, other school and national examinations at an equivalent level are equally acceptable. Whatever system you're being educated in, Cambridge requires top grades in the highest-level qualifications available for school students. Most of the information below has been taken from the Cambridge admissions website (www.undergraduate.study.cam.ac.uk/applying/entrance-requirements). It is always advisable to check the website in case there have been any changes since the publication of this book.

If you are taking any other examination system (including the Advanced International Certificate of Education offered by Cambridge Assessment), it is a good idea to make early contact with the Cambridge admissions office to check that it provides an appropriate preparation for the course you hope to study.

AS exams and new reformed specifications

If you are applying to Cambridge you should usually study four subjects in your first year of A levels, although it is not unheard of for students to study five. However, taking three or four subjects does not put you at a disadvantage to those students taking five. Both Cambridge and Oxford are aware of the very different responses to A level reform taken by schools and colleges and will ensure that candidates are not disadvantaged as a result. It should be noted that with unreformed A levels you do not have to cash in your AS grades, but the Supplementary Application Questionnaire for Cambridge requires you to put down the results of all AS and A level examinations taken. Such information is not required of Oxford candidates. However, with reformed AS subjects you do have to declare your AS grades, if you have sat the AS examinations at the end of your first year of A level studies but you will not get a conditional offer based solely on your AS grades. This is especially the case for 2018 entry, because at this time the vast majority of A level specifications will be operating on the reformed two-year linear courses, although some very popular subjects, for example mathematics and politics, will still be operating on the legacy specifications, with modular AS units still required.

A levels

While most applicants to Cambridge are taking three or four A level subjects, the usual conditional A level offer for entry in 2018 is A*AA. The subject in which the A* is to be achieved is unlikely to be specified in most cases. As mentioned already, the usual conditional A level offer for arts subjects and for psychological and behavioural sciences for 2018 entry is A*AA, while the usual conditional offer for the other sciences is A*A*A.

Colleges may alter offers depending on an individual's case. For instance, mitigating circumstances may be taken into account if an Extenuating Circumstances Form has been completed; conversely, higher offers may be made if there is some doubt about a student's potential.

Extended Project Qualification

The Extended Project Qualification (EPQ) is taken by some students in addition to their A levels, which focuses on planning, research and evaluative skills – skills that are valued by higher education bodies such as Cambridge as well as by future employers. The EPQ is worth half the UCAS Tariff points of a whole A level. Although neither Oxford nor Cambridge will use the EPQ in its offers, Cambridge has stated that the EPQ may be used for discussion at interview and it may even form the basis of written work, in some circumstances. Cambridge further states that it welcomes the EPQ as it helps to develop independent study and the research skills valued in higher education.

AQA Baccalaureate

The AQA Baccalaureate may be used as an entry qualification for Cambridge, but offers are dependent on the results of individual A levels within the qualification rather than the whole award.

Cambridge Pre-U

Both Oxford and Cambridge take the Pre-U into account as a qualification, but they do not prefer it above other qualifications. They value the skills it inculcates, such as independent research skills, as well as the promotion of critical, lateral and contextual thinking.

Cambridge Pre-U students, as well as students who are studying a combination of Pre-U and A levels, may apply to Cambridge. Conditional offers are made on a case-by-case basis; however, these are usually dependent on students achieving Distinctions (D2 or D3) in their Principal Subjects.

International Baccalaureate diploma programme

Conditional offers are frequently made on the International Baccalaureate, with scores between 40 and 41 points out of 45, with 7, 7, 6 in the Higher level subjects being required. For certain subjects, students may need to achieve 7. Students should look on the Cambridge website for precise requirements and the best IB subject combinations. It should be borne in mind that Standard level subjects are comparable to lower sixth exams, while Higher level subjects are akin to the full A level.

Scottish Highers and Advanced Highers

Cambridge will usually require Scottish applicants to have gained at least four A grades at Higher grade, plus Advanced Highers. Conditional offers are normally made on the basis of AAA in three Advanced Highers. Two Advanced Highers and an additional Higher may be allowed in certain circumstances. For further details, candidates are advised to peruse the Cambridge website. It should be borne in mind that Highers are roughly the same as lower sixth exams, while Advanced Highers are comparable to the full A level.

Applicants who are studying for the Scottish Baccalaureate will usually be required to get three Advanced Highers as part of it.

If applicants cannot study more than two Advanced Highers through no fault of their own, they should consult the colleges to which they are thinking of applying. At the time of writing there is a major secondary reform taking place in Scotland. It is recommended that prospective undergraduates check with the individual college being applied to for advice.

Advanced Welsh Baccalaureate

Students taking the Advanced Welsh Baccalaureate should normally be taking three subjects at A level as part of their qualification. Conditional offers will be made on the basis of how well they are likely to do in the individual A levels rather than on the overall award. The details of any modular legacy A levels being studied as part of the Baccalaureate should be stated as part of the Supplementary Application Questionnaire (SAQ).

Irish Leaving Certificate

Republic of Ireland applicants who are taking the Irish Leaving Certificate would typically receive offers based on A1/H1 in three relevant subjects at Higher Level.

Applicants for medicine and veterinary medicine may also be required to take an IGCSE or equivalent in the science subject they have not covered as part of the Irish Leaving Certificate.

Access to HE Diploma

Cambridge applicants on the Access to HE (Higher Education) Diploma are normally required to reach a standard akin to conditional A level offers. As a consequence the usual offer will be distinctions in all of the requisite subject units within the Access to HE Diploma.

Applicants may also have to meet certain subject-specific requirements; for example, an extra A level in mathematics or evidence of proficiency in languages may be required. A list of extra requirements for each subject can be found at: www.undergraduate.study.cam.ac.uk/courses.

European Baccalaureate

Successful applicants on the European Baccalaureate are usually required to attain 85–90% overall, with 90% in the areas in closest proximity to the course they are applying to read at Cambridge.

French Baccalaureate

Applicants studying for the French Baccalaureate (including the International option) are usually required to achieve 16 or 17 ('mention très bien') out of 20. In addition, such applicants are normally required to attain 16 or 17 in specified subjects.

German Abitur

German Abitur applicants are usually required to gain an overall score of between 1.0 and 1.3, with 14 or 15 in the subjects in closest proximity to the course they are applying to read at Cambridge.

SATs, ACT and Advanced Placement Tests

If you are from the USA or Canada and you are preparing for Advanced Placement Tests or SATs (Scholastic Aptitude Tests), you should note that applications are considered on an individual basis. You are unlikely to receive an offer based solely on the SAT alone; however, the SAT may be considered if you are also taking other qualifications. Note that the SAT scoring system changed in March 2016. If you took the SAT before these changes, you need a score of at least 1400 in Critical Reading and Mathematics and 700 or more in Writing, giving a total score of 2100. For applicants who have taken SAT since March 2016, you need a minimum of 730 in Evidence-Based Reading and Writing and 730 in Mathematics, giving a total score of at least 1460. If you took the American College Testing (ACT), a score of at least 32 out of 36 may be acceptable in place of the SAT.

Diplomas

Advanced Diplomas in engineering and environmental and land-based studies are considered for entry as they are viewed as preparing candidates satisfactorily for some courses at Cambridge. You would normally be required to have taken two appropriate A levels in addition.

- You can apply for engineering at Cambridge with the Principal Learning components of the Advanced Diploma in engineering on the condition that you have taken A levels in physics and mathematics.
- You can apply for geography and natural sciences (biological) with the Advanced Diploma in environmental and land-based studies on the condition that you have taken the relevant subjects in the Additional Specialist Learning component. For natural sciences (biological), these must be an A level in chemistry and one of biology, mathematics or physics A level. The geography and land economy requirements are more open.

VCE and Applied A Levels, GNVQs and BTECs

Vocational qualifications are not considered an appropriate route to Cambridge, because of the vocational rather than academic focus. That being said, if preferred subjects at A level have been covered, applicants may take an applied A level in lieu of a third A level or as a fourth subject to demonstrate breadth of learning. It is always worth checking with the college admissions tutor about what is acceptable, as indeed it is if you are taking any of the non-standard offers from this section.

Oxford requirements in detail

- Many students who apply to Oxford are taking A levels but any candidate who has already taken, or who is currently studying, any other equivalent qualifications is also most welcome to apply.
- Oxford will assess a student's application on their ability, regardless of their age.
- The information below outlines the general entrance requirements. The Oxford website should also be consulted: www.ox.ac.uk/admissions/undergraduate/courses/entrance-requirements.

A levels

Conditional offers of between A*A*A and AAA, depending upon the subject and course being applied to, are made to Oxford applicants. General studies is ruled out as an approved A level, but Oxford admissions officers say that almost any other subject may be considered, on the proviso that you meet the requirements laid out by the colleges. Colleges make their offers based on your predicted final A level grades.

Extended Project Qualification (EPQ)

While Oxford sees the merit of the EPQ for the skills it develops, it will not make any offers based on it. However, if you have gained skills and experience from working on an EPQ, it is always worth discussing this in your personal statement. In the coming years an EPQ could become a further important piece of evidence for your personal statement with the move to A level linearity and with less data from AS results on which admissions officers can base their decisions. The EPQ demonstrates the independent approach to study and the research skills that Oxford sees as very important attributes in a student. In addition, the UCAS Tariff points for an EPQ are worth 50% of a whole A level.

14–19 diplomas

- While the Advanced Diploma in engineering (Level 3) may be accepted as an entry qualification for engineering science courses at Oxford, applicants have to attain an A level in physics and the new Level 3 Certificate in mathematics for engineering in addition.
- Diplomas in other subjects may be considered as acceptable entry qualifications as long as applicants have chosen Additional Specialist Learning in two appropriate A levels.

Pre-U

The Pre-U diploma is deemed to be an acceptable entry qualification. It depends on the subject, but if you are made an offer it is likely to be in the following range: D2, D2, D3 and D3, D3, D3. If in doubt, you should check the precise requirements with the faculty to which you are applying. Oxford says that D2 is regarded as similar to an A* grade at A level and D3 to an A grade. It also says that applicants may study Pre-U principal subjects instead of A levels.

Young Applicants in Schools Scheme (YASS)

Oxford welcomes applicants who have studied YASS modules. These modules are taught by the Open University, and Oxford says that they may prepare students appropriately for higher education. YASS students are advised to discuss what they have gained from their study of these modules in their personal statements, but it is likely that offers will still be made on the basis of A levels or similar qualifications, as most YASS students will also be taking these.

For students taking only Open University qualifications, an application may still be considered. Strong candidates should have achieved a minimum of 120 points at level 1, in relevant subjects with at least pass grade 2.

English Baccalaureate

This has had little impact at present. It should be noted that it is more important to have achieved a strong set of GCSE grades in the top two bands.

Vocational qualifications

While Oxford is happy to receive applications from students with vocational qualifications that are similar in standard to A levels, such students may also be asked for extra academic qualifications in order to reach the standards set by the admissions officers.

International Baccalaureate

International Baccalaureate students typically receive offers of 38–40 points, including core points; in addition, they need to attain 6s and 7s in the Higher level. You should visit the course page for the subject for which you are applying for details of the individual requirements (www. ox.ac.uk/admissions/undergraduate/courses-listing).

Scottish qualifications

At the moment, the typical offer is AAAAB or AAAAA in Scottish Highers with the addition of two or more Advanced Highers. AAB is normally required if a student is in a position to study three Advanced Highers; if a student is not able to do this, he or she would normally be required to achieve AA in two Advanced Highers, as well as an A grade in a third Higher course studied in the sixth year.

American qualifications

For the old-style SAT (taken before March 2016) Oxford typically requires minimum SAT Reasoning Test scores with at least 1400 in Critical Reading and Mathematics and 700 or higher in Writing, giving a total of at least 2100. On the new SAT, (if you took the test from March 2016), you will need to achieve a total score of 1470 out of 1600 (the optional essay in the redesigned SAT is not a requirement). Alternatively students could apply with an ACT score of at least 32 out of 36.

Other international qualifications

For more detailed information on this, please see Chapter 10, which deals with non-standard applications.

4 | The early stages of preparation

Choosing the right course is the most important decision you will have to make during the whole application process. It is primarily your enthusiasm for your subject that will be attractive to the admissions tutors and interviewers and, if you are accepted, your love for your subject will sustain you through all the hard work you will undoubtedly have to do. When considering which course to take and when preparing for interview, reading is another, and absolutely essential, form of preparation. You need to read widely and in depth. Knowing the school syllabus is not enough. You should be able to think and talk about ideas beyond the scope of school work and above the level of your peers.

The importance of reading

Remember that the academics who teach at Oxford and Cambridge, and who interview prospective students, have dedicated their whole lives to their subject. They believe passionately in the importance of their research and expect you to do the same. If you have read around your subject this shows that you are dedicated and passionate and this will be very attractive to interviewers.

In addition, if you are accepted, the majority of your time as an undergraduate will be spent studying. Whereas students on an essay-based course at UCL, for example, may be asked to write four 2,500-word essays over the course of a 10-week term, Oxbridge students are expected, in some subjects, to write two essays a week, and sometimes more, making a total of around 16 essays per eight-week term. Students who study science subjects at Oxbridge will have a large amount of contact time per week. These hours are made up of lab sessions, supervisions or tutorials, seminars and lectures that fill up most of the week and may run into your weekends. There is little time off, and most of it is taken up studying for assignments and essays. You need to be excited by this work and find the pressure enjoyable rather than a burden.

The method of working at Oxbridge is very different from school. Students who study humanities subjects (English literature and history, for example) typically have very few hours of contact time in the week; perhaps six to eight hours of lectures, tutorials or supervisions and one hour-long seminar per week. However, they are expected to work as many hours as the scientists. This requires them to be independent in their study practice. Humanities students need to be dedicated, focused and able to follow through their own research without getting distracted. Like the scientists, therefore, humanities students need to show that they are able to research independently.

Finally, in order to make the right choice, it is important to gather as much information about a course and its content as possible. Prospectuses for Oxford and Cambridge give detailed course guides, including information on course content and A level requirements, as well as some other equivalent qualifications. In addition, Oxford produces individual prospectuses for each subject. Read this information and the criteria very carefully, making sure your qualifications fulfil the requirements specified.

If you want to be really thorough, contact the individual faculty secretaries at the university. Remember that, while the college administers the teaching, it is the faculty (i.e. the subject department within the university) that controls the syllabus. The faculty secretary will have much more detail on course content than is available in the prospectuses. Information about faculty addresses, including website addresses, is available in the prospectuses.

When you talk with the faculty secretary, ask him or her for an up-to-date reading list for new undergraduates. This will list the books that students are expected to read before they come up to Cambridge or Oxford for the first time. If you dip into some of these books you will get an idea of the sort of information you will be tackling if you study the subject. In addition, if you have time to visit Cambridge or Oxford again, you could spend the afternoon in the university bookshop (Blackwell's in Oxford or Heffers in Cambridge). The staff at both bookshops will be very familiar with the texts used by undergraduates. Of course, if you know any current undergraduates at either university, discuss their work with them. It might also be an idea to read books on your subject from the Oxford University Press's *Very Short Introduction* series, which usually give a good overview. The *London Review of Books* is also a good source.

Collecting this information will boost your confidence and reassure you about your subject decision. Remember, in order to argue your case at interview, and to cope with the workload if you get a place, you must be deeply committed to your subject.

Recommended reading

On the following pages is a list of suggested books and films that may help you to start your research. This list is not definitive and not officially endorsed by the Oxbridge faculties. As already stated, most faculties will have a recommended reading list on their websites and you should be familiar with this.

If you need further ideas, consult the list below. Don't feel you must read every book on this list either. Dip into one or two to start with and see what particularly interests you. If your subject is not included here, or if you want to find out more, ask your teacher at your school or college for further guidance.

Archaeology and anthropology

Social anthropology

- Fox, K., *Watching the English*, Hodder & Stoughton, 2007.
- Keesing, R. and M. Strathern, *Cultural Anthropology*, 2007.
- Monaghan, J. and P. Just, *Social and Cultural Anthropology: A Very Short Introduction*, OUP, 2000.

Biological anthropology

- Clack, T., *Ancestral Roots: Modern Living and Human Evolution*, Palgrave Macmillan, 2008.
- Lewin, R., *Human Evolution: An Illustrated Introduction*, Blackwell, 2005.

Archaeology

- Gamble, C., *Archaeology: The Basics*, Routledge, 2000.
- Diamond, J., *Collapse: How Societies Choose to Fail or Survive*, Allen Lane, 2005.
- Renfrew, C. and P. Bahn, *Archaeology: Theories, Methods and Practice*, Thames & Hudson, 2008.

General books

- Barley, N., *The Innocent Anthropologist: Notes from a Mud Hut*, Waveland, 2000.
- Carrithers, M., *Why Human Beings Have Cultures*, OUP, 1992.
- Dunbar, R., *Gossip, Grooming and the Evolution of Language*, Faber, 1996.
- Fagan, B., *People of the Earth: An Introduction to World Prehistory*, Longman, 2004.
- Gosden, C., *Anthropology and Archaeology: A Changing Relationship*, Routledge, 1999.
- Harrison, G.A., *Human Biology: An Introduction to Human Evolution, Variation, Growth, and Adaptability*, OUP, 1992.
- Haviland, W., *Cultural Anthropology*, Harcourt Brace, 2003.
- Hendry, J., *An Introduction to Social Anthropology: Other People's Worlds*, Macmillan, 1999.

- Keesing, R. and A. Strathern, *Cultural Anthropology: A Contemporary Perspective*, Harcourt Brace, 1998.
- Kuper, A., *The Chosen Primate: Human Nature and Cultural Diversity*, Harvard University Press, 1996.
- Layton, R., *An Introduction to Theory in Anthropology*, CUP, 1998.

Architecture

Also look at the reading list for art history.

- Curtis, W., *Modern Architecture Since 1900*, Phaidon, 1982.
- Davies, C., *Thinking about Architecture: An Introduction to Architectural Theory*, Lawrence King Publishing Ltd., 2011.
- Gelernter, M., *Sources of Architectural Form: A Critical History of Western Design Theory*, Manchester University Press, 1995.
- Le Corbusier, *Towards a New Architecture*, Architectural Press, 1946.
- Mallgrave, H.F. and C. Contradiopoulos, *Architectural Theory: An Anthology from 1871 – 2005* , Blackwell Publishing, 2010.
- Vitruvius, *The Ten Books on Architecture*.

Art history

- Baxandall, M., *Painting and Experience in Fifteenth Century Italy: A Primer in the Social History of Pictorial Style*, OUP, 1988.
- Beard, M. and J. Henderson, *Classical Art: From Greece to Rome*, OUP, 2001.
- Berger, J., *Ways of Seeing*, Penguin,1972.
- Boardman, J., ed., *Oxford History of Classical Art*, OUP, 1993.
- Camille, M., *Gothic Art: Glorious Visions*, Pearson, 1996.
- Campbell, S.J. and M.W. Cole, *A New History of Italian Renaissance Art*, Thames & Hudson, 2012.
- Clark, T.J., *The Painting of Modern Life: Paris in the Art of Manet and his followers*, Thames & Hudson, 1995.
- Crow, T., *The Rise of the Sixties: American and European Art in the Era of Dissent*, Laurence King, 1996.
- Elsner, J., *Imperial Art and Christian Triumph: The Art of the Roman Empire, 100–450*, OUP, 1998.
- Gombrich, E.H., *The Story of Art*, Phaidon, 1995.
- Greenhalgh, M., *The Classical Tradition in Art*, Duckworth, 1978.
- Harbison, C., *The Mirror of the Artist: Northern Renaissance Art in its Historical Context*, Pearson, 1995.
- Haskell, F., *History and its Images: Art and the Interpretation of the Past*, Yale University Press, 1993.
- Hockney, D., *Secret Techniques: Rediscovering the Lost Techniques of the Old Masters*, Thames & Hudson, 2006.

- Honour, H. and J. Fleming, *A World History of Art* (7th edition), Laurence King, 2005.
- Johnson, G.A., *Renaissance Art: A Very Short Introduction*, OUP, 2002.
- Kemp, M., *Behind the Picture: Art and Evidence in the Italian Renaissance*, Yale University Press, 1997.
- Nochlin, L., *Women, Art and Power and Other Essays*, Thames & Hudson, 1989.
- Pollitt, J.J., *Art and Experience in Classical Greece*, CUP, 1972.

Another useful resource is BBC Four, which broadcasts a wide range of high-quality and engaging documentaries that provide a useful background for the aspiring art historian, such as *The Art of China* by Andrew Graham Dixon, *The History of Art in Three Colours* by Dr James Fox and *The Power of Art* by Simon Schama.

Biochemistry (Oxford)

- Alberts, B. et al., *Molecular Biology of the Cell* (5th edition), Taylor & Francis, 2008.
- Campbell, M. and S. Farrell, *Biochemistry* (6th edition), Cengage Learning, 2008.
- Dawkins, R., *The Selfish Gene*, OUP, 1976.
- Devlin, T., *Textbook of Biochemistry with Clinical Correlation* (6th edition), Wiley-Liss, 2005.
- Elliott, W. and D. Elliott, *Biochemistry and Molecular Biology* (3rd edition), OUP, 2004.
- Fox, M. and J. Whitesell, *Organic Chemistry* (3rd edition), Jones & Bartlett, 2004.
- Garret, R. and C. Grisham, *Biochemistry* (3rd edition), Cengage Learning, 2005.
- Jones, S., *Y: The Descent of Man*, Abacus, 2003.
- Lewin, B. et al., eds, *Cells* (1st edition), Jones & Bartlett, 2007.
- Lodish et al., *Molecular Cell Biology* (6th edition), W.H. Freeman.
- Stryer et al., *Biochemistry* (6th edition), W.H. Freeman, 2004.
- Sykes, P., *Guidebook to Mechanism in Organic Chemistry* (6th edition), Prentice Hall, 1986.
- Voet, D., J. Voet and C. Pratt, *Fundamentals of Biochemistry* (3rd edition), Wiley, 2008.

Biological sciences (Oxford)

- Aydon, C., *Charles Darwin: His Life and Times*, Robinson, 2008.
- Burton, R., *Biology by Numbers: An Encouragement to Quantitative Thinking*, CUP, 1998.
- Chalmers, A.F., *What is This Thing Called Science?*, Open University Press, 1998.

- Collins, H.M. and T. Pinch, *The Golem: What You Should Know About Science* (2nd edition), CUP, 1998.
- Coyne, J., *Why Evolution is True*, OUP, 2009.
- Dawkins, R., *The Selfish Gene*, OUP, 1976.
- Freedman, D., R. Pisani and R. Purves, *Statistics* (3rd edition although any edition would do), W.W. Norton and Company, 1997.
- Gribbin, J., *Science: A History, 1543–2001*, Penguin, 2002.
- Jones, S., *Almost Like a Whale*, Black Swan, 2001.
- Southwood, R., *The Story of Life*, OUP, 2003.
- Wood, B., *Human Evolution: A Very Short Introduction*, OUP, 2005.

Although Oxford does not specifically require any of these resources to be read, it does recommend that prospective students read *New Scientist*, *National Geographic* or any other relevant materials to stimulate interest in the subject area.

Chemistry

- Atkins, P. and J. de Paula, *Atkins' Physical Chemistry* (9th edition), OUP, 2010.
- Cotton, F.A. and G. Wilkinson, *Advanced Inorganic Chemistry* (5th edition), Wiley, 1999.
- Emsley, J., *Molecules at an Exhibition: Portraits of Intriguing Materials in Everyday Life*, OUP, 1998.
- Keeler, J. and P. Wothers, *Why Chemical Reactions Happen*, OUP, 2003.
- Morrison, R.T. and R.N. Boyd, *Organic Chemistry* (6th edition), Prentice Hall, 1992.
- Stephenson, G., *Mathematical Methods for Science Students* (2nd edition), Pearson, 1978.

Oxford also suggests that students may wish to read *Chemistry World* magazine and look at other resources on Chemnet (www.chemnet.rsc. org/home).

Chemical engineering (Cambridge)

- Azapagic, A. et al., *Sustainable Development in Practice: Case Studies for Engineers and Scientists*, Wiley, 2004.
- Duncan, T.M. and J.A. Reimer, *Chemical Engineering Design and Analysis: An Introduction*, CUP, 1998.
- Felder, R.M. and R.W. Rousseau, *Elementary Principles of Chemical Processes*, Wiley, 2003.
- Field, R., *Chemical Engineering: Introductory Aspects*, Palgrave Macmillan, 1988.
- Freshwater, D., *People, Pipes and Processes*, IChemE, 1998.
- Solen, K.A. and J.N. Harb, *Introduction to Chemical Engineering*, Wiley, 2010.

The final book in this list by K. A. Solen and J.N. Harb is particularly recommended by Cambridge as it states that many other published books are not of a suitable level for prospective students.

Classics

- Beard, M. and J. Henderson, *Classics: A Very Short Introduction*, Oxford, 1995.
- Davies, J.K., *Democracy and Classical Greece* (2nd edition), Fontana, 1993.
- Goodman, M., *The Roman World 44 BC – AD 180*, Routledge, 1997.
- Graves, R., *The Greek Myths*, Penguin, 2000.
- Herodotus, *The Histories*, Penguin Classics, 2003.
- Homer, *The Iliad*, Penguin Classics, 2003.
- Homer, *The Odyssey*, Penguin Classics, 2003.
- Irwin, T., *Classical Thought*, OUP, 1989.
- Parker, R., *On Greek Religion*, Cornell University Press, 2013.
- Ste Croix, G.E.M. de, *Class Struggle in the Ancient Greek World*, Duckworth 1982.
- Scullard, H.H., *From the Gracchi to Nero: a History of Rome from 133 BC to AD 68*, Routledge, 2010.
- Sophocles, *The Three Theban Plays*, Penguin, 2000.
- Thucydides, *History of the Peloponnesian War*, Penguin Classics, 2000.

Both Cambridge and Oxford recommend that candidates familiarise themselves with a range of prose texts including Thucydides' *History of the Peloponnesian War* (especially books 1–2), Plato *Republic* and Tacitus *Annals* (especially books 1–4) if they have not already been covered in an A level course.

In addition, it is also recommended that prospective students visit websites with excellent links to materials about the ancient world, such as the British Museum or the BBC Radio 4 archives, for example for the programme *In Our Time* covering material from Ancient Greece and Ancient Rome. There are also many social media sites that can be joined, such as Classics Confidential, Classics Outreach and Classics International.

Economics

Although economics here is subdivided into microeconomics and macroeconomics, both Cambridge and Oxford very much emphasise the synergies between the two 'parts' and require students to easily adapt and consider models both internal and external to the economy. It is also important to understand that in a degree course in economics a considerable amount of mathematical skill is required and so there is recommended reading in this area also.

Introduction to economics

* Chang, H.J., *Economics: The User's Guide*, Pelican Books, 2014.
* Dasgupta, P., *Economics: A Very Short Introduction*, OUP, 2007.
* Piketty, T., *Capital in the 21st Century*, Belknap Press, 2014.

Microeconomics

* Begg, D.K.H., S. Fischer and R. Dornbusch, *Economics* (latest edition), McGraw-Hill.
* Dixit, A. and S. Skeath, *Games of Strategy* (2nd edition), Norton, 2009.
* Morgan, W., M. Katz and S. Rosen, *Microeconomics* (latest edition), McGraw-Hill.
* Varian, H., *Intermediate Microeconomics* (latest edition), Norton.

Macroeconomics

* Heilbroner, R., *The Worldly Philosophers* (latest edition), Penguin.
* Mankiw, N.G. and M.P. Taylor, *Macroeconomics* (European edition), W.H. Freeman, 2007.

Quantitative methods in economics

* Bradley, T. and P. Patton, *Essential Mathematics for Economics and Business* (latest edition), Wiley.
* Lind, D., W. Marchal and R. Mason, *Statistical Techniques in Business and Economics* (latest edition), McGraw-Hill/Irwin.
* Jacques, I., *Mathematics for Economics and Business*, Pearson, 2012.
* Pemberton, M. and N. Rau, *Mathematics for Economists* (2nd edition), Manchester University Press, 2006.

Political and sociological aspects of economics

* Chang, H.J., *Economics: The User's Guide*, Pelican, 2014.
* Donkin, R., *Blood, Sweat and Tears: The Evolution of Work*, Texere, 2001.
* Dunleavy, P. et al., *Developments in British Politics* (latest edition), Macmillan.
* Hutton, W., *The Writing on the Wall: China and the West in the 21st Century*, Abacus, 2007.

British economic history

* Broadberry, S. and S. Solomou, *Protectionism and Economic Revival: The British Inter-war Economy*, CUP, 2008.
* Floud, R. and P. Johnson, eds, *The Cambridge Economic History of Modern Britain* (three vols), CUP, 2004.
* Hudson, P., *The Industrial Revolution*, Hodder, 1992.
* Mathias, P., *The First Industrial Nation*, Routledge, 2001.

UK, European and world history

- Diamond, J., *Guns, Germs and Steel*, Vintage, 2005.
- Hobsbawm, E., *Age of Extremes: The Short Twentieth Century 1914–1991*, Abacus, 1995.
- Landes, D.S., *The Wealth and Poverty of Nations: Why Are Some So Rich and Others So Poor?*, Norton, 1999.
- Mazower, M., *Dark Continent: Europe's Twentieth Century*, Penguin, 2008.
- Thomas, D. and A. Goudie, eds, *The Dictionary of Physical Geography* (3rd edition), Blackwell, 2000.

Both universities stress the importance of being able to relate economic theory to modern, relevant and up-to-date information. As such they recommend that prospective students regularly read *The Economist* as well as quality newspapers for stories of economic interest.

English

Your personal statement should identify your knowledge and appreciation of authors outside those of the English A level syllabus. It is sensible also to display an interest in different genres and periods; a student who only referred to twentieth-century American literary texts would not be overly impressive. You should not simply be reeling names off but explaining why your chosen authors mean so much to you. Also, if you display an interest in the work of an author it is only sensible to have read more than one work by him or her and to have considered the cultural context in which he or she wrote.

- Barry, P., *Beginning Theory: An Introduction to Literary and Cultural Theory*, Manchester University Press, 2009.
- Bate, J., *The Soul of the Age: Life, Mind and World of William Shakespeare*, Viking, 2008.
- Culler, J., *Literary Theory: A Very Short Introduction*, OUP, 2011.
- Culler, J., *On Deconstruction: Theory and Criticism after Structuralism*, Routledge, 2008.
- Culler, J., *Structuralist Poetics*, Routledge, 2002.
- Daiches, D., *Critical Approaches to English Literature*, Kessinger, 2007.
- Eagleton, T., *Literary Theory: An Introduction*, University of Minnesota Press, 1983.
- Eagleton, T., *The English Novel: An Introduction*, Blackwell Publishing, 2005.
- Guerin, W.L. et al., *A Handbook of Approaches to Literature*, OUP, 2010.
- Hopkins, C., *Thinking About Texts: An Introduction to English Studies*, Palgrave Macmillan, 2009.
- Kerrigan, J., *Revenge Tragedy: From Aeschylus to Armageddon*, Clarendon Press, 1997.

- *Norton Anthology of Poetry, The*, W.W. Norton & Co, 2005.
- Nuttall, A.D., *Why Does Tragedy Give Pleasure?*, OUP, 2001.
- Nuttall, A.D., *A New Mimesis*, Methuen, 1983.
- Young, T., *Studying English Literature: A Practical Guide*, CUP, 2008.

History

The key piece of advice for would-be Oxbridge historians is to ensure that you have read widely around your A level topics. You need to show an awareness of recent historical debate and to understand different interpretations of the same events. The books listed below either deal with historiography or are particularly well written and deserve attention.

- Bartlett, R., *The Making of Europe: Conquest, Colonization and Cultural Change, 950–1350*, Penguin, 1994.
- Blanning, T., *Pursuit of Glory: Europe 1648–1815*, Penguin, 2008.
- Burleigh, M., *Earthly Powers*, Harper Perennial, 2006.
- Cannadine, D., *In Churchill's Shadow*, Penguin, 2003.
- Davies, C.S.L., *Peace, Print and Protestantism 1450–1558*, Paladin, 1977.
- Elton, G., *The Practice of History*, Wiley-Blackwell, 2001.
- Evans, R.J., *In Defence of History*, Granta, 2001.
- Ferguson, N., *Civilization*, Penguin, 2011.
- Hobsbawm, E., and T. Ranger, eds, *The Invention of Tradition*, Cambridge University Press, 1983.
- Hobsbawm, E., *On History*, Weidenfeld and Nicolson, 1997.
- Judt, T., *Postwar: A History of Europe since 1945*, Vintage, 2010.
- Mazower, M., *Dark Continent: Europe's Twentieth Century*, Penguin, 1999.
- Nasar, S., *Grand Pursuit: The Story of the People who Made Modern Economics*, Fourth Estate, 2012.
- Pagden, A., *The Enlightenment and Why it Still Matters*, OUP, 2013.
- Worden, B., *Roundhead Reputations*, Penguin, 2002.

Students would also be advised to search out relevant articles in the *London Review of Books*, *Literary Review* and *History Today*.

Law

- Appleton, C., *Life after Life Imprisonment*, OUP, 2010.
- Berlins, M. and C. Dyer, *The Law Machine*, Penguin, 2000.
- Lord Denning, *The Discipline of Law*, OUP, 1979.
- De Schutter, O., *International Human Rights Law: Cases, Materials, Commentary*, CUP, 2010.
- Griffith, J.A.G., *The Politics of the Judiciary*, Fontana, 2010.

- Grove, T., *The Juryman's Tale*, Bloomsbury, 2000.
- Grove, T., *The Magistrate's Tale*, Bloomsbury, 2003.
- Holland, J.A. and J.S. Webb, *Learning Legal Rules*, OUP, 2010.
- Klarman, M.J., *Brown v. Board of Education and the Civil Rights Movement*, OUP, 2007.
- McBride, N., *Letters to a Law Student*, Longman, 2010.
- McLeod, I., *Legal Method*, Palgrave Macmillan, 2011.
- Pritchard, J., *The New Penguin Guide to the Law*, Penguin, 2004.
- Shaw, M., *International Law*, CUP, 2008.
- Smith, A.T.H., *Glanville Williams: Learning the Law*, Sweet & Maxwell, 2010. (This is a popular introductory book. It will not give you any specific, substantive legal knowledge, but it will provide you with useful information ranging from how to read cases to what the abbreviations mean.)
- Vidal, J., *McLibel: Burger Culture on Trial*, Pan Books, 1997.
- Waldron, J., *The Law*, Routledge, 1990.

Linguistics

- Akmajian, A., *Linguistics: An Introduction to Language and Communication*, MIT Press, 2001.
- Atkinson, M. et al., *Foundations of General Linguistics*, Unwin Hyman, 1988.
- Fromkin, V. et al., *An Introduction to Language*, Thomson/Heinle, 2003.
- Murray, N., *Writing Essays in English Language and Linguistics: Principles, Tips and Strategies for Undergraduates*, CUP, 2012.
- Newmeyer, F.J., ed., *Linguistics: The Cambridge Survey*, CUP, 1998.
- Pinker, S., *The Language Instinct*, William Morrow and Company, 1994.
- Radford, A., *Linguistics: An Introduction*, CUP, 1999.

Management

- Dixit, A. and B. Nalebuff, *Thinking Strategically: The Competitive Edge in Business, Politics, and Everyday Life*, W.W. Norton and Co., 1991.
- Handy, C., *Understanding Organisations* (4th edition), Penguin, 1993.
- McCraw, T.K., *Creating Modern Capitalism: How Entrepreneurs, Companies, and Countries Triumphed in Three Industrial Revolutions*, Harvard Business School Press, 1998.
- Pfeffer, J., *The Human Equation: Building Profits by Putting People First*, Harvard Business School Press, 1998.
- Pfeffer, J. and R. Sutton, *Hard Facts, Dangerous Half-Truths and Total Nonsense: Profiting from Evidence-Based Management*, Harvard Business School Press, 2006.
- Tedlow, R., *New and Improved: The Story of Mass Marketing in America*, McGraw-Hill, 1996.

Mathematics

- Gower, T., *Mathematics: A Very Short Introduction*, OUP, 2002.
- Körner, Tom W., *The Pleasures of Counting*, CUP, 1996.
- Petzold, C., *The Annotated Turing*, Wiley Publishing, 2008.
- Russell, B., *Introduction to Mathematical Philosophy*, George Allen and Unwin, 1919.
- Sivia, D.S. and S.G. Rawlings, *Foundations of Science Mathematics*, OUP, 1999.

Elementary mathematics

- Foster, P.C., *Easy Mathematics for Biologists*, CRC, 1999.
- Huff, D., *How to Lie with Statistics*, Penguin, 1991.
- Rowntree, D., *Statistics Without Tears – an Introduction for Non-mathematicians*, Penguin, 2000.

Medicine

- Asimov, I., *New Guide to Science*, Penguin, 1993.
- Bryson, B., *A Short History of Nearly Everything*, Black Swan, 2004.
- Calvin, W.H. and G. Ojemann, *Conversations with Neil's Brain*, Basic Books, 1995.
- Greenfield, S., *The Human Brain: A Guided Tour*, Weidenfeld & Nicolson, 1997.
- Goldacre, B., *Bad Science*, Fourth Estate, 2008.
- Goldacre, B., *Bad Pharma*, Fourth Estate, 2012.
- Jeffreys, D., *Aspirin*, Bloomsbury, 2005.
- Konner, Dr M., *The Trouble with Medicine*, BBC Books, 1993.
- Medawar, P.B., *Advice to a Young Scientist*, Basic Books, 1981.
- Noble, D., *The Music of Life: Biology Beyond Genes*, OUP, 2008.
- Nuland, S., *How We Die*, Vintage, 1997.
- Nuland, S., *How We Live*, Vintage, 1998.
- Revill, J., *Everything You Need to Know about Bird Flu*, Rodale, 2005.
- Ridley, M., *Genome*, Fourth Estate, 2000.
- Sacks, O., *The Man Who Mistook His Wife for a Hat*, Picador, 2011.
- Seedhouse, D. and L. Lovett, *Practical Medical Ethics*, Wiley-Blackwell, 1992.
- Thomas, L., *The Youngest Science*, Penguin, 1995.
- Watson, J., *DNA: The Secret of Life*, Arrow, 2004.
- Weatherall, D.J., *Science and the Quiet Art*, W.W. Norton & Co., 1995.
- Wilham, Dr D., *Body Story*, Channel 4 Books, 1998.

Modern languages

French: reading

- Simone de Beauvoir, *L'Invitée*.
- Samuel Beckett, *En attendant Godot*.
- Albert Camus, *Caligula* or *La Chute*.
- Marie Cardinal, *La Clé sur la Porte*.
- Marguerite Duras, *Moderato Cantabile*.
- Gustave Flaubert, *Trois Contes*.
- André Gide, *La Porte étroite*.
- Julien Gracq, *Le Rivage des Syrtes*.
- Victor Hugo, *Le Dernier jour d'un condamné*.
- Guy de Maupassant, *Bel-Ami*.
- Molière, *Le Misanthrope*.
- Marcel Proust, *Du Côté de chez Swann*.
- Jean Racine, *Phèdre* or *Bérénice*.
- Alain Robbe-Grillet, *La Jalousie*.
- François de La Rochefoucauld, *Maximes*.
- Jean-Paul Sartre, *La Nausée*.
- Stendhal, *Le Rouge et le Noir*.
- Voltaire, *Candide* or *Micromegas* (short story).

French: films

François Truffaut, Robert Bresson, André Téchiné, Eric Rohmer and Louis Malle are important figures in French cinema. Read the following texts if possible:

- Bresson, *Notes Sur le Cinématographe*.
- Truffaut, *Les Films de Ma Vie*.

German: reading

- Heinrich Böll, *Die verlorene Ehre der Katharina Blum*.
- Bertolt Brecht, *Der kaukasischer Kreidekreis*; *Mutter Courage*.
- Friedrich Dürrenmatt, *Die Physiker*; *Der Besuch der alten Dame*.
- Max Frisch, *Andorra*.
- Günther Grass, *Die Blechtrommel*; *Katz und Maus*.
- Franz Kafka, *Die Verwandlung*; *Sämtliche Erzählungen*.
- Thomas Mann, *Tonio Kröger*; *Der Tod in Venedig*.
- Bernhard Schlink, *Der Vorleser*.
- Patrick Süskind, *Das Parfum*; *Die Taube*.

German: art

Taschen books are readily available and cheap. Read in English or German. Books are available on the following subjects:

- Bauhaus

- Expressionism
- Wiener Werkstätte.

German: films

Films about the Second World War:

- *Das Boot*
- *Europa, Europa*
- *Die Fälscher*
- *Heimat*
- *Sophie Scholl*
- *Der Untergang.*

Films about the former East Germany:

- *Goodbye Lenin!*
- *Der Himmel über Berlin*
- *Das Leben der Anderen*
- *Sonnenallee*
- *Der Tunnel.*

Italian: reading

- Italo Calvino, *Se una notte d'inverno un viaggiatore.*
- Natalia Ginzburg, *Lessico famigliare.*
- Giuseppe Tomasi di Lampedusa, *Il gattopardo.*
- Primo Levi, *Se questo è un uomo.*
- Luigi Pirandello, *Sei personaggi in cerca d'autore.*
- Leonardo Sciascia, *A ciascuno il suo.*
- Italo Svevo, *La coscienza di Zeno.*

Italian: films

- *Il Gattopardo*
- *Ladri di Bicilette*
- *Roma, citta aperta*
- *Il vangelo secondo Matteo*

Portuguese: reading

- Lloyd, J. and C. Sousa, *Basic Portuguese: A Grammar and Workbook*, Routledge, 2003.
- Hutchison, A. and J. Lloyd, *An Essential Grammar*, Routledge, 2003.
- Tyson-Ward, S., *Portuguese Verbs and Essentials of Grammar: A Practical Guide to the Mastery of Portuguese*, Passport Books, 1997.
- Whitlam, J., *Modern Brazilian Portuguese Grammar*, Routledge, 2017.

Russian: reading

- Anna Akhmatova, *Requiem*.
- Iosif Brodsky, *Collected Poems in English 1972–1999*.
- Mikhail Bulgakov, *The Master and Margarita*.
- Ivan Bunin, *Life of Arseniev*.
- Anton Chekhov, *Uncle Vanya*.
- Fyodor Dostoevsky, *The Brothers Karamazov*; *Notes from the Underground*.
- Nikolai Gogol, *Taras Bulba*; *Diary of a Madman*.
- Mikhail Lermontov, *A Hero of our Time*.
- Boris Pasternak, *Doctor Zhivago*.
- Alexander Pushkin, *Eugene Onegin*.
- Aleksandr Solzhenitsyn, *One Day in the Life of Ivan Denisovich*.
- Leo Tolstoy, *Anna Karenina*.
- Ivan Turgenev, *A Month in the Country*.

Spanish: reading

- *Lazarillo de Tormes*.
- Leopoldo Alas, *La Regenta*.
- Pedro Calderón de la Barca, *La Vida es Sueño*.
- Pio Baroja, *El árbol de la Ciencia*.
- Camilo José Cela, *La Familia de Pascual Duarte*; *La Colmena*.
- Miguel de Cervantes, *El Quijote*.
- Julio Cortázar, *Rayuela*.
- Miguel Delibes, *Cinco Horas con Mario*.
- Rafael Sánchez Ferlosio, *El Jarama*.
- Carmen Martín Gaite, *Lo Raro es Vivir*.
- Juan Goytisolo, *Señas de Identidad*.
- Mario Vargas Llosa, *La Tía Julia y el escribidor*.
- Federico García Lorca, *Poeta en Nueva York*; *La Casa de Bernarda Alba*.
- Carlos Marcial, *El Surrealismo y Cuatro Poetas de la Generación del 27: Ensayo Sobre Extensión y Límites del Surrealismo en la Generación del 27*.
- Javier Marías, *Corazón Tan Blanco*.
- Gabriel García Márquez, *Cien Años de Soledad*.
- Luis Martin-Santos, *Tiempo de Silencio*.
- Ana María Matute, *Olvidado Rey Gudú*.
- Eduardo Mendoza, *La Ciudad de los Prodigios*.
- Pablo Neruda, *Confieso Que he Vivido*.
- Fernando de Rojas, *La Celestina*.
- Miguel de Unamuno, *La Tía Tula*.

Spanish: films

- Pedro Almodóvar, *Todo Sobre mi Madre*

- Jaime Chávarri, *Las Bicicletas son Para el Verano*
- Víctor Erice, *El Espíritu de la Colmena*
- Alejandro González Iñárritu, *Amores Perros*
- Carlos Saura, *Cría Cuervos; La Caza; Elisa, Vida Mía.*

Music

In addition to reading you should become familiar with the Dover scores of string quartets and symphonies by Haydn, Mozart and Beethoven. Aim to get to know several quartets and symphonies by all three composers.

- Aldwell, E. and C. Schachter, *Harmony and Voice Leading* (3rd edition), Wadsworth Publishing Co., 2002.
- Bohlman, P., *World Music: A Very Short Introduction*, OUP, 2002.
- Caplin, W.E., *Classical Form: A Theory of Formal Functions for the Instrumental Music of Haydn, Mozart, and Beethoven*, OUP, 1998. (This will be invaluable, not only for your analysis studies but also for your understanding of classical-period harmony.)
- Clayton, M., T. Herbert and R. Middleton, eds, *The Cultural Study of Music: A Critical Introduction*, Routledge, 2003.
- Cook, N., *A Guide to Musical Analysis*, OUP, 1994.
- Cook, N., *Music: A Very Short Introduction*, OUP, 2000.
- Ledbetter, D., ed., *Continuo Playing According to Handel*, Clarendon Press, 1990.
- Morris, R.O. and H. Ferguson, *Preparatory Exercises in Score Reading*, OUP, 1931.
- Parker, R., ed., *The Oxford Illustrated History of Opera*, OUP, 1994.
- Ross, A., *The Rest is Noise*, Fourth Estate, 2008.
- *The New Harvard Dictionary of Music*, Harvard University Press, 1986; or *The Grove Concise Dictionary of Music*, Macmillan, 1988. (Both are useful reference books.)

Harmony and counterpoint

Play and study the following.

- *The Chorale Harmonisations of J.S. Bach*. Recommended edition: Breitkopf and Härtel, ed. B.F. Richter; less good but adequate: Chappell, ed. Albert Riemenschneider.
- 'Fugal Expositions' by J.S. Bach in *The Well-Tempered Clavier* (the '48'). Recommended edition: Associated Board, ed. Richard Jones.
- *Schubert Lieder*. Recommended edition: Dover (either *Schubert's Songs to Texts by Goethe* or *Complete Song Cycles*). The lieder of Beethoven, Mendelssohn and Schumann are also recommended for your attention.
- *Renaissance polyphony*. Listen to some of the many fine recordings of the music of Palestrina and his contemporaries (the Gimell and Hyperion labels are a rich source).

Natural science (Cambridge)

Biology of cells

- Alberts, B. et al., *Molecular Biology of the Cell*, Taylor & Francis, 2008.

Chemistry

- Atkins, P. and J. de Paula, *Atkins' Physical Chemistry*, OUP, 2009.
- Boyd, Robert N. and Robert T. Morrison, *Organic Chemistry*, Prentice Hall, 1992.
- Cotton, F. Albert et al., *Advanced Inorganic Chemistry*, Wiley, 1999.

Computer science

- Dewdney, A.K., *The New Turing Omnibus*, Computer Sciences Press, 1993 (reprinted 2001, Henry Holt).
- Körner, Tom W., *The Pleasures of Counting*, CUP, 1996.

Evolution and behaviour

- Barton, N. et al., *Evolution*, Cold Spring Harbour Laboratory Press, 2007.
- Dawkins, R., *The Ancestor's Tale: A Pilgrimage to the Dawn of Life*, Weidenfeld & Nicolson, 2004.

Geology (earth sciences)

- Benton, M.J., *When Life Nearly Died*, Thames & Hudson, 2005.
- Ince, M., *Rough Guide to the Earth*, Rough Guides/Penguin, 2007.

Materials science

- Ball, P., *Made to Measure: New Materials for the 21st Century*, Princeton University Press, 1999.
- Cotterill, R.M.J., *The Material World*, CUP, 2008.
- Gordon, J.E., *New Science of Strong Materials*, Penguin, 1991.

Physiology of organisms

- King, J., *Reaching for the Sun*, CUP, 1997.
- Widmaier, E.P., *Why Geese Don't Get Obese (And We Do)*, W.H. Freeman, 2000.

Philosophy

- Ayer, A.J., *The Central Questions of Philosophy*, Penguin, 1976.
- Blackburn, S., *Being Good*, OUP, 2004.
- Blackburn, S., *Think*, OUP, 2001.
- Blackburn, S., *The Big Questions*, Quercus, 2009.
- Cottingham, J., *Western Philosophy: An Anthology*, Blackwell

Philosophy Anthologies, 2008.
- Crane, T., *The Mechanical Mind*, Penguin.
- Davies, B., *An Introduction to the Philosophy of Religion* (3rd edition), OUP, 2004.
- Descartes, R., *Discourse on the Method and the Meditations* (many translations).
- Guttenplan, S., J. Hornsbym and C. Janaway, *Reading Philosophy: Selected Texts with a Method for Beginners*, Wiley-Blackwell, 2002.
- Hodges, W., *Logic* (2nd revised edition), Penguin, 2001.
- Hollis, M., *Invitation to Philosophy*, Wiley-Blackwell, 1997.
- Hospers, J., *An Introduction to Philosophical Analysis* (4th edition), Routledge, 1997.
- Hume, D., *An Enquiry Concerning Human Understanding*, OUP, 2008.
- Kenny, A., *A Brief History of Western Philosophy*, Blackwell, 1998.
- Mill, J.S., *On Liberty* (many editions), available with *Utilitarianism*, etc. in J.S. Mill, *On Liberty and Other Essays*, Oxford World's Classics, Oxford Paperbacks.
- Nagel, T., *What Does it All Mean?*, OUP, 2004.
- Priest, G., *Logic*, OUP, 2000.
- Russell, B., *The Problems of Philosophy*, OUP, 1997.
- Sainsbury, R.M., *Paradoxes*, CUP, 1988.
- Scruton, R., *A Short History of Modern Philosophy*, Routledge, 2001.
- Shand, J., *Philosophy and Philosophers*, Acumen, 2014.
- Warburton, N., *Philosophy: The Classics*, Routledge, 2006.

Physics

- Cullerne, J.P. and A. Machacek, *The Language of Physics*, OUP, 2008.
- Feynman, R.P., *Six Easy Pieces*, Penguin, 1998.
- Feynman, R.P., *Six Not So Easy Pieces*, Penguin, 1999.
- Gribbin, J., *In Search of Schrödinger's Cat – Quantum Physics and Reality*, Black Swan Books, 1991.
- Hawking, S., *A Brief History of Time*, Bantam Press, 1988.

For those with an interest in engineering

- Gordon, J.E., *Structures, or Why Things Don't Fall Down*, DaCapo Press, 2003.
- Gordon, J.E., *The New Science of Strong Materials*, Penguin, 1991.
- Petroski, H., *Invention by Design*, Harvard University Press, 1998.

Politics

- Curtis, M., *The Ambiguities of Power: British Foreign Policy Since 1945*, Zed, 1995.
- Elliott, F. and J. Hanning, *Cameron*, HarperCollins, 2012.

- Hasan, M. and J. Macintyre, eds, *The Milibands and the Making of a Labour Leader*, Biteback, 2011.
- Heffernan, R. et al., eds, *Developments in British Politics 9*, Palgrave Macmillan, 2011.
- McCormick, J., *European Union Politics*, Palgrave Macmillan, 2011.
- McCormick, J., *Contemporary Britain*, Palgrave Macmillan, 2012.
- Vieira, M.B. and D. Runciman, *Representation*, Polity Press, 2008.
- Woolf, J., *An Introduction to Political Philosophy*, OUP, 2006.

Psychology

- Carter, R., *Mapping the Mind*, University of California Press, 2010.
- Coolican, H., *Introduction to Research Methods and Statistics in Psychology*, Psychology Press, 1997.
- Freud, S., *The Psychopathology of Everyday Life* (various editions).
- Goleman, D., *Emotional Intelligence*, Bloomsbury, 1996.
- Gross, R.D., *Psychology: The Science of Mind and Behaviour*, Hodder, 2010.
- Hayes, N., *Foundations of Psychology: Introductory Text* (3rd edition), Cengage Learning EMEA, 2000.
- Hewstone, M., F. Fincham and J. Foster, *Psychology: British Psychology*, Wiley, 2005.
- Hogg, M. and G. Vaughan, *Social Psychology: An Introduction*, Prentice Hall, 2010.
- Pease, A., *Body Language*, Sheldon Press, 1997.
- Winston, R., *The Human Mind*, Chartered Institute of Personnel and Development, 2006.

Sociology

- Alexander, J.C. and K. Thompson, *A Contemporary Introduction to Sociology: Culture and Society in Transition*, Paradigm Publishers, 2008.
- Crompton, R., *Class and Stratification* (3rd edition), Polity Press, 2008.
- Giddens, A., *Sociology* (6th edition), Polity Press, 2009.
- Sennett, R., *The Culture of the New Capitalism*, Yale University Press, 2006.

TIP!

The Psychologist, a monthly publication of the British Psychological Society, has back issues freely available on its archive at www.thepsychologist.org.uk.

Statistics

- Graham, A., *Teach Yourself Statistics*, McGraw-Hill, 2008.
- Huff, D., *How to Lie with Statistics*, Penguin, 1991.
- Rowntree, D., *Statistics Without Tears – an Introduction for Non-mathematicians*, Penguin, 2000.

Theology

General

- Armstrong, K., *The Case for God*, Vintage, 2010.
- Dawkins, R., *The Blind Watchmaker*, Penguin, 2006.
- Dawkins, R., *The God Delusion*, Black Swan, 2007.
- McGrath, A., *The Dawkins Delusion*, SPCK Publishing, 2007.
- Shortt, R., *Rowan's Rule: The Biography of the Archbishop*, Hodder, 2014.

Biblical

- Bellis, A. Ogden, *Helpmates, Harlots and Heroes*, Westminster/John Knox Press, 2007.
- Clines, D., *The Theme of the Pentateuch*, Sheffield Academic Press, 1997.
- Lambek, M., ed., *A Reader in the Anthropology of Religion*, Wiley-Blackwell, 2008.
- Painter, J., *The Quest for the Messiah*, Abingdon Press, 1994.
- Vermes, G., *The Changing Faces of Jesus*, Penguin, 2001.

History and doctrine

- St Augustine, *City of God*.
- St Augustine, *The Confessions*.
- Duffy, E., *The Stripping of the Altars*, Yale University Press, 2005.
- Gunton, C.E., *The One, the Three and the Many*, CUP, 1993.
- McCulloch, D., *Silence: A Christian History*, Allen Lane, 2013.
- McGrath, A., *Reformation Thought* (4th edition), Wiley-Blackwell, 2012.
- McGrath, A., *Modern Christian Thought*, Wiley-Blackwell, 1995.

Further resources

In addition to the suggestions above, remember to:

- read around your subject in the press
- search for podcasts and videos
- check out blogs and online articles
- if possible, discuss your reading with friends, family and teachers.

Case study: Pippa, Oxford

When I am asked how best to prepare for Oxbridge, two things spring to mind: read and debate as much as you possibly can. I set myself the target of reading at least one book or journal article which was not set by my A level teacher every week throughout sixth form. I cannot say I achieved this every single week, but it was an excellent target to aim for. It definitely meant I had read far more by the time I walked into my Oxford interview than had I simply told myself I would do it 'when I had time'. There is never enough time, you need to make time.

In terms of debating, I mean more than just going to a debating society (though that is an excellent thing to do too!). I tested my ideas and thoughts about history, and particularly the historical periods I was studying at A level, with as many people as possible – even calling in favours from friends regarding connections they had to specialists in the field. I managed to secure an informal chat with a scholar who worked on 17th-century England and she helped me to identify alternative points of view, weaker areas of my knowledge and ways that I might tackle questions on them. This gave me a great deal of confidence as it allowed me to accept that there was no 'right' answer and that the way I approached thinking about a question mattered more than having a huge store of knowledge. She also reassured me that the interviewer would keep asking questions until they found an area where I had a lack of knowledge in order to see what I would do next. When that happened in my actual interview, I was expecting it and made extra effort to explain my train of thought. I'm sure that helped secure my place.

5 | Choosing your university and college

So you've decided that you want to apply. You're studying the right A levels, you are predicted or already have the appropriate grades and you've been reading around your subject. What next?

As an undergraduate, you may only apply to either Oxford **or** Cambridge, and therefore you need to decide which. You should try to make an educated choice; ideally, do your research and visit both, have a look around the various colleges and university buildings and absorb the atmosphere. Talk to friends who are currently at Oxbridge and teachers who have been there. You also need to understand the courses each university offers; for example, Cambridge offers natural sciences in place of physics, chemistry or biology; politics, philosophy and economics (PPE) is on offer at Oxford, while human, social and political sciences (HSPS) is on offer at Cambridge. A very good guide on some of the similarities and differences between Cambridge and Oxford universities can be found on the Oxford website here: www.ox.ac.uk/admissions/undergraduate/applying-to-oxford/supporting-an-applicant/resources-teachers/oxford-and-cambridge-similarities-and-differences.

Which university?

There are several reasons to choose one university over the other but the most important aspect to consider is whether it offers you the right course. Oxford and Cambridge agree that the most important decision a prospective applicant has to make is the degree they wish to study, not which university they want to apply to. Both universities are committed to recruiting the most talented students regardless of their background and both are world class in teaching and research in both arts and science subjects.

First, choose your course

It is essential to check that the university you prefer teaches the subject you wish to study. There are various subjects that Oxford offers that Cambridge does not and vice versa.

Subjects you can study at **Cambridge** but not at Oxford include:

- Anglo-Saxon, Norse and Celtic
- architecture
- Asian and Middle Eastern studies
- economics (as a stand-alone subject; at Oxford economics is offered only as a combined course with management, history or as an element of the PPE degree course)
- education
- human, social and political science (HSPS)
- land economy
- management studies (as a stand-alone subject; at Oxford you do management as a combined course with economics)
- natural sciences (at Oxford all the sciences are offered but not in the same combination)
- philosophy (as a stand-alone subject; at Oxford you do philosophy as a combined course such as PPE or physics and philosophy)
- veterinary medicine.

Subjects you can study at **Oxford** but not at Cambridge include:

- archaeology and anthropology (as a stand-alone subject; at Cambridge you can choose to do the subjects as part of the HSPS course)
- biochemistry, molecular and cellular (as a stand-alone subject; at Cambridge you can choose to do the subjects as part of the natural sciences course)
- human sciences (as a stand-alone subject; at Cambridge human sciences is incorporated into the HSPS course)
- the languages Sanskrit and Czech with Slovak
- Oriental studies
- philosophy, politics and economics (PPE)
- psychology, philosophy and linguistics (PPL)
- separate sciences (although you may have to take modules in other science subjects as well).

Subjects you can study at **both** universities include:

- classics
- computer science
- engineering
- English language and literature (Cambridge offers English)
- geography
- history
- law
- modern and medieval languages
- music
- psychology (Cambridge offers Psychological and Behavioural Sciences)
- theology and religious studies.

It is important to note that, although many subjects are the same, their components may differ between the two universities and you should take time to compare the courses in detail.

For more information go to the websites listed below:

* Cambridge: www.undergraduate.study.cam.ac.uk/courses
* Oxford: www.ox.ac.uk/admissions/undergraduate/courses

Course flexibility

At Oxford, most subjects include compulsory courses for the first year, and then give students the opportunity to choose options in subsequent years. At Cambridge, courses cover the subject very broadly in the initial years and then become more specialised within a wide range of options in the later years.

Comparing the Tripos system at Cambridge with the two-part system at Oxford can be another way to help you decide which university is better suited to you. One of the great attractions of Cambridge is the flexibility of its Tripos system (the name Tripos is said to have been derived from the three-legged stool that undergraduates in the Middle Ages sat on at graduation ceremonies). The Tripos system at Cambridge gives you the opportunity to gain a broad overview of the subject and to discover areas of interest before specialising later on in the course.

Each course, or Tripos, is usually divided into two parts: Part I and Part II. After each part there is an exam that counts towards your final undergraduate mark. A Part I can take one year (in economics, for example) or two years (in English). A two-year Part I is divided into Part IA and Part IB. Once you have completed Part I (A and B), you have the option of continuing to specialise in the same subject, or swapping to a related but different subject for Part II. There is also an optional Part III offered in some subjects, such as Mathematical tripos.

The exact details vary from subject to subject but in theory, this gives students quite a bit of flexibility, and there have been students who have studied three different but related subjects during the course of their three years at Cambridge and have come out with a First Class degree. In reality, however, you should not go to your interview thinking that you will be able to change courses easily. Admissions tutors, particularly those interviewing for humanities, arts and social sciences, will see this as a sign that a student is not committed to their subject, and give the place to someone who is. If students want to change subject when they get to Cambridge they have to work very hard at convincing their current director of studies (DOS) that they want to change for the right reasons. Then students have to convince the DOS in their new subject to take them on.

On the other hand, there are subjects where elongated undergraduate degrees are encouraged. Natural sciences and mathematics students have the option of adding a Part III, while engineering students take Parts IA, IB, IIA and IIB over four years, leading ultimately to the award of MEng.

The system works slightly differently at Oxford. As at Cambridge, students have to pass exams in two parts. However, students do not have to take examinations at the end of each year, as is the case in many Cambridge courses. The Preliminary Examinations (or 'Prelims') are taken at the end of the first year (apart from a few exceptions) and the Final Examinations ('Finals') are taken at the end of the third year. In some courses, such as Classics, the first set of examinations are called Honour Moderations (or Mods) but the structure for subsequent study remains the same. Most arts and social science undergraduates at the University of Oxford do not take exams in their second year; maths and science students take exams at the end of each year.

In general there are more courses at Oxford that are designed to take four years. The Joint Honours courses of mathematics and philosophy and physics and philosophy, as well as classics, take four years. Mathematics itself, physics and earth sciences can take either three or four years (your choice), but in the case of molecular and cellular biochemistry, chemistry, engineering and metallurgy, students are normally expected to progress to the fourth, research-based year leading to the award of a master's degree.

You should research the similarities and differences that apply to your particular subject choice carefully, and then be prepared to discuss your discoveries when it comes to the interview stage.

Case study: Silvester, Cambridge

What I really appreciate about studying at Cambridge is the opportunities I have been given to develop my passion for my subject, archaeology and anthropology. For example, this year I was fortunate enough to be able to participate in an excavation in Tajikistan. What follows is a report of my time on the dig, which also gives an idea of the type of work a Cambridge student may be expected to produce.

The archaeological site, Panjakent, is a mud brick city dating from the fifth to eighth centuries AD situated in the Sugd Province of north-western Tajikistan. The geography of the area is defined by snow-capped mountains (exceeding 5,000 metres in elevation), cut through by the high-velocity Zarafshan River. At Panjakent, the Zarafshan eventually incorporates a floodplain prior to its disappearance/evaporation in the deserts of Uzbekistan. The local climate is of a 'dry continental' nature, with warm summers, cold winters and limited precipitation. As a result, irrigation was and still is key to human settlements in the region, allowing for the cultivation of grain, the tending of orchards and grazing animals.

Until the expansion of Islam, the Zarafshan valley, together with the neighbouring Samarkand and Bukhara regions of Uzbekistan, was run by various semi-autonomous Sogdian polities. These can trace their origins back to the fifth-century Achaemenid expansion. As a result, the ancient inhabitants of Panjakent are associated with Iranian people, their Sogdian language being classified as a Persian dialect.

The city itself was in use at a time when trade along the 'Silk Road' was at its height. With regard to this, Russian archaeologists who worked in the region often interpret a situation in which Sogdian polities acted as 'middle-men', exchanging Mediterranean/Middle Eastern goods for Uighur (the indigenous people of what is now the Xiangjiang province of China) as well as Chinese trade items, from the Far East (Vaissière 2005). This is not only supported by Panjakent's strategic position along the east–west Zarafshan axis, but also by numerous Chinese and Arabic Texts – the writings of the Chinese Buddhist Pilgrim Monk Xuanjaung being such an example (Vaissière 2005). Furthermore, the uncovering of Sogdian texts, listing economic transactions (the exchange of Sasanian silver ware, alfalfa, Baltic amber for Chinese silk) found in places as far away as Kashgar, truly supports this merchant image, and suggests that the Sogdian dialect was the 'lingua franca' of the Silk Road.

This 'golden' Sogdian era lasted until the early eighth century, when the Arabic conqueror Said al-Harashi laid siege to various Sogdian towns as part of the spread of Islam. Thus, in the year AD722 Panjakent was besieged and burnt. The following centuries saw Persian/Sogdian culture becoming increasingly 'mixed' with Arabic, Muslim traditions.

The destruction (through fire) and relatively quick abandonment of the city has facilitated its superb preservation, uncompromised by human intervention. The easily erodible clay (transported by wind and colluvium) from nearby mountainsides was able to quickly cover the settlement area in the state in which it was left. This has helped keep streets, arches, towers, wall reliefs, carbonised organic material, and houses up to two storeys high sheltered from the elements. Thus when the site was rediscovered by Soviet archaeologists, Panjakent was nicknamed the 'Pompeii of Central Asia'.

The Panjakent excavations have been undertaken by the St Petersburg Hermitage museum every year since 1947. Due to this, almost 50% of Panjakent has already been uncovered, thereby allowing for the estimation that Panjakent was originally 20 hectares in size, with a population of 5,000 people. A lot of the finds and data obtained so far reflect the city's unique location and role in central Asia. For instance, the walled town and fortified citadel of Panjakent, together with further outposts extending eastwards along the Zarafshan Range, demonstrate how the Sogdians were in strong control of the trade caravan routes and high mountain passes. In addition, the uncovering of Buddhist texts, and wall paintings depicting Shaivist deities, show how Panjakent was incorporated in the cultural spread of ideas throughout Asia (e.g. Sogdians also operated as translators, for example, translating the Buddhist Sutra texts from the Indian subcontinent into Chinese (Vaissière 2005). Nevertheless, this year's substantial uncovering of funeral pyres once again suggests that Zoroastrianism was the main religion, thereby affirming the close Persian cultural link.

A major feature during the excavation was distinguishing deposited clay from clay/mud bricks, which formed the built structures of the town. As a result, techniques were significantly different from those used in British archaeology. For instance, this year the volunteers would frequently work with hammers and adzes in order to gradually 'knock' away naturally deposited layers from mud-brick structures. At the beginning it is often difficult to distinguish between the two; however, with practice one was able to gradually feel, and hear, the difference.

The Russian team stressed the importance of uncovering pottery, and every afternoon we occupied ourselves with the restoration of ceramic artefacts. This desire to complete the excavation with as many intact pieces as possible may once again have reflected the team's interest in typology, in order to identify different artefacts arguably coming from different cultural groups. This would highlight the importance of trade. However, it also shows how cultural-historical interpretations have a much stronger voice outside of Anglophone archaeology.

In the former Soviet Union, Panjakent's claim to fame was its elaborate wall paintings and frescoes. These were once again of great importance during this year's excavation, since a substantial number were uncovered. A lot of time was thus spent painstakingly cleaning, drawing, removing these images from uncovered walls and artificially preserving them through various chemical treatments. Since, however, Tajikistan is now independent, this raised serious questions about Russian and Tajik heritage. One was frequently confronted with the fact that Russian archaeologists were the first to discover Panjakent, at a time when Tajikistan was part of the Soviet Union – thereby explaining why the majority of frescoes are now exhibited in the St Petersburg Hermitage museum. At the same time, while frescoes uncovered today are required to remain in Tajikistan, both local and Russian academics still doubt as to whether or not the Dushanbe Museum is capable of ensuring adequate protection and preservation. This strengthens the case that such artefacts should be once again taken care of by Russia. From one point of view this would see the heritage value shift, from something as symbolic of Tajik/Persian/Sogdian identity, to a symbol of the project achievements of the Hermitage museum.

In terms of built structures, this year involved digging test pits near the Eastern Gate of the town. This eventually led to the uncovering of what was interpreted as two granaries and a house. During this process, geochemical surveying played a significant role, contributing to the identification of earlier destruction/burnt layers prior to AD722. Occurring on a small scale at the east side of Panjakent, these layers make clear 'earlier continuation' harder to identify, thereby raising the possibility that the built structures we uncovered could have originally had a different use.

In conclusion, Panjakent as an archaeological site stands out due to its strategic location in central Asia, connecting the Far East to the Middle East and Mediterranean worlds. It is also unique in that its destruction, abandonment and quick burial under clay deposits allowed for great preservation. This allowed our team to once again access a great amount of data.

Bibliography

de la Vaissière, E., *Sogdian Traders: A History*, Leiden, Brill, 2005

Other factors to consider

The location

Oxford is located about 100km (62 miles) north-west of London, with excellent links to the capital and the rest of the country by car, coach and train. It is a lively, medium-sized city with a total student population of over 30,000 (including students at both Oxford and Oxford Brookes). Most university and college buildings are located in the centre and are easily reached on foot or by bike.

Cambridge lies 88.5km (55 miles) north of London, off the M11 motorway, and is a 45-minute journey by train from the capital. There are also excellent rail links to Scotland and the north of England (via Peterborough), with direct regional services from Birmingham, the Midlands, East Anglia and the north-west of England. The city is also very well served by bus services to and from other cities. Stansted Airport is 48km (30 miles) away. The city has also become the centre of the hi-tech 'silicon Fen' industries. It is smaller than Oxford and this can make Cambridge feel claustrophobic for some, but there are plenty of open green spaces in this undeniably beautiful place.

The student mix

Oxford currently has an undergraduate ratio of 53% male and 47% female. The percentages for undergraduate students are 72% home , 9% EU and 19% overseas (undergraduates: 83% home; 17% overseas). The University's intake from state schools is 56% of undergraduates.

Cambridge's profile is very similar: currently 52% male, 48% female; a state school intake (undergraduates) of 63% with 67% domiciled in the UK, 12% in the EU and 20% of students are international.

Teaching

Teaching methods are very similar at both universities, as students will attend lectures, classes and laboratory work, as appropriate for their course. Unlike at many other universities, students at Oxford and Cambridge also benefit from one-to-one teaching from world experts in their field; the only difference is in the name: Oxford refers to these sessions as 'tutorials' while Cambridge calls them 'supervisions'.

Assessment

Students at Oxford and Cambridge are assessed informally throughout their course by producing work for their tutors/supervisors for weekly tutorials/supervisions. Formal assessment is almost entirely based on examinations, although in the final year of many courses one examination paper can be replaced with a dissertation. For certain subjects, such as music, additional coursework papers and performance options can replace examination papers.

At Oxford, the final degree classification result is usually based on the examinations taken at the end of the final year, though for some science subjects, such as biology, the final classification is based on results achieved in both the second- and third-year examinations. Cambridge students are assessed through examinations in more than one year of their courses.

Research standards

Oxford has more world-leading academics than any other UK university and was ranked number one in the 2014 national Research Excellence

Framework; 48% of Oxford's research was rated 4* ('world-leading') in 2014, while 39% was rated 3* ('internationally excellent'). It has consistently boasted the highest research income from external sponsors of any UK university (in 2015–16 40% – £537.4 million – of income came from this source), and receives the highest level of quality research funding from the Higher Education Funding Council for England (HEFCE).

Cambridge is equally blessed financially, and performance league tables consistently place Cambridge among the world's top-ranking institutions. Academics associated with Cambridge have been awarded more Nobel prizes in recognition of their research than any other university, nationally and internationally. In the Research Excellence Framework in 2014, 47% of the research submissions from Cambridge was judged to be 4*, while 40% was rated as 3*.

International reputation

In the 2016 Academic Ranking of World Universities published by the Shanghai Jiao Tong University, Cambridge was placed fourth globally for academic and research performance and Oxford was positioned in seventh place, placing both institutions at the forefront of the most prestigious universities in the world.

Availability of part-time work

Oxford offers opportunities for a limited amount of paid work within college, for which you may need your tutor's permission, and colleges sometimes offer employment during the vacations. The University Careers Service facilitates summer internship and work opportunities through the Oxford University International Internship Programme and on-campus employer events and fairs.

Cambridge states that since the university terms are short and highly demanding on students' time and intellectual capabilities, it strongly discourages students from taking on part-time work. However, as a Cambridge undergraduate, you will find it relatively easy to procure internships and holiday work if you are prepared to put enough effort into researching and applying.

Which college?

Your next decision is which college to choose. Many students are thrown into a complete quandary about this and at first sight it seems hard to know how to decide. Your college will be the centre of your academic and social life so it is worth putting a bit of thought into why you might prefer one over another. On the other hand, at both universities there is the very real possibility of being moved to another college before, during or after (in the case of Cambridge) the interview process.

So while you should put some thought into which college to apply to, you shouldn't agonise over it too much. Rest assured that whichever college you end up in, by the end of your first term you will think it's the best one! Detailed information on the colleges at both universities is provided in the College profiles section on page 172.

Oxford and Cambridge are comprised of 44 (38 colleges and six permanent private halls) and 31 colleges respectively although not all of them will offer undergraduate courses (currently there are 35 undergraduate colleges at Oxford and 29 at Cambridge). Oxford and Cambridge colleges are independent, self-governing communities of academics, students and staff. The collegiate system gives students and academics the benefits of belonging to both a large, internationally renowned institution and a smaller, interdisciplinary, academic college community. Colleges and halls enable leading academics and students across subjects and year groups and from different cultures and countries to work and socialise together. This system gives you the opportunity to discuss your work in college tutorials and seminars, over meals in the dining hall or in your college accommodation late into the evening, and it will provide you with the chance to establish a new circle of friends quickly, and to access a range of varied social and sporting activities.

Your college will have a senior tutor whose role includes general oversight of all undergraduate members of the college, although your academic studies will be directed by your department or faculty. The relatively small number of students at each college allows for close and supportive personal attention to be given to the induction, academic development and welfare of individual students. At some Oxford colleges each student has a college adviser, who is a member of the college's academic staff and will be able to offer support and advice. This person is almost always the student's personal academic tutor. At Cambridge, a director of studies has oversight of academic welfare, while a tutor can help with issues to do with finance or other personal matters. Colleges at Oxford and Cambridge may also have college counsellors.

Open application

If you cannot decide which college to apply to, it is possible to make an open application. An open application is where you do not choose a college; instead, you are assigned to one by the admissions board. Allocation is often to 'less popular' colleges; this does not make them bad colleges, simply colleges that have fewer applicants than others in the current cycle of applications. Both universities stress that making an open application in no way disadvantages you.

You may decide to make an open application if you really don't mind what your college life will be like. However, college life is such a great and unique aspect of Oxbridge that it's well worth at least putting some thought into it. As making an open application does not disadvantage you, don't be afraid to take this route if you really feel it is best for you.

If you decide not to make an open application, the next step is to narrow down the list of 29 undergraduate colleges at Cambridge and 35 colleges (and six permanent private halls) at Oxford to make your personal shortlist from which you will make your final choice.

How do I choose a college that is right for me?

You might consider any or all of the following factors when making your decision.

Does it offer the right course?

Not every college will offer every course offered by the universities. To find out which colleges offer your course, you can see a comprehensive list at www.ox.ac.uk/admissions/undergraduate/colleges/college-listing for Oxford and www.undergraduate.study.cam.ac.uk/colleges for Cambridge.

Do you want to be with a certain type of student?

A minority of colleges admit only certain groups of students, so if you want to be in a women-only college or with more mature or graduate students your options are limited.

Women only: Murray Edwards (formerly New Hall), Newnham and Lucy Cavendish at Cambridge.

Mature students (over 21 at matriculation) only: Hughes Hall, Lucy Cavendish, St Edmund's and Wolfson at Cambridge; Harris Manchester at Oxford.

Graduates only: Clare Hall and Darwin at Cambridge; Green Templeton, Kellogg, Linacre, Nuffield, St Antony's, St Cross and Wolfson at Oxford.

Does it have the right character?

There's no question that each college has its distinct character, whether it is highly academic, sporty or literary. Certainly, there is an element of 'horses for courses', if you'll pardon the pun. Being with like-minded students may make you work harder, but if you're the kind of person who would rather come out with a 2.i and have captained a sports team or run student societies than strive for a First, then you may want to pick somewhere that will be sympathetic to your aspirations.

Every year, Oxford publishes the Norrington table and Cambridge the Tompkins table (see pages 212 and 245), which rank the colleges in order of the number of First Class degrees achieved by their students in their final exams. This may give you some indication of the colleges' academic prowess. But beware of placing too much importance on this; colleges go up and down the tables at an alarming rate and those at the top of the tables one year may find themselves halfway down the next.

What are the admissions criteria?

The colleges all have different admissions criteria for the subjects they offer. In addition to the information provided by your UCAS application, some colleges will request some sample work and some will require candidates to sit a test at interview. If you are applying to Oxford, you should check your course webpage to see what is required for your course. At Cambridge, most applicants will be asked to sit a written admissions test, either pre-interview or at interview (there are exceptions, for example for mathematics and music). Colleges may also set their own additional requirements: some may ask you to submit a few examples of school essays, which may form part of the discussion at interview; check the college to which you are applying for individual requirements. For further details, see Chapter 8. You need to read the admissions criteria for your course very carefully and this may help you decide. You might find that there are admissions criteria you aren't comfortable with or colleges whose criteria particularly appeal to you.

Is the location convenient?

It's definitely worth locating your faculty buildings and lecture halls and seeing which colleges are nearby. This may sound faintly ridiculous when most of the colleges are located quite centrally, but you will be delighted to be able to fall out of bed and be at your lecture within 10 minutes of waking up after a hard night of working or playing. Bear in mind that a lot of people cycle around Oxford and Cambridge, so you may wish to consider cycling distance and walking distance.

Equally important is the college's location generally: consider what facilities are nearby, and whether you'd rather be right in the middle of it all or somewhere with more space to yourself.

Does it have the right facilities?

At this stage it might be useful to consult the alternative prospectus provided by students at each university (these can be found on almost every college website). Students already at Oxbridge are expert at discussing their own college's good and bad points. Once you have read them, you can eliminate colleges that don't have a particular facility (such as provision for sports or music). If you're unsure, contact the college directly for clarification. You may think now that all you will do at university is study, but you will be grateful that your college has extra facilities such as a decent JCR bar with ping-pong tables or playing fields nearby or a fantastic music venue. You may not necessarily want to row for the university but you might have fun rowing for your college, for example. It's worth doing a bit of research into what colleges offer before you make a decision.

Should I visit the college and check it out?

If you can, you should. Just a wander around the grounds and a look at the current students will probably give you a feeling that a college is or isn't right for you, and you are bound to prefer some over others. If you are unable to attend an open day, it is still possible to get a feel for a college by visiting at another time, although you may be restricted in terms of which areas you can explore. You can also ask questions of current students and professors. Each college has its own printed prospectus, which will provide more detailed information than its entry in the university prospectus.

Should I think about the accommodation?

You'll be spending three or four years at university and the standard and range of college accommodation varies quite dramatically from college to college. If the size and standard of room matters to you, a bit of research will pay dividends. What's more, some colleges offer accommodation for the whole of your course, whereas at others you may find yourself competing against everyone else in the private rental sector (and 'living out' can prove more costly as you will have to rent a flat or house for the whole of the academic year, not just during term time).

Should I make a tactical decision?

So you're nearly there. You're close to deciding on your choice of university and your course. Lots of people now try to make a tactical choice based on which colleges are less popular, less centrally located, less well endowed; the theory being that somehow they'll be easier to get into. But don't be fooled. There is no clever way around the system. Don't waste any time worrying about it.

Just because a college is smaller or out of the way (such as Girton at Cambridge) or has fewer applicants per place offered (such as St Hilda's at Oxford), you should not think that this will give you a higher chance of a place. Although a few colleges often receive less than one applicant per place offered (check the Oxford admissions website, for example), it does not mean that every direct applicant is offered a place, merely that many of their successful applicants come from the pooling system. Both Oxford and Cambridge put a lot of effort into inter-college 'moderation' to ensure that your chances do not depend on which college you applied to. You might be the only applicant to your chosen college for your chosen course and still not be offered a place. Choose your first preference based on where you think you might be happy, rather than on where you think you have the 'best' chance.

Case study: Ray, Cambridge

My experience of applying to Cambridge was similar to a roller-coaster ride. Having completed secondary school in Hong Kong (but with grades much lower than those I was capable of), I came to the UK to complete one-year intensive A levels at MPW Cambridge in English Literature, Sociology, Chinese and History. During that year I applied to Magdalene to read Law. After an intense but enjoyable interview, I waited for the result. Finally, on 3 January, a response: I had been pooled. In some ways this was more frustrating than a rejection as it meant yet more of an agonising wait, but on the other hand it meant I still had a chance. I had been deemed a suitable candidate. I remained hopeful. Then, sadly, on 8 January I was rejected. I was crushed.

I busied myself with my other university offers. I secured a place at KCL, winning the Dickson Poon undergraduate law scholarship, as well as an offer from a prestigious Hong Kong University. On results day I was thrilled to secure A*A*AA but this was tinged with sadness as I knew I would have been able to meet a Cambridge offer had I managed to secure one. After much soul-searching, I decided to take a huge risk. I rejected my university offers and took a gap year during which I reapplied to Cambridge. Thankfully, my gamble paid off and I received an unconditional offer.

I am now in my second year at Wolfson College reading Law. I am so glad I persevered. I love my college and my course, although it is very hard work (I am currently writing my fourth essay this fortnight!). I had heard lots of rumours about how little chance I had of securing a place: firstly because I had retaken my final school exams and secondly because I had been rejected the previous year. However, I am proof that these rumours are unfounded. If you are good enough, Oxbridge will take your application seriously. However, I do recognise that luck does play a part. I certainly took a big gamble and I would only encourage others to follow the same path if, like me, they could cope with a second rejection.

6 | Experience to support your application

Everything about your Oxbridge application needs to be convincing if you are to present yourself in the best possible light. We have already discussed the importance of being able to show that you have read around your subject and that you have delved far beyond the standard exam texts in your desire to find out more about your subject. But what else can you do that will set your application apart?

Work experience is essential if you think you want to study a vocational subject such as medicine, and it is important that you explore how you are going to organise this well in advance. It is naïve to think that you can arrange work experience at short notice; you will need to ask the advice of your parents, friends and school to help you arrange something worthwhile and you must plan ahead. Ideally you will have arranged several stints of relevant work experience. Be aware, however, that both Cambridge and Oxford are very academically focused.

It is important to keep your eyes and ears open to relevant events that you could attend in your area, newspaper articles that relate to your subject, blogs, radio programmes and any other sources of information that might give your application an additional dimension. A whole range of companies have in the past offered gap-year programmes; for example, the big four accountancy firms (PricewaterhouseCoopers, KPMG, Deloitte, Accenture), as well as IBM, the Bank of England and Rothschild. There is also The Year in Industry, which specialises in a broad range of year-long gap-year placements.

Increasingly, Oxbridge admissions officers talk in terms of 'super-curricular' activities that support your application, rather than extra-curricular. If you have done something to investigate and explore your interests beyond the school curriculum and if these activities are relevant to your degree course, this could provide substantial evidence that you are really committed to your subject area. This could be something that shows that you have really engaged with your subject. However, the main criterion remains academic excellence in the case of both universities.

Gap years

There has been much debate recently about the value of gap years. You will need to decide whether to make an application for deferred entry (this is when you apply while doing your A levels, two years in advance of your first term at university) or to apply a year after your school friends do, while you are on your year out. When making this decision you should ring your college of choice to discuss its preferences.

Can I take a gap year and defer my entry?

Some Cambridge and Oxford colleges do not like making offers to deferred entrants for some courses, simply because this means they have to commit a place before they have met competing applicants for the following year. In this case, colleges encourage you to wait a year and apply while on your gap year. If you ask their advice and make the most of your time out, you will find that most colleges are happy for you to have a gap year. In allowing yourself time to mature you may even make a better application and become a more attractive candidate. You should be aware, however, that if you apply pre-A level and ask for a gap year, you may be swaying your odds of being offered a place against you. It is always best to check with the college to which you are thinking of applying as to its policy before deciding on deferred entry or not.

Cambridge states that about one in 10 students take a gap year before starting their studies. It acknowledges that a year out can be a very useful time in which to improve skills, earn money, travel and generally gain maturity and self-reliance. It asks that you state on your UCAS application if you wish to defer entry. You'll almost certainly be asked about your plans at interview, so you need to be prepared to talk about what you hope to do and achieve in your gap year.

If you're applying for mathematics, most colleges have a preference for immediate entry as the skills you acquire in A level study can be quickly forgotten. However, if you're applying for engineering, many colleges generally prefer applicants to take a year out, to gain some experience in industry. You will not be able to defer entry for the graduate course in medicine.

What about Oxford? Some commentators will say that it isn't true that you can't get in if you take a gap year; for instance, in 2016 for medicine, Oxford made 4.2% of offers to gap-year students, with 2.8% of applicants applying to start post-gap year. This is an insignificant difference, demonstrating that taking a gap year may do your chances of getting an offer no harm. However, if you do opt to take a gap year, it is important that you choose to do something worthwhile which, ideally, emphasises your enthusiasm for the subject. Note that if you are applying to read history of art or fine art at Oxford, you will not be able to apply for deferred entry.

It's important to understand that each college has a different point of view about gap years and you must check the college's website to ensure that you know what its opinion is.

Some science tutors do not encourage deferred entry, largely because lack of practice can affect the mathematical competence achieved at A level or equivalent. They will, however, consider applications in certain special circumstances, e.g. where a candidate sponsored by industry is spending a year in a laboratory.

It is very helpful if all applicants planning a gap year explain briefly what their plans entail on their application form.

Work experience

What kind of work experience is best?

Any kind of work experience will be useful. Just getting used to the routine of working in an office, shop, restaurant or factory can come as quite a shock. Getting to work on time, dressing appropriately, getting on with your work colleagues, coping with boredom as well as stress are all valuable lessons in life skills.

Ideally, though, you should try to find work experience that relates to the subject you hope to study at university. Experience within the work environment is particularly important if you want to study a vocational subject, for example law or medicine. It is often only in a work situation that one can fully understand the stresses, responsibilities and pleasures that go along with a particular career, and only then can you really commit. Work experience can provide admissions tutors with strong evidence that candidates are committed, determined and have thought through their applications carefully. It can also provide you with a goal that keeps you motivated even through the toughest periods of study.

Apart from giving a real idea of where you might be in five years' time, work experience can expose you to ideas relating to the subject you are about to study in exciting ways. For example, if you want to study a science subject at Oxford or Cambridge, you might try to get a week during school holidays helping or observing at a laboratory where the scientists are working on something you are particularly interested in. You will be able to sit in on lab meetings and hear for yourself the problems that they face and the solutions they come to. You can also ask them personally for reading suggestions. No one will be as ahead of the game as they are, and this will give you some really exciting things to discuss at interview.

If you are really serious about studying and learning, find a way to get more information within the work environment. This will not only give you greater knowledge and confidence, it will also show the admissions tutors that you are really interested.

How do I organise my work experience?

It's never too early to start planning your work experience and the really ambitious student will aim to organise several sessions.

It may be difficult in the current economic climate to persuade companies to let you join them, but if you are persistent and imaginative you will find openings.

First, do your research. Search online to find out about companies and institutions that operate in your field of study. What about think tanks and other, more academic organisations or publishing houses that produce literature for your chosen subject?

Next, find someone in your chosen organisation to contact. Never send a letter to a company or organisation without finding an appropriate person to address it to; the more senior, the better. Letters that are sent without a specific recipient usually end up in the accounts department!

Write a winning introductory letter. Say exactly what you're looking for in terms of job opportunities, when you want to join and what you feel you can offer the company.

Attach the perfect CV. Brief, accurate, with no typing errors or grammatical or spelling mistakes.

Include a couple of references. Perhaps one from a teacher at your school and one from another responsible adult who has been impressed by your resourcefulness or past endeavours.

Email a few days after you've posted your letters. Quite often, your email will go straight to the relevant person if you type their full name with a stop in the middle and then their company name, e.g. joe.brown@ multinational.com. It is worth a try!

Follow up. If you haven't had a response, phone a week later and ask if they received your application. Be very polite. Good luck!

Case study: Julia, Oxford

I have always been very interested in archaeology and anthropology, but in the years preceding my university application I had mostly just read about the subject. However, in my first year of A levels, as I was deciding that the subject was one that I definitely wanted to study at university, I thought it would be best for me to get some practical experience to see whether it was definitely for me. I also knew that the practical element was important.

During that summer, I returned to my home country of China. My town is an ancient one with a great deal of history and tradition, so before I returned I wrote to my local cultural museum to see whether they needed any volunteers, especially English-speaking ones who could work with the many tourists from England and other countries where English is spoken. Fortunately, I was a good fit for the museum as they needed English-speaking guides. I was really in my element.

I also entered a competition for a travel fund that my college was running. I wrote about a special project I wanted to do, working in a village in Cambodia, observing the customs of the local ethnic group and reporting back on these. I was awarded a sum of money to pay for some of my costs and in return I had to write up some of my findings for the college magazine.

I found both of these experiences to be very rewarding and they really helped to prepare me for my course at university.

Events in your subject area

If you want to study a humanities subject, particularly a subject that is not vocational, keeping up to date with current affairs and events in your area is perhaps even more important than work experience. If you are really passionate about your subject, and dedicated to getting a place at Oxford or Cambridge, you should be constantly on the look-out for local events that are relevant to the subject that you want to study. Local libraries often host talks by renowned authors, the Royal Institution and the Science Museum in London host regular science lectures, the Royal Geographical Society organises regular discussions with eminent geographers and the Royal Academy of Arts has an ongoing art history lecture series. In addition, the universities in your area may hold lectures that could interest you. Speak to your teachers for ideas or go online to search for relevant events.

Ideas you might consider include:

- politics: go on a tour of the Houses of Parliament
- law: sit in the public gallery of your local magistrates' or Crown court

- history and archaeology: visit the British Museum or local archives to conduct some research in interesting areas
- art and history of art: visit every gallery and museum you can get to, including the galleries local to Oxford and Cambridge, such as the Ashmolean in Oxford and the Fitzwilliam in Cambridge.

You should also be aware of news stories that relate to developments in your field. Try to get as big a picture as possible of your subject: about how it relates to the rest of the world and why it might be important to know about it. Keep up to date with relevant blogs, social media and think tanks, read the newspapers online and listen to podcasts.

Case study: Rachel, Cambridge

Having been educated in London, I made the most of every opportunity to visit art galleries and exhibitions. At first this was not only because I was genuinely interested in furthering my knowledge about history of art, but also because I was aware that it would enhance my profile for my personal statement. The more places I visited, however, the more I enjoyed the visits in themselves, so that this side of my preparation for university became a pleasure in itself.

On family trips to Europe, I began to make a point of visiting art galleries and museums, such as the Musée D'Orsay in Paris and the Rijksmuseum in Amsterdam. These experiences really focused my mind on my chosen university degree course, history of art. My other subject areas, English literature and ancient history, really complemented my history of art A level and my teachers helped me by always encouraging me to make links between the subjects.

7| The UCAS application and the personal statement

So finally you are ready to apply. The next stage is arguably the one that causes students the most anxiety, until they are invited to interview of course. Your UCAS application will need to be submitted by the closing date for all Oxbridge applications of 6 p.m. on 15 October.

Let's go through the practicalities step by step.

Step one: preparing your UCAS application

The online form will be the same as for every other university: through the University and Colleges Admissions Service (UCAS). The UCAS form is a long document that is completed online and sent to all five of your chosen universities. It asks you to include details of your school(s), exam grades, employment experience, your choices of university and a personal statement: a 4,000-character written document that outlines the reasons for your choice of subject.

We will look more closely at what makes a winning personal statement later in this chapter.

You will need to specify a campus code in your 'courses' section. For most universities, this will be 'main site', but for collegiate universities such as Cambridge and Oxford, you need to state the college you wish to apply to from the list, or select 'Open' if you are not concerned about naming a specific college.

Step two: references

You will need to tell your school or college that you wish to apply to Oxbridge as soon as possible. If it has had lots of candidates who have applied before, the staff will be aware of what the colleges are looking for from the academic reference. If your school has little experience of making Oxbridge applications, the universities will probably be aware of this anyway and base their decision more on your personal statement and grades. But it is worth reminding your referees of the early deadline and making sure they'll have your reference ready on time. It is also worth remembering that although it may only be one person, such as a Personal Tutor or Director of Studies, who will be writing your reference, they will be talking to all of your subject tutors so it is in your best interests to keep them all very happy and impressed with your work.

You will also need to confirm that your school has submitted the Extenuating Circumstances Form to Cambridge, if you are eligible to apply through this scheme (see pages 17–18).

Step three: external tests

You must check the deadlines for any special tests that you may be required to sit, such as the BMAT or the LNAT. Oxford admissions tests will take place on 2 November 2017. The subjects at Cambridge that require a test pre-interview will also take place on the same day as the Oxford tests. See Chapter 8 for more information.

Step four: supplementary questionnaires

Cambridge

Once you've submitted your UCAS form, you will receive an acknowledgement almost immediately from Cambridge by email, along with its Supplementary Application Questionnaire (SAQ), which will require completion by the following week. The following link gives some very helpful advice about completing the SAQ, which can be a bit daunting for some students www.undergraduate.study.cam.ac.uk/applying/saq/faq. The link also contains the phone number for the admissions office and they are very happy to help students who have queries about how to complete the form.

The SAQ is filled out online, costs nothing to send and gives Cambridge more information about you and your application. If you do not have access to email you can contact the Cambridge admissions office for a paper version.

The initial email will give you all the information you need in order to complete the form correctly, as well as a deadline (usually the end of October).

The SAQ includes the following eight sections.

1. **Photograph.** You will need a passport-sized colour photograph of yourself, preferably in digital format, which can then be uploaded onto the form.
2. **Application type.** This section asks questions about your application, such as whether you have applied for an organ scholarship, if

you are taking a gap year or whether you are including the Extenuating Circumstances Form.

3. **Personal details.** This covers information about you and your own situation, such as where you live, what your first name is, etc.

4. **Course details.** Here you need to declare your preferred course options (if applicable); for example, if you are applying to read modern and medieval languages, you state which languages you wish to study in this section.

5. **Education.** In this section, you will need to give information about your school(s), such as class sizes and descriptions of any extra help you may have received towards your application.

6. **Qualifications.** In this section, you need to give details of your AS and/or A level modules (for any qualifications sat under the 'legacy' modular specifications), or their equivalents, and your marks.

7. **Additional information.** This is where you can add an additional personal statement. You will also need to discuss your career plans and give some proof of your interest in your chosen subject (for example, details of your work experience).

8. **Submission.**

The additional personal statement is the perfect opportunity for you to explain to the admissions tutor how excited you are about the course and it is also recommended that you give any reasons for applying to a particular college. Do take advantage of this extra space to make an impression.

Remember, however, not to duplicate anything you have said on the UCAS form. While your UCAS personal statement will be seen by every institution you apply to, the SAQ is for the admissions tutors at Cambridge only. This means that you can discuss particular elements of the course content or programme at Cambridge without putting any other university off. Make the most of this and explain why its course and teaching staff are perfect for you, and why you will fit in particularly well there.

Remember also that by mentioning your areas of special academic interest you will encourage predictable questions at interview, making it easier to prepare thoroughly.

Oxford

Your chosen college at Oxford will usually be fairly swift in confirming that it has received your application and it will write requesting any further information it requires. If you have made an open application, the college to which you have been allocated will respond.

Oxford no longer requires any additional forms, apart from the following two exceptions:

1. candidates for **choral or organ awards**
2. graduate applicants for the **accelerated medical course**.

Step five: submitting written work

Another way in which admissions tutors decide whether or not to interview you – if you are applying for an essay-based subject – is by looking at a sample of your written work. This is something that you need to consider once you have submitted your application form(s). By looking at your work, the admissions tutors will be able to assess your ability to research, organise information, form opinions and construct a coherent and cogent argument in writing. These are essential skills to have when studying an essay subject at Oxbridge, and the admissions tutors need to see that you have these skills, and the potential to improve.

Normally the work that you send will have been written as part of your A level course. It would not normally be expected to be more than 2,500 words. Make sure that you send a particularly good example of your work. Normally, this should be original work which has been marked by your teachers, but not corrected or re-written based on your teachers' feedback.

Do not, however, submit anything that could not have been written by you. Plagiarism will be very obvious to admissions tutors and could potentially get you into some tricky situations at interview, since submitted written work is often discussed then.

> 'The submitted essay is often used as the starting point for discussion in the interview. The essay can show us whether the candidate has the ability to argue and has academic confidence.'
>
> Admissions tutor, Cambridge

At Cambridge, each college has a different policy on written work, but you are more likely to be asked to send in work if you are applying to read an arts or social sciences subject. For example, to study HSPS at Selwyn College you will be required to submit two essays from relevant areas of your A level studies. The college will contact you directly if it requires work from you.

The Oxford prospectus gives clear instructions about what you need to send and when. Remember to inform your teachers in advance that you will need to send marked work.

If you have applied to Oxford, there are a number of courses that will require you to submit written work and you should check the course page at www.ox.ac.uk/admissions/undergraduate/courses-listing to see if it is the case with your subject. At the time of writing the following subjects require written work to be submitted:

- archaeology and anthropology
- classical archaeology and ancient history
- classics
- classics and English
- classics and modern languages
- classics and oriental studies
- English and modern languages
- English language and literature
- European and Middle Eastern languages
- fine art (portfolio submission)
- history
- history (ancient and modern)
- history and economics
- history and English
- history and modern languages
- history and politics
- history of art
- modern languages
- modern languages and linguistics
- music
- oriental studies
- philosophy and modern languages
- philosophy and theology
- theology and religion
- theology and oriental studies.

As with Cambridge, Oxford says that you should submit marked written work that you have completed over the course of your school or college studies. Each piece of written work should be no more than 2,000 words and should be submitted together with an accompanying written work cover sheet, which is available from the University of Oxford website.

Step six: await the call for interview!

See Chapter 9 for more advice on interviews.

How to write your personal statement

This part of the application process can be tortuous if you allow yourself to overcomplicate matters. The quest for the 'perfect personal statement' is like searching for the Holy Grail. There's no such thing; or, if there is, you will have died of exhaustion before you find it.

Before you start you might want to remind yourself of what admissions tutors are looking for.

'Cambridge is looking for very capable students, academically. It has to be selective as there is such stiff competition for places. On average, there are six applicants per place per year. Cambridge works its students very hard once they are here, so students need to be able to keep up with the pace and intensity. Cambridge wants motivated and committed students. Students need to spend time in the library and time thinking about their subject, so they need to be self-disciplined, well-organised and independent in their approach to their studies. Students need to be really interested in their subject. The advice is to pick a subject you really like and that you will really enjoy studying. Students should think carefully before choosing a subject.

'Oxford and Cambridge will look at prior grades. Good grades at AS [where legacy specifications are still being taken] are the best indicator of how students will perform. Regarding the personal statement, students should write about why they have chosen their subject and what they have found out about their subject outside school, such as research, public lectures, wider reading and work experience if applicable. Interviews are usually subject-based and problem-solving. Oxford and Cambridge want to see how students can work things out, how they think and whether they can work on their own.

'As part of their preparation for a Cambridge application, students should work hard. They should do as well as they can in their AS examinations [if taken], as they will need good grades. They should carry out independent research into their subjects. Finally, they should practise talking about ideas.

'With specific regard to international students, they need Band 7.5 in IELTS overall, with 7 in every component. By the time of the interview, applicants would need to be operating at Band 6, in order to be able to cope with the interview. International students should work especially hard on improving their English.'

Admissions Department, Sidney Sussex College, Cambridge

Think of things from the admissions tutor's point of view. What constitutes a great personal statement as far as they're concerned? Most candidates will present with excellent grades, predicted or actual, and glowing references from their teachers. They may also have taken specific admission tests or submitted written work. The personal statement is one more element that the staff can use to judge whether or not a candidate will be suitable for their courses. Most admissions tutors are keen to stress that all candidates' applications are viewed 'in the round'. Be assured that they are not expecting your personal statement to be a literary masterpiece or a work of stunning originality. They want to hear about you, and, in particular:

- what interests you about your chosen subject (and why)
- why you want to study the subject(s) you've applied for
- what you have learned or done outside your college or school syllabus
- which activities you've participated in that have added to your knowledge of your subject
- what you do apart from studying and why this is important to you, especially if it relates to your subject
- what you hope to do after you've finished university, if you currently have an idea.

Your personal statement should convey a fascination with your subject with evidence of good reading around and beyond your current studies. Work experience and what you have learned from it should be stated if relevant, especially for more vocational courses such as medicine. There should be no clichés in your personal statement and it should be a minimum of 80% academic content. You can mention your interests but Oxford and Cambridge don't really care about these, they just want to know that you are a well-rounded individual with diverse interests.

How to get started – some dos and don'ts

Do take time to submit something that is well written; i.e. the grammar and spelling should be correct, and you should write in sentences rather than a list. Ask your teacher or someone you trust to read it through carefully for mistakes.

Do go into detail. It's better to write in detail about a few topics than try to cite lots of interesting topics in a cursory way. Use examples to demonstrate your understanding of your subject so far and your desire to explore your subject further.

Do justify everything that you put down on paper. 'I found going to lectures at the LSE fascinating' only begs the question 'Why?'

Don't be tempted to just list the books that you have read; explain how reading them enriched your learning or excited you and made you want to read around your subject. Similarly, please don't tell them that you've read the obvious choices; when the twentieth economics applicant says that they've enjoyed *Freakonomics*, even the most well-disposed tutor will marvel at a student's lack of imagination.

Don't use long, convoluted sentences that are hard to follow; the admissions tutor may lose concentration before he or she reaches the end of the paragraph. Your writing should be clear, concise and precise.

Don't lie; you will be found out. If you are lucky enough to be called for interview you will be asked about your personal statement, and although you may not remember that you said that you read and enjoyed Nietzsche's *Twilight of the Idols*, the tutor interviewing you will. Be warned!

Don't be tempted to spend too much time listing your achievements outside school. No more than a fifth of your personal statement should be devoted to non-academic matters. Always try to demonstrate the relevance of your outside experience to your chosen subject; some of it may not be directly relevant but you are likely to have acquired useful, transferable skills that can be highlighted.

Another important consideration is the fact that your personal statement needs to be no more than 4,000 characters including spaces; this is a strict limit and so you need to ensure that you stay within this.

Many schools who are very successful at getting their students into Oxbridge adopt a fairly formulaic approach to writing personal statements. This is certainly one way of making your life a little easier and it might help you on your first draft. But remember, the key to writing your personal statement is that it should be personal; if you allow lots of people to read yours, you will receive lots of different opinions on its strengths and weaknesses. This can be confusing, to say the least. In the end, the best advice is to decide what you want to say and say it with conviction, in your own words, not those of your parents, teachers or other advisers. A typical personal statement takes time and effort to get right; don't expect perfection after one draft.

A model Oxbridge personal statement

There are no hard and fast rules about how to structure your personal statement. Below, however, is an example of how a well-organised statement might be written, with a synopsis, paragraph by paragraph. Below each synopsis is an example of a paragraph written by a candidate who did get a place at Oxford to study history and ancient history. Read the example carefully, but **do not copy it**.

The **first paragraph** should explain what sparked your interest in your chosen subject and why you wish to study it at university.

My passion for history and ancient history began, perhaps unusually, in the genre of historical novels, and the more general histories of those such as Norwich and Goldsworthy. These originally caught my imagination with their sweeping narratives of the Roman military world, and the world of late antiquity. This swiftly sparked an interest in more specific and more scholarly works, such as Syme's *The Roman Revolution*, which made me think differently about my assumptions of the power of individuals; in this case Augustus' role as the product of a talented new ruling class, rather than as a lone genius, as well as Scullard's *From the Gracchi to Nero*, on the challenges that Rome faced internally, as she externally became a superpower, and the necessary changes that the fall of the republic would later bring about.

In **paragraph two** you could discuss your particular interests in relation to your university subject choice. This is your chance to write about specific ideas you have developed as a result of reading beyond your A level syllabus.

What perhaps fascinates me the most is the way in which history, particularly in the distant past, is perceived by the succeeding generations of scholars, either through a difference of opinion in scholarly debate, or as a natural result of their environment. For example, Gibbon's demonisation of the Byzantine Empire, despite hardly being based in historical fact, is easy to understand in the context of the founding of the European world empires and the Enlightenment. Another example of this is the illusion of the founding of nations during the Dark Ages, and the tendency of historians to link the kingdoms of the Dark Ages with the modern states they were to form later on. Christopher Wickham's discussion of this phenomenon, in his *The Inheritance of Rome*, interested me immensely, as it made me question the blind belief I had shown before when reading the narrative history of this period. Perhaps in a less orthodox way, I was also heavily influenced by Terry Jones' protestations at the misinterpretation of Celtic culture in his study *Barbarians*. Though clearly it is difficult to make assertions about an empire without trusting your sources to some degree, it is nevertheless hugely interesting to read history from a contrary viewpoint.

The **third paragraph** can start to incorporate your personal experiences and how these have shaped your academic interests and choice of university subject.

Another stimulating part of studying both history and ancient history is the way in which one can see how different cultures have left their mark on a particular place. A good example of this, particularly in an ancient context, is in Tunisia, where the Phoenicians, the Carthaginians, the Romans, the Vandals, the Byzantines and the Arabs have all left their mark in the numerous sites, which are fascinating in the context of both ancient and modern history. To follow this up, therefore, independently, I undertook a week-long trip, in which I covered a route retracing Cato's last march, as well as looking at the ruins of Jugurtha's capital at Beja, which has since seen many conquerors, the Byzantine fortress at Kelibia, the remarkable Arabic city of Kairouan, and the Roman ruins at Dougga. One piece of extended work which I have done this summer has been on the Jugurthine war, and the other was on Justinian's capture of Africa from the Vandals. I have also used my trip to supplement my research, as well as to develop much further my knowledge of post-Almohad Tunisian history.

The **fourth paragraph** can include a brief summary of your extra-curricular activities. Remember, the admissions tutor will have to work with you for three years if you get in to his or her college. You need to come across as a responsible, interesting person who will be an asset to the college.

Outside of the academic sphere, my main passion is music. I play the double bass to grade seven standard, and have recently started the jazz double bass, as well as enjoying collecting vinyl records. I have also attended many Model United Nations meetings, which I have enjoyed and have excelled in, particularly those set in historical situations. I am also interested in journal-ism, in which I have done work experience, and I would hope to contribute to magazines at university. My reading, though mostly focused on history, also encompasses literature, and I am particularly interested in the great American novel, having been moved by the work of Fitzgerald, Hemingway and Capote, as well as the works of Leo Tolstoy, Maxim Gorky and Fyodor Dostoevsky.

Examples of successful Oxbridge personal statements

Through many revised editions of this book one of the things that stu-dents have said they found most useful are examples of really good personal statements. What follows, therefore, is a set of excellent personal statements collected over recent years. It is important to stress that it's worth reading not just the one specific to your subject. I hope that you can see several common factors that have impressed Oxbridge tutors.

- They explain clearly why the student wants to study the subject they have applied for.
- They are well written; there are no spelling mistakes or grammatical errors.
- They show that the candidate has the ability to think logically, critically and independently.
- They show enthusiasm and clear motivation through their detailed examples of how the student has explored their subject beyond the A level syllabus – by extra reading, through work experience or through attendance on extra-curricular courses.
- They show that the student has the skills necessary for studying at a university where the tutorial system reigns; that they are organised, committed and able to put forward a point of view and justify it.
- They show that the candidate is the sort of person the tutors would like to teach.
- If the student has gap-year plans, they relate them to the chosen area of study.

It is a useful exercise once you have finished a first draft to see how many of the above qualities your personal statement encompasses.

PPE – Oxford (3,990 characters, with spaces)

I enjoy engaging with issues where there is a debate to be had. Working for an MP showed me how rare certainty is, with complex economic and political questions being approached from a number of differing philosophical standpoints. One such discussion that often dominates modern politics is the question of the role of civil liberties in society, introduced to me by Foucault's disconcerting account of Bentham's Panopticism. Despite being built on the aim of common security, I saw the suggested intensity of the surveillance apparatus as an inevitable precursor to eradicating a free society.

While Kafka's The Trial revealed to me the importance of the judiciary in defending civil liberties, Bingham's The Rule of Law seemed to suggest this function has been limited through the USA's continuing war on terror. Despite the Supreme Court's extension of the writ of Habeas Corpus to Guantanamo Bay inmates in Boumediene 'v' Bush (2008) and the right against warrantless search to mobile technology in Riley 'v' California (2014), detention without trial and mass surveillance continue to be a problem. Even though some limitations to these programmes have been introduced under the Freedom Act, the USA's reactions to terrorism in a post 9/11 world still concern me. The US government appears to have forgotten that constitutional freedoms were intended to be universal, as asserted by Justice Kennedy in his majority opinion in Boumediene that they should continue to exist 'in extraordinary times'. Additionally, the precarious nature of such fundamental liberties being decided by a single swing justice on the Supreme Court through numerous 5-4 decisions is inherently troubling.

The development of international political mechanisms that promote and encourage economic security, such as Bretton Woods, must be an important aim of governments. While a member of the Perse's winning Target 2.0 competition team, I became interested in the impact of monetary policy on the global economy, with the recent unpredictability of Chinese and Swiss monetary policy highlighting a need for greater coordination between central banks. Governor Rajan's calls for greater international cooperation are particularly compelling to me, as it is EMEs that are often hardest hit by the spill over effects of these decisions. It is clear to me that the Bretton Woods institutions have failed to support balanced global growth through cooperation, instead they have furthered the influence of the US and its economic allies. The rise of the Renminbi as a second reserve currency, while a significant change with very uncertain consequences, offers little in the way of hope for EMEs. I still think substantial reform is required to give smaller economies an international voice.

As a Christian, I have struggled with the concept of mind-body dualism. In search for a defence of this belief I turned to Plato, but find his arguments lacking. I specifically question his recollection argument, stating that we must have innate knowledge of concepts like equality of length as these are not observable in the physical world.

I would suggest that despite these concepts not existing perfectly in nature we could still obtain them by extrapolating from observable data. Therefore, I see little basis for the suggestion that these ideas must arise from our recollection of knowledge of their ideal Forms. However, the notion posed in the affinity argument that there exist fundamental differences between the mind and body intrigues me. Through his half brain transplant thought experiment, Swinburne has largely convinced me that it is impossible to know everything about someone through physical obser-vation alone due to the existence of mental states, which one can only know through introspection. Although this seems to lead to the Christian notion of substance dualism, I remain interested in exploring alternative explanations of the mind-body problem as this idea is not yet immune from objection.

English – Oxford (3,999 characters, with spaces)

Literature has always fascinated me for its ability to transform human experience by expressing it with beautiful language. I love reading; being absorbed in another world found between pages of a book has continually supplemented my perceptions and own experiences and has allowed the pursuit of existences quite dif-ferent from my own. Here stems my love for Victorian poets: through the manipulation of words they escape an arts-sparse era to worlds oozing reverie and wonder: Browning's Renaissance Florence in 'Fra Lippo Lippi' or Arnold's 'dreamy woods' in 'The Stray Reveller'.

The threads that inter-connect works most captivate me, where one concept can be carried across centuries by the written word. That literature can transcend temporal bounds has impressed on me the desire to study it as distinct from my desire to read it, to value a work not only in its own right but for its role in a flux of convention, genre and style. Having read *The Mayor of Caster-bridge* this summer, the novel's importance is in its role as a 'trag-edy' while also having estimable independent value.

One reading sees Henchard's hubristic dismissal of his wife reflected in themes unravelled in *King Lear*; though separated temporally both downfalls are rooted in an early rejection of famil-ial bonds. Swept into the scandal of Hardy's challenge to sexual mores I read *Far from the Madding Crowd* and *Tess of the d'Urbervilles*, with Tess' descent to insanity again mirroring the underpinning theme of madness in *King Lear*. Reading 'Maud, a Monodrama' furthered this study; Tennyson's sparsely simple but powerful repetition conveys a profound depth of sorrow with which the narrator is to 'weep and weep and weep'. Maud is empowered yet helpless, vulnerable and villain simultaneously; with ambivalence of the female Tennyson creates a platform for a more conscious exploration into the discordance of sexual politics in the subsequent Modern 'period'.

Having written on female isolation from mental illness in Kaysen's *Girl, Interrupted* for coursework, I became interested in woman's displacement in literature; Jean Rhys' employment of the stream-of-consciousness technique in *Good Morning, Midnight* expresses the female mind fractured between the past and present in haphazard ragged thought. This portrayal of a scorned and isolated woman with the addictions symptomatic of patriarchal oppression fulfils the societal female role as the 'constitutive Other', a concept I explored in Simone de Beauvoir's *The Second Sex*. Here, the notion that 'One is not born, but rather becomes, a woman' forges the distinction between biological sex and constructed gender, and questions the root of these imbalances of gender, ideas supplemented by a philosophy module which posed questions of how and when a human obtains 'Personhood'. Reading Rhys' collection of short stories *Sleep It Off Lady*, as well as from the collections of Katherine Mansfield and Alice Munro, demonstrated how a form can be metaphorical of its content: the short story, itself a fleeting snapshot of time, seems intrinsically displaced somewhat and is thus so effectively used to represent the lost female, Mansfield's Miss Brill an example as well as particular favourite of mine.

Used to being transported mentally in this way, my upcoming gap year travels to South America are indeed an exciting prospect. Until then, I have won an internship at Allison and Busby (a publishing house to reveal the technical face of literature) and am earning money waitressing. The commitments undertaken in school and beyond have often taken unconsciously English-driven forms. My dedication to musical endeavour often results in its convergence with writing; performing in a recent opera of 'Dido and Aeneas' or a choral performance of Britten's 'Hymn to St Cecilia' (words from Auden), as well as enjoying music for its own sake, in particular playing solo violin at prestigious venues like St John's Smith Square and Chichester Cathedral.

Computer Science – Cambridge (3,900 characters, with spaces)

The logical approach to solving complicated problems is the main driving force behind my enjoyment of computing and programming. For me one of the stimulating challenges of computer science is searching for ways to optimise my solutions to problems. Computing has many practical uses, leading to a variety of personally fascinating fields such as artificial intelligence and software engineering, while computational physics and robotics appeal to my interest in physics and computer science combined. Recently, reading *The New Turing Omnibus* has introduced me to even more areas of computer science. I have enjoyed reading chapters on detecting prime numbers and program correctness. Furthermore, topics such as binary search trees and the Newton-Raphson method have encouraged me to write my own related programs.

While studying at Allameh Helli School, computing was a large part of my core syllabus. There I learned programming in various languages including C and C++. At every opportunity I took part in the extra computing classes offered, which included topics such as algorithms for data manipulation, computer graphics for games programming, object-oriented programming and computational simulations. My greatest achievement was playing a key role on the 3D soccer simulation project. Our team qualified for the 2012 Dutch Open and Iran Open robotics competitions, even though many university teams did not manage to qualify. This project allowed me to combine my interest in both physics and computing by challenging my ability to produce specific algorithms and programs based on my knowledge of physics and mechanics. Prior to this, my Chemical Clock project won 2nd place in the National Young Researcher's competition in middle school. During lower sixth I completed my mathematics A level and took part in the UK Mathematics Trust's Senior Challenge, securing a gold certificate. This year I am completing A levels in further maths, physics and economics.

Recently, my knowledge of mathematical algebra proved useful in understanding a paper I read in *Communications of the ACM* magazine describing different cake-cutting algorithms. It interestingly went on to explain how these algorithms could help solve real issues such as the equitable division of limited natural resources. In economics, it was intriguing to learn how firms such as Hyde Park Global Investments use computer technology to meet their objectives. This firm uses computers instead of hedge fund managers to buy and sell shares, as being a nanosecond faster than their rivals equates to profits of tens of thousands of pounds. My knowledge of physics has proved invaluable when writing programs. For example, I am currently studying about projectiles in mechanics, which goes perfectly hand in hand with the work I carried out in middle school, creating simulations of freefall and other physics experiments.

I have always brought commitment and enthusiasm to every aspect of my school life. At my previous school I was part of the organisational committee for our science and technology seminars. I was also in charge of organising the first games programming competition between schools at a national level. While being a scholarship student at MPW, I have been appointed as a mentor to international students and elected onto the student council. I am part of the school's debating team and have successfully participated in the Debating Matters public speaking competition. Beyond academics I enjoy playing sports such as football and volleyball. These experiences have strengthened my independence, leadership and teamwork skills, which will help my transition into university education. I believe that my strong ability for logical reasoning and problem solving combined with passion and commitment to the subject offer the prerequisite needed to succeed as an undergraduate computer scientist.

Natural Science – Cambridge (3,912 characters, with spaces)

I see physics as an all-encompassing field covering every natural phenomenon imaginable. I have already been introduced to so many fascinating aspects; from the quantum world, governed by the electromagnetic, weak and strong forces, through to stars and galaxies that are constantly shaped by gravity. This inspires me to look deeper into both Newtonian and Relativistic mechanics.

The language of physics is mathematics so it is obviously a crucial area of study and one that I very much enjoy. It gives me a chance to challenge myself, tackling the toughest questions. I enjoy the sense of achievement which comes from solving a difficult question, even more so when I find a mathematically eloquent solution. Studying further maths gives me more time to develop my abilities; providing an understanding of complex numbers, matrices and advanced calculus.

In chemistry, I tend towards the physical side and being one of the select few chosen to take part in a day of practical work in an undergraduate lab at the University of Leeds was a great experience. We used spectroscopes to study the hydrogen spectra to calculate the Rydberg constant as well as studying the links between temperature and rate of reaction. This provoked me to research the kinetic theory of gases for a maths project.

Since starting A levels I've done as much as I can to drive my passion for physics. I contacted Dr J. Collins, who has been mentoring me since. Over the last year he has suggested reading material, such as The Feynman Lectures, and assisted me with problems. During the year I have attended lectures; one about radio astronomy by Dr T. O'Brian and another about dark matter given by Dr S. Paling, which inspired me to read the thought provoking A Brief History of Time. I attended the Physics Master Class at Cambridge in early 2013; it gave me my first deepened insight into the world of quantum mechanics which was broadened by working through sections of Cavendish Quantum Mechanics Primer. In the summer I completed a week of work experience at the University of York, undertaking experiments ranging from measuring the specific heat capacity of liquid nitrogen through to measuring the charge/mass ratio of an electron using a cathode ray tube. Talking to both theoretical and experimental researchers demonstrated to me the current problems being tackled by physicists.

At school, I, along with three other students, ran the STEM club. We worked with lower school students with the aim of inspiring them to take on physics through GCSE and beyond. The club consisted of fun practical work and we pushed the students to ask questions and think about why and how something happens. This is something I feel passionately about, as physics is seen by some to be one of the least popular sciences and this is something that I would like to help change.

Outside of school, I currently work as a tutor at Explore Learning, tutoring children from the ages of 5 to 14 in maths and English. Sharing my passion for maths is extremely rewarding. It is helping me to develop my communication skills, working with young people of a range of ages and abilities. I also have many hobbies, the main of which is photography. Although it is essentially a creative hobby, the practical understanding of a how a camera works will always create the best results. I have been lucky enough to reach the final of the RSPCA Young Photographer Awards and win the AMP Awards photography competition, as well as being in a business team which organised the event. I have been playing the trumpet since the age of 10 and have played in the school bands throughout my school life.

I am driven simply by, in the words of Feynman, the pleasure of finding things out. I look to build on the concepts that I have been briefly introduced to and then to continually develop my understanding of the physical world throughout the rest of my life. It will be a genuine pleasure to be a part of the era of scientific development.

Economics and Management – Oxford (3,978 characters, with spaces)

Individuals and institutions, private and public, are all faced with making choices in situations where resources are scarce. This is the central problem of economics. In Chinese schools, economics is an insignificant sub-discipline and part of introductory level politics. I was curious early on, and wanted to understand why things happen. In 2014, 1% of the Chinese population possessed over a third of the country's wealth, while at least 82 million people were living under absolute poverty. Why has wealth inequality in China risen sharply in recent years? Consequently, I read *The Economics of Inequality* by Thomas Piketty, and found that socio-economic mechanisms generate inequality, with key issues being the extent of redistribution and how it is achieved.

Once I realised that high school economics was what I lacked, I believed it was a sensible choice to get an advanced education abroad. To give myself a challenge, I also chose geography. As the only non-native English speaker in geography classes, my speaking and essay-writing skills left much to be desired at first, but I quickly improved as the course developed.

Two months after my arrival, I took part in the UKMT Senior Maths Challenge. I won a gold medal, so I represented my school in the UKMT Senior Team Challenge. This allowed me to solve mathematical problems not just alone but as part of a group. Although I enjoy maths, it is the application of mathematics to real life problems that I find really satisfying. Algebra, calculus and statistics have helped me understand economic models. David J. Hand's *Statistics: A Very Short Introduction* explains the ubiquity of statistics. For example the calculation of CPI, during which statistical models are used to combine the prices of different items in the 'basket' to yield an overall number. Another example is calculating opportunity costs and hence applying this to the law of comparative advantage.

In economics classes, I developed a deeper understanding of the economy, sharpened my research skills, and encountered practicums that pushed me to think more creatively through my coursework. I also attended LSE public lectures on all kinds of issues. I particularly enjoyed 'Is the American Century Over?' by Professor Joseph Nye, during which I discovered much about the ramifications of the changes in the international economic environment, such as the relationship between the USA and China. The USA was the largest trading nation when the GATT was created in 1947. Although China overtook the USA in 2013, trade between these two countries remains a large proportion in their current account. I further explored this concept while reading *The Return of Depression Economics and The Crisis of 2008* by Paul Krugman. Although closer integration may bring benefits in terms of increased global production and trade, it also creates vulnerability by allowing for contagion between countries. I also enjoyed reading about the vicious cycle of financial crisis and the speculative attack that generated the crisis in Brazil, 1998. In addition, by reading his babysitting cooperation model, I have developed knowledge relating to strategic and operational aspects of economic models.

In the summer of 2015 I completed a month-long internship in the risk management department of Sinolink Securities investment bank. My main duty was to manage margin trading, which is also a cause of the recent Chinese stock market crash. This experience, a mix of theory and practical application, allowed me to think things through and then apply my ideas in a variety of real life situations. After this internship, my analytical skills and knowledge of statistical modelling programmes were considerably improved.

In the future, I am interested in pursuing margin trading and short selling in investment banking. I look forward to learning more about economics in a vibrant intellectual community, where I can truly live the life of the mind.

Mathematics and Philosophy – Oxford (3,904 characters, with spaces)

The world of mathematics is abundant in extraordinary formulae and applications which have resulted from centuries of work by great thinkers, and so it is humbling and exciting to learn of these ideas. However, the aspect of maths that I find to be the most challenging and valuable is the development of my own mathematical creativity, rather than simply my mathematical knowledge.

Moreover, the study of maths and philosophy collectively has led me to recognise the value of mathematical creativity to maths as a whole. Inventions such as imaginary numbers which defy reason show that it is impossible to deduce all of maths by reasoning alone, and therefore innovation is essential. The square root of a negative number is beyond the limits of human understanding, yet it has solved many mathematical conundrums and become the language of quantum mechanics.

Qualifying for many UKMT Junior, Intermediate and British Olympiad papers has given me the opportunity to solve more advanced problems where there is no obvious method. Moreover, in 2013 I was one of 40 pupils nationally invited to attend the UKMT Summer School following my result in the Intermediate Maths Challenge. There I met topics which presented me with contradictions to the mathematical rules I had learnt in school, such as in spherical geometry where the angle sum of a triangle is not 180 degrees. This taught me to think for myself as opposed to relying on my preconceived ideas of mathematical truths. I investigated innovation in maths through the thoughts of the philosopher Ludwig Wittgenstein, and in a 4000 word essay I found I agreed with his argument that maths is a human invention, and therefore creativity is not merely conducive to progress, but the very nature of maths. Wittgenstein maintained that mathematical truths are not discoverable by indisputable logic, but fluctuate in accordance with the set of 'game rules' (e.g. logical system) we employ, and thus maths is a flexible system which we can manipulate to our convenience. I encountered a fascinating example of one such set of game rules in paraconsistent logic, a recently developed logical system which rejects the principle of explosion, therefore facilitating contradictions and the unavoidable inconsistencies of mathematical systems which Gödel identified.

Euler's Identity, which links the constants e, pi and 1 with the imaginary number, i, exemplifies the phenomenal results of invention of imaginary numbers, and it was my first experience of the mathematical beauty which has inspired me to continue maths to higher education. G. H. Hardy, in 'A Mathematician's Apology', accredits our subconscious appreciation of the identity to its combination of unexpectedness, inevitability and economy, and indeed I had been enchanted by the unexpected union of seemingly unrelated constants in one economically brief equation, alongside the inevitability of the conclusion as I saw it derived step by step.

Beauty is broadly viewed as subjective, and so it seems futile to try to analyse it as a composition of qualities. Yet I surprisingly found echoes of G. H. Hardy's beautiful qualities in my perception of beauty in dance. Having achieved the highest level in ballet, Advanced 2, and taught ballroom and Latin American dance, I was long intrigued by the contrast of aesthetically displeasing shapes and movements of some contemporary dance with the welcome elegance of ballet. I realised that ballet combines unexpectedness of both height in jumps and speed in turns, economy of movement creating unaffected lines, and inevitability produced by graceful movement, contrasting with some disturbing, unnatural and exaggerated elements of contemporary dance. Philosophy provides such analysis of the nature of abstract concepts and thus has allowed me better to understand the unpredictability of maths and the resulting necessity for broad thinking.

Personal statement advice from a student

Here is some very useful advice from a student who has successfully applied to both Oxford and Cambridge for two very different degrees. Flora read geography at St Anne's College, Oxford (2011–13) followed by medicine on a graduate-entry programme at Wolfson College, Cambridge.

- Think about how you can make your personal statement stand out from the others.
- Don't try and pack it with too much information. Tutors like to see your thought process and how you critically analyse things. Explore issues rather than just writing a sentence about it.
- Whatever examples you do provide in your personal statement, make sure you are comfortable and familiar with them as there is a high chance they will bring it up in your interview (and not in the way you may expect them to!) – know the basics!
- Think outside of the box – try to approach scenarios or problems in a unique, interesting and thoughtful way.
- The tutors have to read so many personal statements – make yours thought-provoking and fun – engage the reader!
- Think about how you can link different examples together to make it fluid and interconnected.
- It sounds obvious, but really think about why you want to study your chosen course. What is it about that subject that engages you? What are you passionate about? What does the Oxford/Cambridge course offer that attracts you to it? Look at what modules are on offer, etc. Reflect on your own life (whether academic or personal) and think about why that course is suited to you.

Case study: Jamie, Oxford

When applying for any arts subject at Oxbridge it is important to know your personal statement well. It isn't necessarily going to form the entirety of your interview, if it features at all you're incredibly lucky and the tutors will most likely only base the first few questions on your personal statement in order to put your mind at ease. Despite this, developing the ideas that you introduced in your personal statement – and trust me, with PPE they will have been very brief introductions indeed – is still good practice. The tutors in their questions, whether they be on the philosophy of Hamlet or how you would advise ISIS (yes, someone did get that question!), are testing to see how you think – you will not have ever seen anything like the materials they will give you at interview, but it's fine because no one else will have either. That's why developing your personal statement is so important; it offers a base from which you can leap off in your interview. It also helps you hone those all-important thinking skills. It is pointless trying to anticipate the questions that can come up in interview, but at least if you are well grounded on your personal statement you have something to fall back on and have some knowledge that may be applicable.

As for the personal statement itself there are some very clear dos and don'ts, the first being do not cite *The Prince* by Machiavelli as everyone who has ever applied for a politics based course has had that idea before you (including me). As well as this, starting a personal statement with the words 'the interconnections between politics philosophy and economics' has been done before (again by me). Other than that, there are not many specifics to worry about with your personal statement.

The UCAS application

These are the steps you need to take, and when to take them, to apply through UCAS.

1. Go to www.ucas.com/ucas/undergraduate/register to register in September. In order to do this you will need an email address and will be asked to choose a password. Your password should be easy to remember and ideally one that you don't use for other accounts. If you have a school email address, use it to register. After inputting some basic personal details you will be given your username and UCAS application number which is to be used in all correspondence with UCAS and the universities. Once you have chosen four security questions, in case you lose your details and have to contact UCAS directly, you'll be asked to log in to your application. If you are applying through a school or college then you will have a buzzword to enter (ask your UCAS adviser if you don't know what it is). This will associate your application with that school or college which will allow your reference to be uploaded by them.

2. The entire application is done online. Although it may seem complex and time consuming, you can complete it in stages and come back to it. There are 'help' buttons by the side of most fields that need to be completed in case you get stuck.

3. Fill in the 'Personal details' section, which includes your name, address and date of birth. Some of this information will already be there from when you registered.

4. Next is an 'Additional information' section in which you can list the activities you have done in preparation for further education. These activities specifically refer to attending summer schools in preparation for university, run by either the universities themselves or trusts such as the Sutton Trust. See www.suttontrust.com or contact UCAS for more information (www.ucas.com/corporate/about-us/contact-us).

5. Fill in the 'Student Finance' section, which is where you have to select your fee code. Once again the help buttons will help to explain the options available if you are uncertain. If you are a British national your local authority will be your fee payer.

6. The next section is where you enter your university choices. You can apply to either Oxford or Cambridge but not both. Choose the correct university code from the drop-down menu (CAM C05 for Cambridge or OXF O33 for Oxford). You also need to add what UCAS calls the 'campus code', which is the college code. A drop-down list will appear again. You will also need to choose the subject and select which year of entry you are applying for.

7. The next section asks you for details of your education. You need to write down every GCSE and A level (or equivalent qualification) you have taken and what grade you got under the heading of the school in which you took them. If you are applying post-A level, you need to write down all of your module grades.

8. The next section is 'Employment'. This does not ask you about work experience but about paid employment. It is worth writing down even the most insignificant jobs you have done – washing dishes at the local restaurant, for example – since admissions tutors will value the commitment and maturity you will have shown when holding down a job.

9. Next is the 'Personal statement'. This is your chance to show the admissions tutors how you write and how informed you are about your subject. You should write this in a Word document, spell check it and read it through carefully, then, when it is ready, copy and paste it into the UCAS form. You have a maximum limit of 4,000 characters for your personal statement, including spaces, and the application form will automatically tell you if you have exceeded that limit and by how much.

10. Finally, send the application in the first week of October to be com- pleted by your teachers. If you are applying to UCAS as an individual, for example, a mature student not applying through a

school or college, you will need to provide the contact details of your chosen referee (this would usually be your employer) so that they can log in to your application and fill in the reference page separately; see Chapter 10 for more details. The application fee for 2018 entry is £13 if you're applying to just one university or £24 for multiple courses. This must be paid by credit card (your school may have a policy of paying this for you so you need to check before you part with any money). Your teacher, Personal Tutor or Director of Studies will then be able to open your application on the advisers' part of the UCAS site. They will read it to check everything is correct and will then write their reference and your predicted grades. Your teachers may need some time to write the reference, so do make sure you have your part done well in advance.

11. Your teacher or adviser then needs to submit your UCAS application by 6 p.m. on **15 October**.

8 | Succeeding in written tests

Despite the proportion of top grades achieved by A level students across England, Wales and Northern Ireland falling over the past few years, places at Cambridge and Oxford are still highly competitive and the number of applications for Oxbridge places have increased in this time. In addition to this, the introduction of the new reformed A levels for students sitting qualifications set by English examination boards means that the majority of students will not be sitting external AS exams at the end of their Lower Sixth year, except in subjects they are intending to drop. This has made it even more important for both Oxford and Cambridge to rely upon additional testing systems when selecting candidates for interview. The following chapter aims to give an account of the various written tests students face prior to or during their interviews, including the deadlines for registering for the exams; when and where the tests are sat; details about the structure of the tests, including knowledge requirements; sample questions; and useful links for more information and practice.

These tests include the BMAT for medicine (at both universities), biomedical sciences (at Oxford) and veterinary medicine (at Cambridge), and the LNAT for law at Oxford, two externally administered tests. The History Aptitude Test (HAT) is taken for history at Oxford. As discussed earlier in the book, as of 2017 entry, all Cambridge colleges have introduced common-format written assessments, to be taken by applicants for all subjects except mathematics and music (see under Cambridge admissions tests on page 111). Students applying to Cambridge are required to sit tests either pre-interview in November, or during the December interview period. The Oxbridge exams aim to highlight the natural intelligence and academic potential of the candidate and, in doing so, widen access. Since it is often difficult to revise for the Oxbridge written tests, students have to rely on their innate intellectual ability to complete them. In theory, students whose schools have provided less preparation should not be disadvantaged, although it can help to have at least some understanding of what the tests entail.

The style of testing also differs from what many school leavers will be used to. Whereas A levels often test factual recall, the Oxbridge written exams look for analytical and critical capabilities. It should be noted, therefore, that these tests are likely to be much harder than anything you will have experienced at school. This is taken into consideration, and admissions tutors do not expect students to achieve 100%.

Both Oxford and Cambridge now take a common approach to additional written tests. Both universities set common-format, university-wide tests for certain subjects. The following university websites provide links to all of the tests you would be required to take for certain subjects.

- www.ox.ac.uk/admissions/undergraduate/applying-to-oxford/tests
- www.undergraduate.study.cam.ac.uk/applying/admissions-assessments

Testing happens at various stages during the application process. Some tests are sat in early November at your school. The results of these tests can then play a part in determining whether you are called to interview. Some tests take place when you go up for interview in early December. The results are then used, alongside your interview performance, your personal statement, your school references and your exam grades, to decide whether you should be made a conditional offer.

Don't let taking these tests put you off applying. If you are serious about wanting a place at a top university, you should be able to do well without masses of additional tuition or extra work. It is very important, however, to go online and get full details of what the tests entail and to do some practice papers if they are offered.

Oxford admissions tests

The schedule of tests for 2018 entry should be as shown below.

1 October 2017

- Deadline date for registering for the BMAT. If you register between 2 November and 6 p.m. on 15 October, you will pay a late fee.

15 October 2017

- 6 p.m. is the final deadline for registering for Oxford admissions assessments, including the English Literature Admissions Test (ELAT), the HAT, the Physics Aptitude Test (PAT) and the Thinking Skills Assessment (TSA), and Cambridge pre-interview assessments.
- Closing date for all UCAS applications to Oxford and Cambridge.
- Closing date for receipt of applications for the accelerated medical course.

2017

- LNAT: registrations begin on 1 August. For Oxford, you must register for the test from 5 October and the deadline for sitting it is 20 October.

2 November 2017

- BMAT: Aptitude Test for biomedical sciences and medicine.
- ELAT: Aptitude Test for English language and literature. Students applying for the joint courses classics and English or English and modern languages should also take the ELAT. Students applying for history and English do not need to sit the ELAT.
- HAT: Aptitude Test for history (ancient and modern). Students applying for the joint courses history and economics, history and English, history and modern languages or history and politics should also take the test.
- PAT: Aptitude Test for physics, engineering science and materials science. Students applying for the joint course physics and philosophy should also take the PAT.
- MAT: Aptitude Test for mathematics and computer science. Students applying for the joint courses computer science and philosophy, mathematics and computer science, mathematics and philosophy or mathematics and statistics should also take the MAT.
- TSA: Aptitude Test for chemistry, economics and management, geography, human sciences, PPE, psychology (experimental), and PPL.
- MLAT: Aptitude test for all modern languages courses. Students applying for the joint courses classics and modern languages, English and modern languages, European and Middle Eastern languages, history and modern languages, modern languages and linguistics or philosophy and modern languages should also take the MLAT.
- OLAT: Aptitude Test for oriental studies for students whose course combinations include Arabic, Turkish, Hebrew and Persian. Students applying for the joint courses oriental studies with classics or European and Middle Eastern languages should also take the OLAT. If you are applying for theology and oriental studies (Judaism and Islam strands) and you are intending to study Hebrew, Arabic, Persian or Turkish, you must take the OLAT.
- CAT: Admissions test for classics. Students applying for the joint courses classics and English, classics and modern languages or classics with oriental studies are required to take the test.
- Philosophy Test: Admissions Test for philosophy and theology. If you are applying for modern languages and philosophy, check on the Oxford website which papers are required for your course.

If you are applying for fine art or music and are called to interview, you will be asked to complete a practical test at interview.

There are no written tests for biochemistry, biological sciences, classical archaeology and ancient history, earth sciences (geology), history of art or theology and religion.

Cambridge admissions tests

Cambridge has introduced common-format tests, which students must either take pre-interview on 2 November 2017 or at interview (if short-listed for interview). There are no common-format assessments for mathematics and music; students applying for mathematics are required to take the STEP in June, and music applicants will be asked to complete short tasks at interview, if called to interview.

Courses with a pre-interview written assessment

- Anglo-Saxon, Norse and Celtic: Anglo-Saxon, Norse, and Celtic Admissions Assessment (ASNCAA)
- Asian and Middle Eastern studies: Asian and Middle Eastern Studies Admissions Assessment (AMESSA)
- chemical engineering: students studying chemical engineering via engineering must sit the Engineering Admissions Assessment (ENGAA). Students studying engineering via natural sciences must sit the Natural Sciences Admissions Assessment (NSAA)
- economics: Economics Admissions Assessment (ECAA)
- engineering: Engineering Admissions Assessment (ENGAA)
- English: ELAT
- geography: Geography Admissions Assessment (GAA)
- history: History Admissions Assessment (HAA)
- history and modern languages: History Admissions Assessment (HAA). In addition, students will be required to sit the Modern and Medieval Languages Assessment at interview if called to interview
- history and politics: History Admissions Assessment (HAA)
- human, social and political sciences: Human, Social and Political Sciences Admissions Assessment (HSPSAA)
- medicine: BMAT
- natural sciences: Natural Sciences Admissions Assessment (NSAA)
- psychological and behavioural sciences: Psychological and Behaviour Sciences Admissions Assessment (PBSAA)
- theology, religion and philosophy of religion: Theology Admissions Assessment (TAA)
- veterinary medicine: BMAT.

The Reading Comprehension assessment (60 minutes) is relevant for students applying for Anglo-Saxon, Norse and Celtic, Asian and Middle Eastern Studies, geography, history, history and modern languages, history and politics, human, social and political sciences, theology, religion and philosophy of religion and some students intending to read psychological and behavioural sciences.

The Reading Comprehension normally forms section one of the pre-interview assessment and is followed by a subject-specific critical response to text extracts, which is also 60 minutes. The undergraduate admissions pages are an excellent source of information regarding these texts and each subject has a specimen paper available; see www.undergraduate. study.cam.ac.uk/applying/admissions-assessments/pre-interview.

Courses with an at-interview written assessment

- archaeology
- architecture
- classics
- computer science
- education
- history and modern languages (MML)
- history of art
- land economy
- law
- linguistics
- modern and medieval languages
- philosophy.

There are no common elements to these tests between subjects. Candidates are strongly advised to consult the following web link for information on their specific subject: www.undergraduate.study.cam.ac.uk/applying/admissions-assessments/at-interview.

All test details can be checked at the University of Cambridge website www.undergraduate.study.cam.ac.uk/applying/admission-assessments.

Thinking Skills Assessment

As of 2017 entry, most subjects that used to set the TSA Cambridge as an admissions test are using subject-specific written assessments either pre-interview or at-interview. However, land economy continues to use the TSA. Once again, details can be found on the University of Cambridge website at www.undergraduate.study.cam.ac.uk/applying/admission-assessments. Sample questions are provided at the end of the chapter.

BioMedical Admissions Test

All medicine and veterinary medicine Cambridge applicants must sit the BMAT after they have submitted their application and before their set interview date. The test examines scientific aptitude and concentrates on the skills needed for studying medicine and veterinary medicine. Sample questions can be found at the end of this chapter. The BMAT is used by Oxford for applicants to medicine and biomedical sciences and is also used by some other universities for medical and dental applicants.

Applicants are responsible for ensuring that they check the BMAT website for the relevant dates for registering for BMAT and dates of the test.

There is a cost for the BMAT, details of which may be found on the BMAT website (www.admissionstestingservice.org/for-test-takers/bmat/about-bmat). Certain UK candidates who receive financial support may apply for their BMAT fees to be refunded. Such applicants should get in touch with the BMAT support team for further information.

Cambridge Law Test

The Cambridge Law Test is used in addition to your interview, personal statement and academic performance by the admissions team at Cambridge. You will be given one hour to answer a two-part question; prior knowledge of the law is not required in order to help you respond to the question. The admissions team will not base its decision on your performance in the test alone; your test result will be used within the context of your application as another piece of information for the admissions team to take into account.

The test is taken at interview. Applicants who are interviewed overseas will be able to sit the Cambridge Law Test at an overseas centre and further details about the test will be given by the college handling your application. You do not need to pre-register and the test is free to take. Sample questions are available at the end of the chapter.

Some tips for taking specialist tests

Although these tests cannot be revised for it is advisable to make sure you know what to expect and practise the tests beforehand. Information on BMAT can be found at www.admissionstestingservice.org/for-test-takers/bmat/about-bmat and sample questions are included here. Further information about how the universities view and use the tests can be found on their own websites (www.medsci.ox.ac.uk/study/medicine/pre-clinical/faqs/bmat-gcses-and-short-listing/what-is-the-bmat and www.undergraduate.study.cam.ac.uk/applying/admissions-tests/bmat).

For information on TSA Oxford and TSA Cambridge go to www.admissionstestingservice.org/for-test-takers/thinking-skills-assessment and follow the links for the appropriate institution and test. There are also sample questions at the end of the chapter.

Information on LNAT can be found at www.lnat.ac.uk. Sample questions are also included in this chapter.

Information on HAT and specimen papers can be found at www.history.ox.ac.uk/history-aptitude-test-hat.

For information on ELAT go to www.admissionstestingservice.org/for-test-takers/elat/about-elat and follow the links to find further details of the test. Sample questions are provided at the end of the chapter.

- Remember that Oxford and Cambridge have designed these tests to try to give them another tool to differentiate between students. They are looking for those who are most academically suited to their courses. You should not need to spend hours preparing to take these tests; in fact, if you need to undertake an enormous amount of preparation, it is arguable that you may not be an appropriate candidate.
- The universities give a full description of what the specialist tests entail on their websites:
  - www.ox.ac.uk/admissions/undergraduate_courses/applying_to_oxford/tests/index.html
  - www.undergraduate.study.cam.ac.uk/applying/admissions-tests.
- Past papers or sample questions are available for all tests and it is vital that you practise some of these in mock exam conditions to familiarise yourself with the format of the tests and the time constraints on the test. Some sample questions are included below from a selection of admissions tests used by both universities.
- Do not be upset if you can't answer all the questions. The tests are devised to be stretching and it is important not to panic if you come across something unfamiliar. It is often how you approach a particular problem that will be considered rather than if you actually get a 'correct' answer.

Specimen papers for Oxbridge tests

BMAT sample questions and answers

BMAT® Aptitude & Skills Practice Questions

Have a go at these BMAT Aptitude and Skills practice questions.

DIRECTIONS:

Answer every question. Points are awarded for correct answers only. There are no penalties for incorrect answers.

All questions are worth 1 mark.

Some questions have more than 1 correct answer. Read carefully to ensure that you select the appropriate number of answers. Answers for short-answer questions must fit in the space provided.

Calculators are not permitted during any portion of the test.

1. Media coverage of organ donation has increased as the Government considers making the donor registry 'opt-out', rather than 'opt-in'. Every week, newspapers and TV reports are filled with grim stories and statistics of waiting lists and deaths of those waiting for a transplant. Regardless of any changes to legislation, the media could do more to increase organ donation at present. For example, the frequent news reports on the need for more donated organs rarely mention how, exactly, members of the public can 'opt-in' to the donor registry. This practice stands in stark contrast to the presentation of such stories in other countries, such as the USA and Canada, where stories on the need for more organ donors almost always end with contact details for joining the donor registry. Providing viewers with a phone number or website for joining the registry is seen as a public service, part of the media's responsibility in calling attention to such a problem.

Which of the following best summarises the main conclusion of the argument?

A It's easier to become an organ donor in the USA or Canada than in the UK.

B Sometimes the media can help to solve the problems it identifies.

C The Government wants to make organ donation compulsory.

D Many people die waiting for organs each year as there are too few donors opting-in to the registry.

E Everyone should be required to join the organ donor registry.

2. Shannon and Dave are hosting a dinner party for six friends. The surface of the dining table is circular, with chairs set out equal distances around its circumference, as shown below. Each chair is directly opposite one other chair.

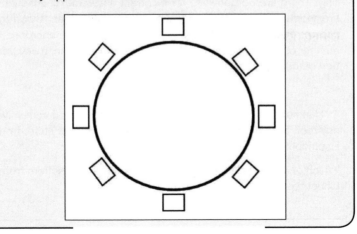

Dave prefers to sit directly opposite Shannon. Rachael and James are a couple, and prefer to sit next to each other. Ben fancies Lola, and he's a bit shy, so he prefers to sit directly opposite her. Dave and Shannon can't stand Patrick, whom Cindy is seeing, so neither of them will sit next to him.

If the seating plan meets everyone's preferences, what is the probability that Cindy will be seated directly opposite Rachael?

A 1/16

B 1/12

C 1/6

D 1/2

Practice questions provided by Kaplan Test Prep, a leading provider of preparation for the UKCAT and BMAT. See www.kaptest.co.uk

Answers

3. B

4. D

Answer explanations for each practice question can be found on Kaplan's website at www.kaptest.co.uk/sites/kaptest.co.uk/files/bmat-answer-book_0.pdf.

BMAT® Scientific Knowledge and Applications Practice Questions

DIRECTIONS:

Answer every question. Points are awarded for correct answers only. There are no penalties for incorrect answers. All questions are worth 1 mark. Some questions have more than 1 correct answer. Read carefully to ensure that you select the appropriate number of answers. Calculators are not permitted during any portion of the test.

1. Haemophilia B (Christmas disease) is an X-linked recessive disorder. Both Jane's father and maternal grandfather suffer from Haemophilia B.

Which of Jane's relatives is neither a carrier of, nor suffers from, Christmas disease?

A Her sister

B Her father's monozygotic twin

C Her maternal uncle

D Her maternal aunt

E Her paternal grandmother

3. Three points in the (x , y) coordinate plane lie at:

(a, b)

$(a+3\sqrt{2}, b)$

$(a+\sqrt{2}, b-4\sqrt{2})$

What is the area of the triangle described by these coordinates?

A $\sqrt{2}$

B 6

C $5\sqrt{2}$

D 12

E $12\sqrt{2}$

Practice questions provided by Kaplan Test Prep, a leading provider of preparation for the UKCAT and BMAT. See www.kaptest.co.uk

Answers

1. C

3. D

Answer explanations for each practice question can be found on Kaplan's website at www.kaptest.co.uk/sites/kaptest.co.uk/files/bmat-answer-book_0.pdf.

BMAT® Writing Practice Questions

Time: 30 MINUTES

DIRECTIONS:

Answer only one task from the choice of four essay titles. You must write your answer by hand, and are limited to a space consisting of one side of A4. You are permitted to make any preparatory notes as needed, but time spent on such notes counts against the 30 minutes allowed for the essay. In this task, you are expected to show how well you can order and explore ideas, and convey these ideas in clear, effective writing. You may not use dictionaries or any other reference books or resources. Essays are assigned a numerical score. To achieve a top mark, you must address all aspects of the question and write compellingly with few errors in logic or in use of English.

1. 'A scientific man ought to have no wishes, no affections – a mere heart of stone.' Charles Darwin

Write an essay in which you address the following points:

Why should those who practise science or medicine have 'no wishes, no affections'? What is the negative impact when scientists or doctors have 'hearts of stone'? How could a scientist or doctor best reconcile these competing concerns?

2. 'The greatest enemy of knowledge is not ignorance; it is the illusion of knowledge.' Stephen Hawking

Write an essay in which you address the following points:

In science, how is the illusion of knowledge an enemy of knowledge? Can you argue that ignorance itself an enemy of knowledge? By what criteria could you assess the comparative impact of these two, to determine which is the greater enemy of scientific knowledge?

Practice questions provided by Kaplan Test Prep, a leading provider of preparation for the UKCAT and BMAT. See www.kaptest.co.uk.

TSA Oxford and TSA Cambridge sample questions and answers

The following questions are provided courtesy of Oxbridge Applications (www.oxbridgeapplications.com).

TSA Oxford and TSA Cambridge tests are the same, with the exception that the TSA Oxford also includes a section at the end requiring students write an essay.

1. In a game, each player scores either 2 points or 5 points. If *n* players score 2 points and *m* players score 5 points, and the total number of points scored is 50, what is the least possible positive difference between *n* and *m*?

A 1

B 3

C 5

D 7

E 9

Answer: B

The quickest solution is to pick numbers for *n* and *m*. Since *n* = 1 and *m* = 1 would amount to 7 points, and since we want to minimise the difference between *n* and *m*, and since 50/7 is just a bit more than 7, it is a good idea to start with values near 7: *m* = 7 and *n* = 7 will give a total of 49 with a difference of 0, very close to what we want to achieve. The key is to discover what values for n, when multiplied by 2 points, will leave a multiple of 5 as the remaining points. As 50 minus a multiple of 5 will leave another multiple of 5, we need *n* times 2 to be a multiple of 5, so *n* itself must be a multiple of 5. The nearest multiple of 5 to our starting point of *n* = 7 from above is *n* = 5 (10 points), which allows for 8 for *m* (40 points). This results in a total of 50 points, and the positive difference between the two values is only 3.

2. Although the schooling of fish is a familiar form of animal social behaviour, how the school is formed and maintained is only beginning to be understood in detail. It had been thought that each fish maintains its position chiefly by means of vision. Our work has shown that, as each fish maintains its position, the lateral line, an organ sensitive to transitory changes in water displacement, is as important as vision. In each species a fish has a 'preferred' distance and angle from its nearest neighbour. The ideal separation and bearing, however, are not maintained rigidly. The result is a probabilistic arrangement that appears like a random aggregation. The tendency of the fish to remain at the preferred distance and angle, however, serves to maintain the structure. Each fish, having established its position, uses its eyes and its lateral lines simultaneously to measure the speed of all the other fish in the school. It then adjusts its own speed to match a weighted average that emphasises the contribution of nearby fish. The passage suggests that, after establishing its position in the school formation, an individual fish will subsequently:

A Maintain its preferred position primarily by visual and auditory means.

B Rigorously avoid changes that would interfere with the overall structure of the school.

C Make sensory readjustments to its position within the school.

D Make unexpected shifts in position only if threatened by external danger.

E Surrender its ability to make quick, instinctive judgements.

Answer: C

Since the school is moving each fish's adjustments must be ongoing and continuous, as (C) states. (A) must be wrong because auditory organs are not mentioned. Lateral lines correspond to a sense of touch, not hearing. (B) and (D) both have words that should strike you as improbable. Nothing suggests that each fish rigorously avoids any disruptive movements, (B), nor that the fish would make sudden, unexpected movements only in the presence of danger, (D). The idea contained in (E) is not mentioned in the passage – it is never suggested that a fish, once part of a school, completely loses its ability to act on its own.

3. Plant Y thrives in environments of great sunlight and very little moisture. Desert X is an environment with constant, powerful sunlight, and almost no moisture. Although Plant Y thrives in the areas surrounding Desert X, it does not exist naturally in the desert, nor does it survive long when introduced there.

Which of the following would be most useful in explaining the apparent discrepancy above?

A Desert X's climate is far too harsh for the animals that normally feed on Plant Y.

B For one week in the autumn, Desert X gets consistent rainfall.

C The environment around Desert X is ideally suited to the needs of Plant Y.

D Due to the lack of sufficient moisture, Desert X can support almost no plant life.

E   Plant Y cannot survive in temperatures as high as those normally found in Desert X.

Answer: E

The best explanation is, as the fifth choice states, that it is the high temperatures Plant Y cannot handle. If the information in (E) were true, conversely, Plant Y would not be able to grow in Desert X at all. (A) does not work because it is not suggested that the plant needs animals to feed on it in order to survive. (B) cannot be right because one week of consistent rainfall does not explain why Plant Y is not in Desert X. The fact that it can easily grow elsewhere does not answer the question of why it does not grow in Desert X; this fact is already known and so it does not resolve the paradox. (D) is wrong because the ability of other plants to survive in Desert X by itself has nothing to do with Plant Y. Plant Y might be one of the few plants that can flourish despite the lack of moisture in the desert.

Source: Oxbridge Applications (www.oxbridgeapplications.com). Reproduced with kind permission from Oxbridge Applications.

TSA Oxford-specific essay questions example

1. Is patriotism morally valuable or is it a stance we should avoid?

2. Should same-sex marriage be legal?

Source: Oxbridge Applications (www.oxbridgeapplications.com). Reproduced with kind permission from Oxbridge Applications.

ELAT

The ELAT always has the same question, which is:

Select two or three of the passages (a) to (f) and compare and contrast them in any ways that seem interesting to you, paying particular attention to distinctive features of structure, language and style. In your introduction, indicate briefly what you intend to explore or illustrate through close reading of your chosen passages.

This task is designed to assess your responsiveness to unfamiliar literary material and your skills in close reading. Marks are not awarded for references to other texts or authors you have studied.

The exam will then select different short passages each year for students to compare and contrast.

Source: Oxbridge Applications (www.oxbridgeapplications.com). Reproduced with kind permission from Oxbridge Applications.

LNAT

1. Greater censorship of violence in the media would help reduce knife crime. Do you agree?

2. Cancer patients who smoke should not receive treatment on the NHS unless they quit. Is this a good idea?

Source: Oxbridge Applications (www.oxbridgeapplications.com). Reproduced with kind permission from Oxbridge Applications.

Cambridge Law Test

1. Are there any circumstances in which security interests, and more specifically those of national security, should be allowed to override legal or human rights?

2. Giving judgement in Coco v. A.N. Clark (Engineers) Limited, Megarry J said:

'In cases of contract, the primary question is no doubt that of construing the contract and any terms implied in it. Where there is no contract, however, the question must be one of what it is that suffices to bring the obligation into being; and there is the further question of what amounts to a breach of that obligation.

'In my judgment, three elements are normally required if, apart from contract, a case of breach of confidence is to succeed. First, the information itself, in the words of Lord Greene, M.R. in the Saltman case on page 215, must "have the necessary quality of confidence about it". Secondly, that information must have been imparted in circumstances importing an obligation of confidence.

'Thirdly, there must be an unauthorised use of that information to the detriment of the party communicating it.'

NB for the purposes of the question:

The term 'quality of confidence' should be taken to mean that the information is secret or confidential in nature.

The party communicating the information is the party to whom the information relates.

The term 'breach of confidence' has more recently been taken to occur when a person comes into contact with information that somebody in their position should know would reasonably be considered confidential.

Giving judgement in Attorney General vs. Guardian Newspapers, Lord Goff said:

'To this broad general principle, there are three limiting principles to which I wish to refer. The first limiting principle (which is rather an expression of the scope of the duty) is highly relevant to this appeal. It is that the principle of confidentiality only applies to information to the extent that it is confidential. In particular, once it has entered what is usually called the public domain (which means no more than that the information in question is so generally accessible that, in all the circumstances, it cannot be regarded as confidential) then, as a general rule, the principle of confidentiality can have no application to it.

'The second limiting principle is that the duty of confidence applies neither to useless information, nor to trivia. There is no need for me to develop this point.

'The third limiting principle is of far greater importance. It is that, although the basis of the law's protection of confidence is that there is a public interest that confidences should be preserved and protected by the law, nevertheless that public interest may be outweighed by some other countervailing public interest which favours disclosure. This limitation may apply, as the learned judge pointed out, to all types of confidential information. It is this limiting principle which may require a court to carry out a balancing operation, weighing the public interest in maintaining confidence against a countervailing public interest favouring disclosure.

'The duty of confidence is, as a general rule, also imposed on a third party who is in possession of information which he knows is subject to an obligation of confidence.'

Consider the application of the information above in each of the alternative situations detailed below.

i. A, a well known celebrity is photographed leaving a rehabilitation clinic and the photographs are published alongside information about her treatment. This is the first instance of anything like this being published about A.

ii. X and Y, two well known celebrities are getting married and want the ceremony to remain private. They grant sole (very restricted) photographic rights to the (fictitious) magazine 'What?' and security is ordered to keep any other press away. A photographer from the (fictitious) magazine 'Who?' sneaks into the ceremony and takes photos which are later published alongside information as to the colour schemes and food served. Later these photographs are republished by several smaller magazines.

iii. S, an MP, submits his expenses claims which include some rather questionable items, including a claim for interest on a fictitious mortgage (as it had already been paid off). Details of S's expenses claims are then published in the (fictitious) newspaper 'Read all about it.'

Source: Oxbridge Applications (www.oxbridgeapplications.com). Reproduced with kind permission from Oxbridge Applications.

9 | Surviving the interview

About four to eight weeks after you have submitted your application, a letter will drop through your door and you will usually be sent an e-mail from the college you have applied to. However, do bear in mind that due to the pooling system you could be receiving a letter or email from a different college, so do read all correspondence carefully. At this stage you will find out whether you have been called for interview.

If you haven't, don't despair. There's always next year or another university. It's really not the end of the world.

If you have been called for interview – congratulations! Now make the most of the opportunity presented to you and do your preparation to make the experience a positive one.

Prepare properly: the practicalities

If you live a long distance from the universities or have an exam to take, the college may ask you to stay over the night before the interview. Being in college for a night or even a few days will give you an opportunity to meet some of the current students and other candidates and, while you may find it hard to get a good night's sleep in a strange bed, you should try to make the most of the experience. Some interviews may also be spread over the course of an entire day, especially if they entail some form of assessment test in addition to the actual interview, so give yourself plenty of time to get there and be prepared. Although it may be a stressful situation for you, try to relax and have fun. Not many people will get to sit these interviews at world leading universities, so congratulate yourself for being in that position and try to make the most of the experience.

Leave plenty of time to get to your first appointment

Arrive at least half an hour earlier than you planned to. You do not want to turn up stressed and sweating. Transport links to both universities are excellent and generally reliable but it's always worth assuming the worst-case scenario and arriving with plenty of time to spare.

Print off a map

Double check that you know your college's location and make sure you have enough money to get a taxi in case you arrive late or get lost.

Have the phone number of the admissions office

Save it on your mobile and write it down (in case your battery runs out) so you can let them know if you're delayed. It is also worth having the number of the Porters' Lodge as you will normally be required to report to them upon arrival for your interview. Each individual college will have its own Porters' Lodge so make sure you know the number for the college you have applied to before your arrival.

Know where your interview is taking place

When you arrive and are given the location of your interview room, go and find out exactly where it is. Oxbridge colleges can be confusing to navigate and many a candidate has arrived 10 minutes late to a 20-minute interview because they couldn't locate the right staircase. Be warned and be prepared. You can often find very good instructions online as to how to get around the colleges usually from students who have been for interviews before.

Dress as if you've made an effort

You don't have to wear a suit but you should look clean and not scruffy. This is not the occasion for jeans, T-shirts and trainers. Brushing your hair is usually a good thing too. Oxbridge colleges can be cold in December (or overheated). It's best to err on the safe side and bring clothes to cover both eventualities.

Make sure you have a book, some money for food and a charged phone – it may even be worth bringing your phone charger

You may spend a lot of time waiting around. As already mentioned, some of the interviews and assessments can be spread over an entire day. For Oxford interviews, you may be seen by several different colleges over a number of days. The cities are expensive and you really don't want to run out of money.

Don't relax too much!

If you meet up with friends, please don't go out and party. You will not do well at your interview the next morning and tutors will be predictably unsympathetic if you turn up the worse for wear.

Prepare properly: the interview

There's no real mystery about what you are likely to be asked at the interview. The tutors are looking for the best-qualified candidates; people whom they will enjoy teaching and who will make a contribution to their academic department. It's worth reminding yourself what qualities they are looking for in a student.

> 'Keble admits about 130 students each year from all types of school and educational backgrounds to study a wide range of subjects. We seek applicants who are academically aspiring and intellectually ambitious. We are looking for potential as much as achievement, and encourage applications from schools that do not regularly send candidates to Oxford … We admit students on the basis of academic merit alone.'
>
> Source: www.keble.ox.ac.uk/admissions/undergraduate
> Reproduced with kind permission.

It's essential, therefore, that you have thought through your answers to the following questions.

- Why have you applied to study your course?
- What have you done to prepare yourself for your course?
- What does your course entail, all three, four or more years of it?
- What did you write in your personal statement and why?

When did you last read your personal statement?

You may not remember all the books that you said you had devoured but the tutor interviewing you will. You are **very** likely to be asked questions about your personal statement, so take a copy with you and be sure you know what you wrote in it. The same applies to any written work and any supplementary answers that you submitted. Make sure you have copies with you and re-read them before the interview.

Do you really know your subject?

Have you read the 'Introduction to …' on the university and college's website? Have you read around your subject beyond the obvious choices?

What else have you done that proves your interest in your subject? Once again your personal statement should reflect your motivation to study on the course that you have applied for and also tell the university what you have done to move a few steps closer to realising that ambition.

Is your body language right?

During mock interviews, practise walking into a room, looking your interviewer in the eyes, smiling and saying hello and shaking their hand. When you are called in to the interview room for real, try to greet your interviewers confidently even if you're feeling very nervous. Sit forward in your seat and look interested. You will score no extra points for slouching or seeming bored. Some candidates will even go as far as to try a technique called 'mirroring' where you copy the body language of the person interviewing you and this helps to build a rapport. Many interviewers will be wise to this technique, and please don't do it every single time, but they may be impressed that you've made the effort to impress them. These techniques are secondary so please don't try them at the expense of forgetting about your personal statement or giving an honest portrayal of yourself.

Do you know the sort of questions you may be asked?

First of all, don't worry about the apocryphal bizarre Oxbridge questions. Some of the strange questions you hear about will have occurred in the context of a particular discussion and may have made perfect sense at the time! Most of the questions asked will be about your A level subjects, any super-curricular activities in which you have engaged and other topics that should give you an opportunity to show your abilities. There is a list of questions below that have been asked by tutors over the past few years. It's useful to look at them to give you an idea of the type of questions that might come up, but that's all. You are much more likely to be asked a straightforward question about your subject than any of the ones on this list.

It's also important to read a decent newspaper and keep up to date with current affairs. You may be asked your opinion on something in the news, so it's definitely worth brushing up your knowledge of current affairs in preparation. Subscribing to the BBC News RSS feeds or social media accounts can be a good way of keeping up to date with current affairs straight to your phone. Subject-specific podcasts and websites have similar facilities, so do your research beforehand and keep on top of current events in your field of study.

What happens if I can't answer their question?

Don't panic. There will often be no 'right' answer to whatever question you've been given. It's perfectly okay to ask for a few seconds to think about what you're going to say; something along the lines of 'That's an interesting question. Can I have a few moments to consider my answer?' makes you seem thoughtful, not desperate. In most cases the interviewer may not be looking for a definitive answer to a question. It is often more about how you approach and think about the question rather than whether you can get a correct answer or not. This of course is not so for the more obvious questions so really think through and rehearse the answers to these questions as even strong candidates can fail to give convincing answers.

- Why do you want to read [insert subject]?
- What is it about the course that interests you? (Have you been online to ensure you know exactly what the course entails, all three, four or more years of it?)
- Why have you chosen [insert college name]? (Do you know the names and special interests of the tutors who will be conducting the interview? It's all there online; make sure you find out. Knowing this makes you seem well prepared and it will make you feel more confident, because you have a little inside knowledge on the people who are interviewing you. Increasingly, students are telling us that they are not being asked this question at interview, but it may still be worthwhile bearing in mind why you have chosen your particular college. There tends to be much more of a focus on the subject, rather than the college or university. While this has always been the case, it is perhaps even more pronounced now.)
- Why should we give you a place to read [insert subject] rather than the nine other candidates whom we are interviewing today?

Remember, no tutor will be trying to make you feel small, trick you or humiliate you. A good interviewer will allow you to demonstrate your interest in your subject and your academic potential. They are most interested in your ability to think logically and express your ideas orally. If you can show how you are thinking and that you can think 'on your feet', that is more important than always getting the right answer. Remember that in certain subjects, there may not necessarily be a 'right answer' anyway. In mathematical and science subjects, how you are attempting to work out problems or how you are working out the answer while you are attempting to solve a problem could be equally important.

The big day

So the moment's finally arrived. What exactly will happen at the interview? Every experience can be different. Some colleges use a panel of interviewers, sometimes you will have consecutive interviews conducted by one individual (often the college admissions tutor, followed by one with a subject specialist) and sometimes interviewers do them in tandem.

In most cases two interviews is the standard but extra interviews may be given, or you may be sent to another college. Again, it varies.

The format will vary widely depending on subject. For some subjects (e.g. English) you may be given some prose or poetry to read before you go into your interview. You will then be asked questions on this by the tutors, who may then want to discuss the content of your personal statement – such as books you've mentioned reading or poetry you've enjoyed. For science subjects this is less common, and it is more likely that you will be given problems to solve or questions to answer. Generally these are designed to require no specific prior knowledge.

You may also be asked to attend a 'general' or 'college' interview. This is conducted by interviewers who don't teach your subject. It is possible that one of the purposes of this interview will be to see how you'll fit in with the college atmosphere and whether you are a well-rounded person who will be an asset to the college. You may be asked questions on your personal statement, about a topic of interest in the news or about your enthusiasm for your chosen subject.

Below are some examples of the sort of questions you may be asked and some students' experiences at their interviews. The case studies presented earlier in this book also cover some of the interview questions asked and how students responded to them. The University of Oxford also provides sample questions by course and these should be checked for updates when you apply at www.ox.ac.uk/admissions/ undergraduate/applying-to-oxford/interviews/sample-interview-questions. Although the University of Cambridge does not have a list of sample questions in the same way, they do give more general advice on how you should prepare for your interview here: www.undergraduate. study.cam.ac.uk/applying/interviews/how-should-i-prepare.

General interview questions

- Why do you want to come to this college?
- What made you want to study this subject?
- What are you intending to do in your gap year?
- Where do you see yourself in five years' time?
- Excluding your A level reading, what were the last three books you read?
- What do you regard as your strengths and weaknesses?
- What extra-curricular activities would you like to take part in at this college?
- Why did you make an 'open application'?

- Give us three reasons why we should offer you a place.
- What will you do if we don't offer you a place?
- Why did you choose your A level subjects?
- How will this degree help in your chosen career?
- How would your friends describe you?
- Tell us why we should accept you.
- Why have you chosen Cambridge and not Oxford (and vice versa)?

Subject-specific interview questions

Anthropology/archaeology

- Name the six major world religions.
- What does Stonehenge mean to you?
- What are the problems regarding objectivity in anthropological studies?
- Why do civilisations erect monuments?
- Why should we approach all subjects from a holistic, anthropological perspective?
- Being given an object and being told where it was found, then being asked what you could deduce from the object.
- Discussing an archaeological find.

Architecture

A large part of the interview is likely to be dedicated to discussing your portfolio. Be prepared to discuss the ideas, purposes and motivations behind your work. Your work should also illustrate a well-developed ability to relate two- and three-dimensional experience through drawing and 3D models. Be aware that portfolio requirements can vary from college to college and it is advisable that you check the relevant college's website at www.undergraduate.study.cam.ac.uk/colleges/college-contacts. You should also be prepared to discuss your work experience. Below are some other questions that might be asked.

- Is architecture in decline?
- Could you describe a building that you recently found interesting?
- Do you have an architect whom you particularly admire? What is it about their work that you find attractive?
- If you could design a building anywhere in the world, and if money, space and time were unlimited, what would you design?

Art history

- What do we look for when we study art? What are we trying to reveal?
- Comment on this painting on the wall.
- Compare and contrast these three images.
- What exhibitions have you been to recently?

- How do you determine the value of art?
- Who should own art?
- What is art?
- Why is art important?
- What role do art galleries and museums play in society today?
- Are humans inherently creative?
- Apart from your studies, how else might you pursue your interest in art history while at university?
- What are some key themes in the history of art?
- How has the depiction of the human form developed through the centuries?
- Who invented linear perspective – artists or architects?
- When was the discipline of art history brought to England and by whom?

Biochemistry

For most questions related to biochemistry it is again not a final answer that interviewers are looking for and they will often understand if students say that they don't know the answer to a question. Once again it is how the candidate approaches the problem that will be assessed. They would expect a hypothesis to be built which can then be tested using the student's own knowledge. They can then discuss this in more detail with the interviewer even using their knowledge to help come to a plausible answer. This approach is generally true of all of the science subjects.

- How do catalysts work?
- Describe the work of enzymes.
- Discuss the chemistry of the formation of proteins.
- Questions on oxidation, equilibria and interatomic forces.
- Questions on X-ray crystallography.
- Why do you wish to read biochemistry rather than chemistry?
- What scientific journals have you read lately? Is there a recent development in the field that particularly interests you?
- Why does most biochemistry take place away from equilibrium? (Or, how important is equilibrium to biochemical processes?)

Biological sciences

- How does the immune system recognise invading pathogens as foreign cells?
- How does a cell stop itself from exploding due to osmosis?
- Why is carbon of such importance in living systems?
- How would you transfer a gene to a plant?
- Explain the mechanism of capillary action.
- What are the advantages of the human genome project?
- How would you locate a gene for a given characteristic in the nucleus of a cell?
- What is the major problem with heart transplants in the receiver?

- Should we be concerned about GMOs? Why or why not?
- Do cellular processes take place at equilibrium?
- How important are primary electrogenic pumps for transmembrane ion transport of organic molecules? Why are these important?
- Why do plants, fungi and bacteria utilise H+ gradients to energise their membranes whereas animals utilise Na+ gradients?

Chemistry

- Questions on organic mechanisms.
- Questions on structure, bonding and energetics.
- Questions on acids and bases.
- Questions on isomerisation.
- Questions on practical chemical analysis.
- Describe the properties of solvents and mechanisms of solvation.

(See also biochemistry questions.)

Classics

Interviewers would generally not ask questions on texts unless the student has specifically said that they have read them first either in the interview or in their personal statement. The interviewer may instead ask the candidate to talk about a piece of classical literature they have enjoyed and developing their questioning on the basis of that piece so it is important that you have some texts in mind and have something pertinent to say about them as your interviewer is going to be an expert in anything that you may have read and more.

- Questions on classical civilisations and literature.
- Why do you think ancient history is important?
- How civilised was the Roman world?
- Apart from your A level texts, what have you read in the original or in translation?

Earth sciences and geology

- Where would you place this rock sample in geological time?
- How would you determine a rock's age?
- Can you integrate this decay curve, and why would the result be useful?
- Questions on chemistry.
- When do you think oil will run out?

Economics

After one or two general questions such as 'what have you enjoyed most about economics' or 'what are you hoping to gain by studying at degree level' interviewers may then move on to more puzzle-based questions. Economics is highly mathematical so don't be surprised to get some challenging puzzles to test your numeracy and logical thinking skills. It is a good idea to remember that no matter how mathematical the puzzle may be, they would be expecting you to link the ideas back to economic theory. Think about how you can use the ideas of utility or return or the allocation of resources to help explain your answers.

- Explain how the Phillips curve arises.
- Would it be feasible to have an economy that was entirely based on the service sector?
- A man pays for his holiday at a hotel on a tropical island by cheque. He has a top credit rating and rather than cashing it, the hotelier pays a supplier using the same cheque. That supplier does the same thing with one of his suppliers and so on ad infinitum. Who pays for the man's holiday?
- What do you know about the interaction between fiscal and monetary policy?
- I notice that you study mathematics. Can you see how you might derive the profit maximisation formula from first principles?
- Tell me about competition in the television industry.
- How effective is current monetary policy?
- What are your particular interests as regards economics?
- Do you think we should worry about a balance of payments deficit?
- If you were the Chancellor of the Exchequer, how would you maximise tax revenue?
- If you had a fairy godmother who gave you unlimited sums of money, what sort of company would you start and what types of employee would you hire?
- What are the advantages and disadvantages of joining the euro?
- What are the qualities of a good economist?
- Why are you studying economics at A level?
- What would happen to employment and wage rates if the pound depreciated?
- Do you think the Chinese exchange rate will increase?
- How does the housing market affect inflation?
- How has social mobility changed in recent times?
- How best can the government get us out of the recession?

Engineering

- Questions on mathematics and physics, particularly calculus and mechanics.
- Questions on mathematical derivations, for example on laws of motion.
- Look at this mechanical system sitting on my desk – how does it work?
- How do aeroplanes fly?
- What is impedance matching and how can it be achieved?
- How do bicycle spokes work?
- How would you divide a tetrahedron into two identical parts?

- What is the total resistance of the tetrahedron if there are resistors of 1 ohm on each edge?
- How would you design a gravity dam for holding back water?

English

It won't just be classical literature that the interviewer will expect you to have knowledge of but the impact of literature in general. Don't be surprised therefore to be asked questions on the Harry Potter books or the recent popularity of urban fantasy as a sub-genre. Of course more specific questions will be related to works that you say you have enjoyed or learnt something from, so again make sure that you are confident of what you have written about in your personal statement as the chances are you will be asked questions on those works mentioned.

- Why might it be useful for English students to read the *Twilight* series?
- What do you consider to be the most important work of literature of the 20th century?
- Who is your favourite author?
- Apart from your A level texts, what book have you read recently, and why did you enjoy it?
- Give a review of the last play you saw at the theatre.
- Critically analyse this poem.
- Comment in detail on this extract from a novel.
- How has the author used language in this text?

Geography

- Why should it be studied in its own right?
- Is geography just a combination of other disciplines?
- How can cities be made sustainable?
- If I were to visit the area where you live, what would I find interesting?
- Would anything remain of geography if we took the notion of place off the syllabus?
- How important is the history of towns when studying settlement patterns?
- Why is climate so unpredictable?
- What is the importance of space in global warming?
- Why do you think people care about human geography more than physical geography?
- What is more important, mapping or computer models?
- If you went to an isolated island to do research on the beach, how would you use the local community?
- Analyse a graph about a river. Why are there peaks and troughs?
- Look at a world map showing quality of life indicators. Explain the pattern in terms of two of the indicators.

(See also land economy questions.)

History

Candidates may be asked to discuss general concepts in history such as the role of the state, nationhood and the role of monarchy and parliament. Interviewers may also expect candidates to draw links between various related disciplines, for example politics and religion and be asked to evaluate the relative impact of these ideas in a historical context. As history is so broad the interviewer won't expect you to have detailed knowledge of many historical events but again if you have referred to something specifically in your personal statement, make sure you have done your research beforehand, as they are likely to ask you about it. Don't be surprised by a more light-hearted line of questioning, such as: 'if you were going to throw one of these historical figures out of a hot air balloon who would it be and why?'

- Discuss a historical movement that you find particularly interesting.
- How can one define revolution?
- Why did imperialism happen?
- Who was the greater democrat – Gladstone or Disraeli?
- Was the fall of the Weimar Republic inevitable?
- 'History is the study of the present with the benefit of hindsight.' Do you agree?
- Would history be worth studying if it didn't repeat itself?
- What is the difference between modern history and modern politics?
- What is the position of the individual in history?
- Would you abolish the monarchy for ideological or practical reasons?
- Why do historians differ in their views on Hitler?
- What skills should a historian have?
- In what periods has the Holy Grail been popular, with whom and why?
- Why is it important to visit historical sites relevant to the period you are studying?

Human sciences

- Talk about bovine spongiform encephalopathy and its implications, and the role of prions in Creutzfeldt–Jakob disease.
- What causes altitude sickness and how do humans adapt physiologically to high altitudes?
- Tell me about the exploitation of indigenous populations by Westerners.
- Why is statistics a useful subject for human scientists?
- Why are humans so difficult to experiment with?
- How would you design an experiment to determine whether genetics or upbringing is more important?
- What are the scientific implications of globalisation on the world?

Land economy

- Will the information technology revolution gradually result in the death of inner cities?
- What has been the effect of the Channel tunnel on surrounding land use?

Law

Interviewers won't be expecting candidates to have detailed knowledge of modern law but will be expecting them to be able to discuss general concepts in law. From many questions candidates will be expected to formulate initial definitions from ideas such a 'steal' or 'duty of care' and use those to respond to hypothetical situations posed by the interviewers.

- Questions on the points of law arising from scenarios – often relating to criminal law or duty of care.
- What does it mean to 'take' another's car?
- A cyclist rides the wrong way down a one-way street and a chimney falls on him. What legal proceedings should he take? What if he is riding down a private drive signed 'no trespassing'?
- X intends to poison his wife but accidentally gives the lethal draught to her identical twin. Would you consider this a murder?
- Questions on legal issues, particularly current ones.
- Should stalking be a criminal offence?
- Should judges have a legislative role?
- Do you think that anyone should be able to serve on a jury?
- Should judges be elected?
- Do judges have political bias?
- To what extent do you think the press should be able to release information concerning allegations against someone?
- Who do you think has the right to decide about euthanasia?
- How does the definition of intent distinguish murder from manslaughter?
- Can you give definitions of murder and manslaughter?
- Should foresight of consequences be considered as intending such consequences?

Material sciences

- Questions on physics, particularly solid materials.
- Questions on mathematics, particularly forces.
- Investigations of sample materials, particularly structure and fractures.

Maths and computation

- Questions (which may become progressively harder) on almost any area of the A level syllabus.

Maths and further maths

- Pure maths questions on integration.
- Applied maths questions on forces.
- Statistics questions on probability.
- Computation questions on iterations, series and computer arithmetic.

Medicine

An intellectual curiosity about the field, strong academic achievement and a realistic view of modern medicine and all that it entails are the most vital pre-requisites for medicine. So expect questions that test your interest and commitment to medicine as well as your understanding of the less glamorous side of the profession. Medicine is tough and they will be looking to weed out candidates who they don't think can stick the course. Expect work experience or volunteer placements to be assessed in terms of what you have learnt from those experiences. Some indication of your ability to work with others will be a big part of what they expect from you at interview.

- What did your work experience teach you about life as a doctor?
- What did you learn about asthma in your work experience on asthma research?
- How have doctors' lives changed in the past 30 years?
- Explain the logic behind the most recent NHS reforms.
- What are the mechanisms underlying diabetes?
- Why is it that cancer cells are more susceptible to destruction by radiation than normal cells?
- How would you determine whether leukaemia patients have contracted the disease because of a nearby nuclear power station?
- What does isometric exercise mean in the context of muscle function?
- What can you tell me about the mechanisms underlying sensory adaptation?
- What is an ECG?
- Why might a general practitioner not prescribe antibiotics to a toddler?
- Why are people anxious before surgery? Is it justifiable?
- How do you deal with stress?
- Why does your heart rate increase when you exercise?
- Questions on gene therapy.
- Questions on the ethics of foetal transplantation.
- Questions on biochemistry and human biology.

Modern languages

Prepare for comprehension and translations and to answer questions on a text given immediately prior to the interview. Also be prepared to have a short conversation in the pre-studied language that you have chosen to study further at university.

- Questions that focus on the use of language in original texts.
- Looking at a poem in the original language and commenting upon it.
- Describe aspects of this poem that you find interesting.
- Interpret this poem, commenting on its tone and context.
- Why do you want to study this language and not another?
- Why is it important to study literature?
- What is the difference between literature and philosophy?
- Questions on cultural and historical context and genre in European literature.
- How important is analysis of narrative in the study of literature?
- How important is knowledge of the biography of the author in the study of their literature?
- What is language?
- Detailed questions on writers, aspects of culture and films mentioned in personal statements.
- Questions on poems in whatever language is going to be studied.
- Questions on, for example, Italian literature in general, including questions on work in Latin, despite that subject not having been studied before.

Natural sciences

- What is an elastic collision?
- What happens when two particles collide – one moving and one stationary?
- What is friction?
- Questions on carboxylic acids.
- What is kinetic energy? How does it relate to heat?
- Questions on mechanisms in reactions of electrophiles and nucleophiles.
- Being shown a picture of an abnormal chromosome sequence and being asked to discuss this.
- Questions on how students will choose their modules in their first year of study.
- Questions on HIV and AIDS.
- Being given a graph showing the amount of a particular virus and the changes in T cells in the body over 12 years and being asked to discuss this.

Oriental studies

- What do you know about the Chinese language and its structure?
- What are the differences between English and any oriental language with which you are familiar?
- Does language have an effect on identity?

- Compare and contrast any ambiguities in the following sentences. 'Only suitable magazines are sold here.' 'Many species inhabit a small space.' 'He is looking for the man who crashed his car.'
- Comment on the following sentences. 'He did wrong.' 'He was wrong.' 'He was about to do wrong.'

Philosophy

As well as discussing classical philosophical ideas such as Plato's Cave and the problem of evil, be prepared to be asked questions drawing links between different disciplines such as politics, economics and even mathematics. The quest of most of philosophy is to 'seek the truth' and candidates must be prepared to be able to break down questions into their constituent parts and use evidence and logical reasoning to present an argument. Listening to podcasts such as Philosophy Bites can be a very good way to get an overview of the main ideas in a very wide range of philosophical debates and arguments in a short, easy to digest format.

- What is philosophy?
- Would you agree that if p is true and s believes p, then s knows p?
- Was the question you have just answered about knowing or about the meaning of the word 'know'?
- Comment on these statements/questions: I could be dreaming that I am in this interview; I do not know whether I am dreaming or not; therefore I do not know whether I am in this interview or not. A machine has a free will. When I see red, could I be seeing what you see when you see green?
- Is it a matter of fact or logic that time travels in one direction only?
- Is our faith in scientific method itself based on scientific method? If so, does it matter?
- I can change my hairstyle and still be me. I can change my political opinions and still be me. I can have a sex change and still be me. What is it then that makes me be me?
- Can it ever be morally excusable to kill someone?

Physics

Be prepared to answer any questions relating to the A level syllabus including the following.

- Questions on applied mathematics.
- Questions on mathematical derivations.
- How does glass transmit light?
- How does depressing a piano key make a sound?
- How does the voltage on a capacitor vary if the dielectric gas is ionised?
- How has physics influenced political thinking during the past century?

Politics

- Can you define 'government'? Why do we need governments?
- Can you differentiate between power and authority?
- What makes power legitimate?
- What would be the result of a 'state of nature'?
- How can you distinguish between a society, a state and an economy?
- Will Old Labour ever be revived? If so, under what circumstances?
- What would you say to someone who claims that women already have equal opportunities?
- What would you do tomorrow if you were the leader of the former Soviet Union?
- How does a democracy work?
- What elements constitute the ideologies of the extreme right?
- What do you think of discrimination in favour of female parliamentarians?
- How would you improve the comprehensive system of education?
- Does the UN still have a meaningful role in world affairs?
- Is further EU enlargement sustainable?
- How important is national identity?
- Should medics pay more for their degrees?

Psychology

Expect to be asked questions covering a wide range of aspects in psychology. Questions on whether psychology is a science or not and hence its usefulness are not uncommon. Questions on the ethics or morality of some psychological research methods can also be asked. A scientific basis and evidence-driven approach to presenting arguments is expected so you may be given the outcome of some kind of research and asked to comment on it. Don't forget that it will be important for you to say you are making assumptions based upon the reliability of the initial data and perhaps question its validity but be prepared to make an argument based upon the evidence as presented to you.

- Is neuropsychology an exact science? If not, is it useful?
- Questions on the experimental elucidation of the mechanisms underlying behaviour.
- Give some examples of why an understanding of chemistry might be important in psychology.
- A new treatment is tested on a group of depressives, who are markedly better in six weeks. Does this show that the treatment was effective?
- There are records of violent crimes that exactly mimic scenes of violence on television. Does this indicate that television causes real violence?
- Can a robot ever think like a human?

- How would you establish the quietest sound that you can hear as opposed to the quietest sound that you think you can hear?
- Why might one be able to remember items at the beginning and end of an aurally presented list better than items in the middle?
- Could a computer ever feel emotion?
- Is it ethically justifiable to kill animals for the purpose of research?
- What is emotional intelligence?
- Being given data from an experiment and being asked to analyse it.

Sociology

- What is the value of the study of social anthropology?
- Do people need tabloids?
- How would you define terrorism?
- Do you believe in selective education? Are we participating in selective education here?
- Is it possible to pose a sociological problem without sociological bias?
- Does prison work?
- Are MPs only in it for the power?
- How has the study of race and racism changed over the past 20 years?

(See also questions on politics and psychology.)

Theology

- Does moral rectitude reside in the agent, the act or its consequences?
- What, if anything, is wrong with voluntary euthanasia?
- What is the best reason that you can think of for believing in the existence of God?
- Do you think that this course could conceivably be persuasive on the issue?
- What relevance does theology have for art history?
- What relevance does archaeology have for theology?
- Can you comment on the portrayal of Jesus in John versus the other gospels?

(See also questions on philosophy.)

Veterinary medicine

- Has your work experience influenced your future career aspirations?
- Can you discuss an aspect of animal physiology that has struck you as contrasting with what you know of human physiology?
- Would our knowledge of BSE have been of value in controlling foot and mouth disease?
- Tell me about the biochemistry of DNA.
- What animal did this skull belong to?

(See also questions on biological sciences, chemistry and medicine.)

Any questions?

At the end of the interview you may be asked if you have any questions to ask the interviewer(s). It is always a good idea to have a few questions up your sleeve. One or two is a good number; more than three questions is usually too many. Write them down on a notepad and bring it with you. You will appear professional and keen. You may be able to bring up one of your favourite topics that was not discussed during the main part of the interview.

You probably shouldn't ask about anything that you should know already or about information easily available on the website or prospectus as this will seem a bit desperate, rather dull and certainly not well prepared. Questions such as the following are not likely to impress.

- What will my first year course entail?
- Can I change courses once I'm up at university if I don't like the course I've enrolled on?
- What's special about this college?
- Do I have to live in college?
- Can I choose my room?

If, after all your research, you still have questions about your course or college, this is the time to ask. If there was a topic covered during the interview that you didn't understand, you could enquire about where you can read more about it, or get further clarification from the interviewers themselves. You might also ask for clarification on how you choose course options in your second, third or fourth year or where last year's graduates have ended up; for example, are they undertaking further academic studies, are they working in the City, or have they gone on to business school.

The most important things to remember for your interview are to be on time, relax, be yourself and try to have fun!

The pooling system

The pooling system exists to ensure that all strong candidates get a good chance of being accepted to an Oxbridge college, but it means something slightly different at Cambridge and Oxford.

At Oxford, you may be 'pooled' after you have had an interview or interviews at your chosen college. This is the reason Oxford keeps applicants for several days during the interview process. You may be seen by other members of the faculty at different colleges during your stay. If you are a particularly strong candidate, academics at several colleges might ask you to interview, even if they are not at the college of your first choice and even if the academics at your preferred college already know they want to offer you a place. More often, being pooled indicates that, although you are a good candidate, your chosen college does not want to offer you a place but another college may. You will then be called for interview at the college that is considering offering you a place.

At Cambridge, pooling happens after the first interview process. If you are a strong candidate but there has been particularly high competition for places at your college, your interviewers may feel that they cannot offer you a place with them but that you deserve a place at Cambridge. They will then place you in the 'pool': a database that can be accessed by members of their faculty at different colleges. Academics at these other colleges, who may have spare places or weaker candidates, will then 'fish out' their choice of strong 'pooled' students and may ask them to come for interviews at their college. These second-round or 'pooling' interviews take place at the college of the academic who selects you some time in early January and a few weeks after the first round of interviews. If you are pooled, you still stand a chance of being accepted.

At Cambridge, in the 2016 cycle, 853 applicants got an offer from a college that was not the one to which they had applied or from a college to which they were assigned because they had made an open application – representing about 20% of all offers. In the 2015 cycle at Oxford, the percentage was even higher, with around 27% of applicants receiving an offer at a college other than their preferred choice.

Case studies: interview stories from previous applicants

Case study: Rachel, Maths and Philosophy, Oxford

At the time of writing this I have only been at Oxford a few weeks. Matriculation was great fun but now the work has well and truly started and I'm just about surviving! My course is particularly heavy (lucky me!) so trying to keep my head above water means I don't have much time to do other things, but I've learnt so much already and it is a truly amazing place.

As I applied for a combined degree, I was interviewed on both subjects. I was also interviewed at another college I hadn't applied to (as a potential applicant for the pool) but ended up going to my first choice of college anyway – so if this happens to you, don't worry about it. In short, I had a lot of interviews!

For my first interview, I had to arrive 30 minutes before the interview for a test. However, this turned out to be less of a test and more a set of questions which formed the structure of the entire interview. I had four questions on empiricism. One was: *A girl thinks she was born in Scotland and she lives there and her parents say she was born there. She was born there. So does she know she was born there?* Another question was: *A man has had a clock for many years and it has always been reliable. The clock shows 5.30. It is 5.30. Does the man know that it is 5.30?* Then there were two questions on ethics. The first was: *You can plug into a happiness machine that lets you live your dreams. You are not aware that you are plugged in when you are plugged in. Do you agree with the statement: 'It would be a mistake to plug into this machine.'?* The second question was: *We regret that thousands died in World War II but if they hadn't we might not be here today. This suggests we regret our own existence, but we do not – we are glad we are alive. Do you agree with the statement: 'Therefore we should not regret these events.'?*

My advice to future philosophy candidates is that obviously it is important to be able to think on your feet. However, from my reading and research I had a very clear idea on my opinion of what it is to 'know' something, which came in very useful for this interview. I definitely recommend having a good basis of knowledge and opinion on some common topics like epistemology, determinism/ free will and morality. Some more general advice to students applying for other subjects is to use any test you have before the interview to your advantage. Include ideas from your reading, especially those you can back up well. Make clear bullet points to help you argue your view. The interviewer will try to find fault in your argument, so listen and do not be afraid to admit you see an error in your argument, but make sure you try to find some alteration to accommodate it. If you believe something works, assert it with good evidence!

My second philosophy interview did not have any preparatory readings or a test beforehand and actually this made it harder! First of all I was asked a series of questions about validity and consistency. I had to analyse whether a set of statements were valid/consistent and each set got progressively harder. As I wasn't given any paper, this made the questions quite difficult. I certainly recommend a good night's sleep before your interview so you can perform mental exercises well! Then I was asked questions about how we define something, such as 'if I buy a car and call it Herbie, then one tyre is punctured and I have to replace it, is it still Herbie? If I buy Herbie and then take it all apart and put it back together exactly the same – is it still Herbie?'

Another piece of general advice is not to worry if your interviewer tells you there is a fault in your personal statement. I looked at a difficult area of philosophy for an essay outside of the A level specification which I had mentioned in my personal statement, but I hadn't got it quite right. When one of the interviewers mentioned this, I started to get quite worried. However, they weren't criticising me, they just wanted to inform me. If you know all of the ideas in your personal statement well, you can show your depth of knowledge to justify how you interpreted it.

My first maths interview also did not have a test beforehand. They started by asking me questions about how I would deal with struggling in my subject. For instance, what would I do if I were unable to complete a worksheet or were falling behind in a module? They also asked about the links between maths and philosophy and questioned me about my personal statement. One of the problems I remember was: if I have a square board of tiles n by n, and I remove 2 tiles in opposite corners, can I fill the remaining shape with a 2 by 1 tile shape?

Hint: consider the n by n board shaded like a chessboard

The interviews go so quickly that you may only do a couple of questions and you may not complete one of them. Don't worry if this is the case – 23 (!) minutes isn't long.

In my second maths interview I was asked what I thought of Euler's Identity as I had mentioned this in my personal statement.

Make sure you know your personal statement really well. If you mention a mathematical idea, be able to talk about it with depth of knowledge and enthusiasm. Sometimes questions may be easier than you expect. It took me some time to get the question 'what is the cube root of i?' because I thought I was looking for something more complicated than the method I already knew, but this method was what they wanted! Another question I remember was 'how do we define the exponential function?' (this was actually just looking at Maclaurin series).

My final maths interview focused on sketching graphs and was extended in several ways. They put a modulus around y rather than x, which has interesting results. I had to do some implicit differentiation and be able to interpret 1/0 as an infinite gradient meaning a vertical line. You definitely want to revise your first A level year work because they know you've covered those areas. However, also make sure you are on top of C4 and the other parts of second year work you have covered recently as these can come up.

Good luck!

Case study: Flora, Geography, Oxford

At Oxford, I had separate human geography and physical geography interviews. At Cambridge, as a graduate applicant I had multiple-mini interviews; normal sixth-form undergraduate applicants will have longer interviews with college tutors.

My advice would be: practise, practise, practise! The more familiar you are with the setting of an interview and the process, the more comfortable and at ease you will be on the day! Ask friends/family/teachers to help you. Become used to the idea of being pushed out of your comfort zone. A good interview should leave you feeling like you were being challenged and stretched. Read around your subject and think about how you can incorporate this into your interview. Be comfortable with talking about data (tables/graphs/compound structures/pictures of cells) that they might show you. Know your personal statement inside out.

Make sure you go through what you have done in A level so far and that you understand everything – the questions they will ask you will build on that knowledge so you need to know the basics! Research who will be interviewing you. Many tutors will ask you about things that are relevant to their field of research (although this is not always the case!).

Stay calm and THINK. Don't rush into giving an answer. Take a moment, think about what they have asked you and structure your answer in a clear way. If you don't understand the question, then don't be afraid to ask them for help. They aren't trying to catch you out, they are interested in how you approach a problem.

It is a stressful time and you will most likely meet many of those competing for a place on your course. Don't be put off by them! Remember, Oxbridge attracts highly competitive people who like to show off but nine times out of ten they won't gain a place. Just be yourself. Although it's a pressured and stressful time, try to enjoy it! You are being given the opportunity to discuss your chosen subject with people who are at the top of the field!

Case study: Toby, Natural Sciences, Cambridge

It is difficult to say what a typical interview is like with Cambridge as every college does it differently and it depends on the subject. The first time I applied, when I didn't have A level Chemistry, Sidney Sussex gave me an interview focused on biology and one on biochemistry (it would have been straight chemistry but I hadn't studied it). Queens', on the other hand, asked for three topics I was good at beforehand and gave me a biology interview and a maths/chemistry/biochemistry interview. The maths part went very, very badly but I still managed to get in, so it's important to realise that they look at all your different academic attributes and it doesn't all rest on the interview. So the more outstanding your grades, the more you can afford to mess up the interview, basically.

One thing I have found that differed from practice interviews is that Cambridge never quizzed me on my personal statement. They asked questions that assumed the knowledge of what was mentioned in the personal statement but they never said, 'Tell me about this thing you've mentioned'. I should also say, apart from the maths one which was a struggle, I really enjoyed my interviews and came out buzzing afterwards.

Case study: Kathy, Engineering, Oxford

Mine was an unusual situation, in that I only finally made up my mind to apply for engineering at Oxford about a week before I completed my application. It was not that I was not interested in the subject; in fact, I was passionate about it and I had done related work experience and immersed myself in the subject through wider reading. My A level subjects were also compatible with studying engineering at degree level. However, my family had really wanted me to apply for economics. I toyed with the idea of reading economics and engineering, a new course at the time, but I decided in the end to follow my heart and to aim for engineering.

Once the decision was made, I continued to read widely and to engage in discussing related topics with my teachers. I also had some very useful mock interview practice with my college tutors who were also subject specialists. When I went for the interview, I tried to remain calm and I think this helped a lot.

Although I had been prepared to answer lots of questions, I did not have to say very much during the interview itself. This was because the interviewers mainly gave me problems to do with mathematics and physics; my task was to find solutions to these problems. I think this style of interview was ideal for me. I really felt that I was working with the tutors to achieve a common goal.

I am now in my second year at Oxford. Although it is very hard work, I am very pleased that I decided to apply for engineering.

Case study: Maud, English, Cambridge

I applied to study English at Cambridge in 2013 and interviewed at both Queens' College and then Churchill College. I won a place at the latter. If all goes well, you will be invited to interview. Oxbridge interviews have a reputation of being full of impossible idiosyncrasies and outlandishly abstract questions, but my own interviews were fairly standard. All of my interviews were divided into two parts. Firstly, I was given a poem to read, which the interviewer then asked me questions about. If you're applying for English, you can definitely practise for that first section. Take an anthology of poetry, pick one at random, read it and start thinking about what you could say about it. Cambridge will not expect you to have all the answers and you do not need to 'explain' the poem. Instead, you want to demonstrate that you are alive to the nuances of language and that you can read critically and flexibly. Secondly, I was asked questions about my personal statement and broader academic interests. When you're thinking about an Oxbridge application, your teachers might encourage you to 'read around your subject', and it is at interview that this kind of preparation can really benefit you. Reading widely gives you more to talk about, but it also shows the assessors that you are academically self-motivated, that you will go beyond what is asked of you at school. Start early: speed-reading a couple of pages the night before will not do you much good! In this section of the interview, I was asked whether 'social, historical and political contexts are important when you read a poem'. There are an endless number of ways you could answer this question. For example, if you read George Orwell's *1984* and loved it, you might use this question to talk about why you found it fascinating and how it was responding to other political events at the time it was written. During the interview, the assessors want to see how you think, so be flexible and vocal, and most importantly, stay confident!

Case study: Lucinda, Theology and Religion, Oxford

You often hear from Oxford and Cambridge interviewees and advisers that the admissions tutors and dons just want to see whether you can think on your feet and whether you are someone with whom they are able to work. They will say that stories of eccentric interviews are a thing of the past. My interviews at Oxford for Theology were rather different and I have vivid memories of them.

The first interview lulled me into a false sense of security. It was with an affable admissions tutor who had a cosy chat with me about many things; the only thing was that none of them was about the subject I wished to study.

The second interview was more daunting. I entered a long, wainscoted chamber, at the other end of which a don was warming himself at a roaring fire. As I approached the welcoming blaze, I was commanded to remain where I was as I had not been invited further into this sacrosanct place. I kept my coat closely fastened as some protection against the icy blast at my end of the room, but was ordered to remove it. Questions about my personal statement were abrasively fired at me. At last, there was some relief. I answered a question which appeared to satisfy my inquisitor. I was rewarded by a long overdue invitation to sit near the hearth and the interrogation became an interview.

My third interview was also a challenge. I was asked to comment upon an unseen passage in Hebrew. Not knowing the language, I requested a translation. The professor seemed impressed by this, declaring, 'At last – someone who admits they can't read Hebrew!' I can only assume that the other poor candidates had struggled valiantly to discuss the passage in the ancient tongue of which they were ignorant.

My ordeal was over. I secured a place at the hallowed halls of Oxford and have never looked back.

The 'post-mortem'

Try not to dwell on how the interview went. Admissions tutors often say that students who think they have done badly in fact have acquitted themselves very well … and vice versa. Sometimes a lengthy interview and a good grilling will mean that they've given you a fighting chance to show your true colours.

I like to tell students the story of a candidate who came out of her interview and phoned her school teacher to report back on how her interview had gone. She told him that she had been given a poem to read and analyse and when she went into her interview she announced that she wasn't sure who had written it but she knew by the style of the writing that it had to be a woman. She then spent half her interview justifying her position. The teacher was silent on the other end of the line until he finally confessed that he knew the poem very well and in fact it was written by a man. Cue many tears of frustration and embarrassment.

Three weeks later, this student was offered a place to read English at Oxford. Remember, they are not looking at how much you know now but your potential. Tutors want students who display enthusiasm for their subject, along with a natural flair and ability. They want people who aren't afraid of putting forward their point of view, as long as they can justify it. Ultimately, they want students who will be fun and challenging to teach.

10| Non-standard applications

This chapter deals with 'non-standard' applications from international students and mature students.

International students

International students are welcome at both Oxford and Cambridge and are valued members of the student population. At Cambridge, there are currently over 21,000 students at the University, including around 1,300 international students from over 65 different countries reading undergraduate courses.

At Oxford, international students currently come from over 140 countries and make up about 41% of the student body, including 63% of graduate students.

If you have read the previous chapters in this book, you will know that both universities offer a distinctive form of undergraduate education. Students apply for a three- or four-year degree in one to three subjects and they study those subjects exclusively. English universities typically do not have 'general education' or 'core curriculum' degrees that, for example, require humanities students to do science courses. The important admissions criterion is excellent academic achievement. Oxford and Cambridge select on academic ability and academic potential, evinced by secondary school results (examination results and/or predicted grades), a personal statement, an academic reference and, if required, an admissions test or written work.

Teaching is by the tutorial/ supervision system. Students attend lectures and seminars, and have practical laboratory sessions in the sciences, but the heart of the Oxbridge teaching method is a weekly meeting with the student's tutor – typically a leading academic – and one or two other students to engage in an intensive exchange of ideas about the week's work.

All Oxford and Cambridge undergraduates live, eat and study in one of the universities' residential colleges or permanent private halls. These small communities of typically 30–70 academics and 300–500 students from across disciplines are the focus for teaching and for social and sporting life.

Both universities are research intensive, where academics are conducting cutting-edge research in every subject. The collegiate system allows academics and students across subjects and year groups and from different cultures and countries to come together to share ideas.

Oxford and Cambridge qualifications are recognised and valued around the world. Graduates will go on to further study and/or to work in a range of professions in some of the best companies and organisations in the world.

In order to study at Oxford or Cambridge your level of English must be of a high standard. This is measured by your performance in various different examinations, including:

* the IELTS (International English Language Testing System), in which you need a score of at least Band 7.0 in each section (speaking, listening, writing and reading) and an overall score of Band 7.0 (Oxford) and 7.5 (Cambridge) – for information about the IELTS exam and where and when it can be taken, visit www.ielts.org
* the English Language GCSE examination at grade B (for Oxford). For Cambridge, you will need to enquire with your college admissions office. Please note that Oxford does not accept IGCSE English First or Second Language
* for European students a high grade in English taken as part of a leaving examination (for example the European Baccalaureate or the Abitur) may be acceptable
* an A or score of at least 185 in the Cambridge Certificate in Advanced English (Oxford), Cambridge will accept a B grade; or A or B grade or a score of 185 in the Cambridge Certificate of Proficiency in English (Oxford), Cambridge will accept a C grade.

For Oxford applicants it is worth noting that the following situations would exempt you from having to meet the English language requirements: studying the International Baccalaureate (as long as it is taught in English), studying the Singapore Integrated Programme (SIPCAL), being educated full-time in English for the duration of the two most recent years prior to the 15 October application deadline, and staying in full-time education taught in English in your country until the end of the academic year.

The level of English proficiency required depends a great deal on which subject you wish to study. If you want to apply for an essay-based subject (any of the arts or social science subjects including economics, PPE, psychology, history and English literature), your written work must be fluent. On the other hand, English language is much less important for the study of mathematics. (See www.ox.ac.uk/admissions/undergraduate/international-students/english-language-requirements and www.undergraduate.study.cam.ac.uk/international-students/entrance-requirements for further details.)

How much does it cost?

As an international student there are three costs you'll need to consider. These are your tuition fees, college fees and living expenses.

You will have to prove that you can finance yourself for your entire course as it's not possible for you to work during the academic session to pay your way through university. Colleges ask for financial guarantees and proof is also required when applying for a visa.

You will need to be sure of your 'fee status'. Generally speaking, in order to be considered as a 'home' student for tuition fee purposes, you need to either live in an EU member state or have indefinite leave to enter or remain in the UK. In addition, you need to have lived in the European Economic Area (EEA) for the last three years, not solely for educational purposes. Currently, EU students are still classed as 'Home' students and there are no fee implications for students for 2017 entry; EU students starting their course in September 2017 will pay home fees for the duration of their course. EU students starting their courses in September 2017 remain eligible to apply for student funding under the current terms. This was confirmed by Jo Johnson, Minister for Universities and Science, in September 2016.

Once the UK triggers Article 50 of the Lisbon Treaty, this will launch the process of formally negotiating Britain's exit from the EU. Therefore, for the time being, until it is announced otherwise, EU students will continue to pay the same fees as home students.

The cost of studying at a UK university for an international student is much higher than for a home student. The tuition fees at Cambridge for the academic year 2017–18 start from between £16,608 and £25,275 for most courses, rising to £40,200 for courses in medicine and veterinary medicine (both pre-clinical and clinical training). At Oxford, annual tuition fees are between £15,755 and £23,190. Please note that clinical medicine fees for overseas and islands students will be significantly higher. For more information go to the following websites.

Cambridge:

- international students: www.undergraduate.study.cam.ac.uk/international-students
- financial issues for international students: www.undergraduate.study.cam.ac.uk/international-students/fees
- application form: www.undergraduate.study.cam.ac.uk/applying/copa.

Oxford:

- Student Information and Advisory Service: www.ox.ac.uk/students/new/international

- official site, including entrance requirements, international qualifications, etc.: www.ox.ac.uk/admissions/undergraduate/international-students/international-applicants
- fees for international students: www.ox.ac.uk/admissions/under graduate/fees-and-funding/tuition-fees.

College fees

All overseas-fee status students, and those home students who are not eligible for tuition fee support (e.g. because they are taking a second degree), normally have to pay college fees in addition to university tuition fees. The college fee covers the cost to your college of providing a range of educational, domestic and pastoral services and support. The fees vary slightly between colleges but at Cambridge are typically in the range of £5,670 to £7,980 per year and you should allow for increases in subsequent years. At Oxford, the college fees are £7,350 for the academic year 2017–18.

Living expenses

Your living expenses may be higher than for a UK student, for instance if you have to stay in Oxford or Cambridge or the UK during the vacations. The Oxford website provides a table that outlines the likely living costs for overseas students in 2017–18.

The Cambridge website advises that the minimum resources needed per year are estimated to be approximately £9,570, depending on your lifestyle. Of course, many international students are likely to spend more money travelling to and from their home countries.

Applying to Oxford or Cambridge

Applications must be made at least three months early, and, with only minor exceptions (e.g. organ scholars – and even here there are restrictions for applicants for medicine, engineering and law), are mutually exclusive for first undergraduate degrees. This means that, in any one year, candidates may apply to only Oxford or Cambridge, not both.

In addition to the usual UCAS application, you will have to submit a Cambridge Online Preliminary Application (COPA) if you are applying to Cambridge. See the website www.undergraduate.study.cam.ac.uk/applying/copa for more details.

Applicants to Oxford or Cambridge will have to submit a UCAS application, take a test or, occasionally, submit written work specific to their chosen subject.

The interview

Every candidate offered a place at Oxbridge will be asked to interview. Normally conducted by a tutor or don, the interview will be used to check whether the course is well suited to the applicant's interests and aptitudes, and to look for evidence of self-motivation, independent thinking, academic potential and ability to learn through the tutorial system.

Cambridge conducts admissions interviews in Canada, Malaysia, Singapore, Hong Kong and China and for those applicants unable to travel to Cambridge. If it's not possible for you to attend an interview at Oxford in person, it does arrange video conference, telephone and Skype interviews – although this is by no means guaranteed. Applicants for medicine at Oxford must travel to Oxford if shortlisted for interview.

Scare stories about impossible questions are rife but, with some advance practice and preparation, the interview should be treated as an opportunity for students to sell themselves rather than as something to be dreaded. Questions are not designed to catch out or embarrass candidates, but to identify intellectual potential and assess how they think and respond to unfamiliar material. To help feel ready, you should practise being in an interview situation and answering questions based around the subject you are looking to study.

Admissions tests

Admissions tests have come to constitute a vital part of many students' applications and are used by Oxbridge and other universities to separate the increasing numbers of students applying with top grades. Tests are now used for several subjects and include the BMAT for medicine and veterinary sciences, the ELAT for English literature and the LNAT for law. Again, the best way for students to prepare for these is practice. Details of these tests are provided in Chapter 8.

Entry requirements vary for international students, so it's always a good idea to read the international pages of each website to ensure you don't miss out. If you don't make the final cut, don't despair. Studying at Oxbridge may be a passport to the realm of the academic elite, but unsuccessful Oxbridge applicants will easily find satisfying and equally challenging alternatives in the UK.

Mature students

A mature student at Oxford or Cambridge is classed as anyone over 21 at the start of October in their first year. Both universities welcome applications from mature students and, like everyone else who wishes to join these highly selective institutions, candidates will need to demonstrate academic ability and a firm commitment to study.

Your work experience and life skills will be considered to be relevant to your application but you must have also undertaken some type of formal academic qualifications within the three years before you apply. You will need to prove to your tutors that you will be able to cope with the demands of academic study and that you have sufficient study skills to commit to an undergraduate degree course. Many different academic qualifications are acceptable. For further information on the qualifications you would need to apply, please consult the universities' websites.

The application procedure for mature students is the same as for other students and you will have to submit an application through UCAS. At Oxford, some subjects require you to take a written test or to submit written work as part of your application. At Cambridge, mature applicants will not have to sit any pre-interview tests, apart from the BMAT, which must be taken by all students applying for medicine or veterinary medicine. If your course has an at-interview assessment, you will be asked to take a common-format written test in Cambridge, if you are called to interview. Your college will be sympathetic if you are unable to supply appropriate written material but you will need to discuss this with it directly.

Oxford does not accept transfer students under any circumstances and Cambridge would only consider them under exceptional circumstances. However, you can apply to take a second undergraduate degree at both universities. If you're a graduate with an approved degree from another university, you can apply to take a Cambridge BA course as an affiliated student. This means you could take the degree in a year less than usual. At Cambridge, most colleges admit some affiliated students. However, please note that it is not possible to study architecture as an affiliated student on a two-year programme – a three-year degree would be required. It should also be noted that only Lucy Cavendish (women only), St Edmund's and Wolfson consider affiliated applications for medicine or veterinary medicine.

How to apply

Most Cambridge colleges accept some mature students and many have large fellowships and graduate communities that make for a very welcoming and supportive environment. Some students may prefer to apply to one of the four mature-student colleges (Hughes Hall, Lucy Cavendish, St Edmund's and Wolfson). Some colleges will not accept mature students for certain subjects, so you must check their websites carefully.

At Oxford, as a mature student, you can apply to any college. One college (Harris Manchester) and three of the permanent private halls (Blackfriars, St Stephen's House and Wycliffe Hall) take only mature students.

Both universities will be looking for academic potential and motivation just as they do for younger students and they assess each application individually. Mature applicants should not be concerned that their profile will be different. Most mature students who have the right academic background will be called for interview and will be compared fairly against applicants from very different educational backgrounds.

You will need to show evidence of your current academic or work-related performance and give assurance that if you have taken a break from education you are fully back in the routine of dealing with a heavy and challenging academic workload.

Ideally, you will present conventional academic qualifications. If this is not possible or appropriate in your case, the colleges may accept Access, Open University and other Foundation courses. You will need to provide full details of the courses you have taken and the grades achieved and/or predicted when you apply. If you cannot find a way to provide the information on your UCAS form you will need to send appropriate documents (transcripts, mark schemes, etc.) by post at the time you apply.

You will also need to present a reference; this can be written by anybody who is familiar with your current academic work. If you are not currently studying, your referee may be a current or former employer but they must be able to comment on your application and potential.

Mature students from outside the UK should check carefully the information for international students. Because of recent visa changes, if you are considering bringing dependants with you to the UK, it is likely that your dependants will not be eligible for a visa.

Mature students can get information and advice from the admissions offices, as well as details about events and activities run by the universities for prospective mature applicants. See the following websites for more information:

* www.ox.ac.uk/students/new/mature
* www.undergraduate.study.cam.ac.uk/applying/mature-students-and-second-undergraduate-degrees
* www.ucas.com/ucas/undergraduate/getting-started/mature-undergraduate-students.

Lady Margaret Hall Foundation Year

The Lady Margaret Hall Foundation Year has been designed to enable students from under-represented backgrounds to have a chance of higher education at the University of Oxford. The development of academic skills is emphasised and each year a small number of students are given the chance to make an application to LMH for degree courses.

Potential students eligible to apply for the Foundation Year include:

- Students from schools or colleges which historically have had little or very few students progressing on to study at Oxford
- students from disadvantaged socio-economic backgrounds
- students whose local area has a low participation rate to higher education.

Further details on the application process can be found at the website www.lmhfoundationyear.com/welcome/course/.

11 | Getting the letter

Once you've had your interview you will probably have mixed emotions about how well you have done. The majority of students have no strong feeling for whether they are likely to be successful. This is perfectly normal! It's worth remembering that admissions tutors have reported to us that often candidates feel they performed badly at interview when in fact they did very well.

Don't forget, too, that your interview is just one part of your 'package'; before the tutors make a final decision they will consider your application as a whole, which means they will look at your UCAS application and any supplementary questions, school reference, written work and specialist test, as well as your performance at the interview. One tutor told me that at Cambridge they spend about 90 minutes considering every application. They really do their utmost to pick the best candidates and make the whole process as fair as possible.

Oxford decisions are usually sent by the end of January, and conditional offers are nearly always A*A*A–AAA depending on the subject.

Cambridge decisions are usually received at the beginning of January, although officially they will be posted by the end of January 2018 for those interviewed in 2017. Conditional offers are nearly always A*A*A–A*AA depending on the subject. If you have applied with an extenuating circumstances form (ECF) you may be made an offer that will take into account your special circumstances.

If you have applied to study mathematics at Cambridge, your offers will be dependent on your grades in two STEPs (Sixth Term Examination Paper) – three-hour maths exams taken at the end of the A level exam period which test advanced problem solving and mathematical ingenuity rather than basic knowledge and technique.

Pooled applicants

Some students who applied to Cambridge may find that they have been pooled. This will indicate that they are strong candidates for a place at Cambridge but that there is no place available for them at their chosen college. Approximately 800 to 900 out of around 3,300 of pooled applicants are subsequently awarded a place at Cambridge. Applicants are pooled for a variety of reasons, and are categorised by the pooling college as A (strongly recommended), B (probably worth an offer), P (outstanding on paper but less impressive at interview) or S (applicant in need of reassessment).

Sometimes a college wishes to see other applicants from the pool before it fills all of its places with direct applicants – this sometimes results in several applicants being pooled and subsequently being awarded places at their original college of choice. Some are subsequently invited for interview at other colleges; if this happens the college concerned will contact you to ask you to come for an interview early in January. If another college wishes to offer you a place following the pool, you should hear from it at the start or middle of January. Otherwise, your original college will write back to you by the end of January informing you that you have been unsuccessful.

At Oxford, pooling occurs while students are in Oxford for their interview with the college they applied to. It is quite normal for an Oxford candidate to be interviewed in multiple colleges and this should not be interpreted negatively. Quite the opposite is true; candidates should see this as further opportunity to impress and secure a place.

Rejection

If you are unsuccessful at either university, you will receive a rejection letter in the post between December and mid-January. If this is the case for you, do not despair. Remember that there is incredible competition to get a place at Oxbridge. Although for many subjects one in five students interviewed are accepted, for other subjects 10 students are interviewed for one place. More than 5,000 of the unsuccessful applicants per year will have been predicted three As or higher at A level, and are clearly intelligent and successful students.

If you are rejected, despite having a set of perfect grades and impeccable references, and you want to know why, ring the admissions tutor at your chosen college and ask for feedback. If your grades are good and you are really set on claiming a place at Oxbridge, think about why you did not succeed the first time and consider trying again. Neither Cambridge nor Oxford looks badly on students who apply twice. You may have been too young the first time or too focused on school exams to dedicate enough time to the application process. Alternatively, you may not have made an appropriate subject choice and were not passionate enough about your field. If once was enough, however, focus on your other university choices and draw on your Oxbridge experiences to help you in your preparation for future interviews.

Case study: Julia, Cambridge

I have always been fascinated by the interaction of people, politics and cultures and enjoy the logic of subjects like languages and mathematics. This curiosity and interdisciplinary interest led me to choose my slightly unusual A level combination of History, French and Maths. It also led me to choose an unusual course, ASNC (a BA in Anglo-Saxon, Norse and Celtic), for my Cambridge application.

I found the mock interview practice my college provided extremely helpful in identifying my strengths and weaknesses. While I had completed a lot of extra reading around my subjects, I found that I needed to interrogate these texts more to be able to adapt and apply them to the questions an interviewer might pose. This feedback did not just help me prepare for my Cambridge interview but other interviews and assessments at some of my other university choices.

I was very nervous at the interview itself but when it was over I realised I had enjoyed it. I also came away feeling that I had learnt more not only about the course but about different ways of thinking. When the decision came and I had not been successful, naturally I was disappointed but I focused on my other university options and took a place at KCL to read International Relations. In hindsight, I am sure that the interview experience itself was an excellent life experience – I do not believe that I will be as nervous as some other applicants when it comes to job interviews!

Ultimately, there are so many other wonderful universities out there that it is important not to get stuck believing that 'Oxbridge is the best'. I truly feel that King's suits my personality, so it turns out that the Cambridge admissions office knows what it is doing.

If you don't get the grades required

If you did not get the grades required by Oxbridge (for example you got an AAB rather than A*AA), your conditional offer will be withdrawn. You may wish to contact the admissions tutor at your college at this point, but you should be prepared for the fact that it is unlikely you be accepted.

If there is a real and significant reason why you did not fulfil your potential in the exams (for example, illness or a bereavement in the family) you should ensure that the admissions tutor is aware of this (ideally this information will be corroborated with evidence and by your referee) as it may affect their decision. Traditionally, students have been discouraged from retaking exams to try and secure a place at Oxford or Cambridge, but there are examples of students who have done so successfully at both institutions. If you do not secure your offer, it is worth asking the admissions tutor whether you would be considered next year if you were to retake and/or reapply.

UCAS has an 'Adjustment' system where students who get above their predicted grades can go back to universities who rejected them and try for a place again. However, it is unlikely that this system will apply to Oxford and Cambridge since they are always extremely oversubscribed. What you can do if your exam results exceed your expectations is to reapply the following year with your excellent grades.

Remember, if you are a motivated and focused student, then you will excel at whatever university you go to, and if you love your subject, then your interest will flourish wherever you are.

Case study: Charlie, Oxford

I initially applied to a college in Oxford to read history. I performed well in the interview, but did not get an offer, although the rejection letter still reassured me that I had been a strong candidate; it was simply that I was out-performed by the other applicants. I went on to get excellent A level grades.

The rejection gave me a chance to reflect on what I really wanted to study at university. I had always been interested in English literature, but had not studied it at A level. Poetry has always been my favourite genre and I have been writing poetry in earnest since my early teens. In fact, I had a volume of poetry published during my enforced gap year. This led to a series of visits to schools and even prisons, where I gave readings from my book and discussed my work. Clearly, this augmented my confidence; it also crystallised my desire to study English language and literature at university and to reapply to Oxford in order to achieve this aim.

The following year I enrolled on a one-year intensive A level course in English Literature. I thoroughly enjoyed the inspiring lessons given by my teacher and got on really well with my classmates. I finished the year with the top grade. Before reapplying to Oxford in the autumn term, I rang around the various colleges to see how they would view me as a candidate applying the second time around. Having heard about my profile, a surprising number said they would view my application favourably. I got my place; I am so glad I persevered.

Appendix 1: timetables

The year before you apply

Throughout the year, make sure that you have engaged with your subject by reading widely around it and by participating in super-curricular activities.

March

- Request an undergraduate prospectus and the alternative prospectus from the student unions of Cambridge or Oxford.
- Research other universities to which you are considering applying.

April

- Write the first draft of your personal statement.
- Book a place at an open day at Cambridge; you don't have to book an open day at Oxford, but you could arrange to visit a tutor.

June/July

- Sit your AS exams (if offered by your school).
- Oxford open days on 28 and 29 June.
- Cambridge open days on 6 and 7 July.

Summer holidays

- Ask friends and family to read your personal statement and make revisions.
- Gain relevant work experience, if you have not done so already.
- Participate in super-curricular activities, if you have not done so already.
- Read widely around your subject, if it is appropriate.

The year in which you apply

September

- Finalise your personal statement with your teachers.
- Visit the UCAS website (www.ucas.com) and register.
- Fill in the UCAS form – UCAS applications may be submitted from 6 September (www.ucas.com/apply-and-track/key-dates).
- Register and book a place to sit the LNAT between 15 and 20 October (if you want to study law at Oxford) – (www.lnat.ac.uk).
- Register for the BMAT if you are applying for biomedical science (at Oxford), medicine (at Oxford or Cambridge) or veterinary science (Cambridge only) – (www.admissionstestingservice.org/for-test-takers/bmat.dates-dates-and-costs).
- Register for other subject-related pre-interview tests for Oxford and Cambridge. See Chapter 8 for a complete list of Cambridge courses that require a pre-interview assessment.
- Oxford open day on 15 September.

October

- For Oxford applicants register and book LNAT test on 5 October. Deadline for sitting the test is 20 October at the latest (although 2017 deadline may change).
- The deadline for UCAS receiving your application, whether for Oxford or Cambridge, is 6 p.m. on 15 October.
- The registration deadline for pre-interview subject-related tests is 15 October.
- Fill in the separate Cambridge SAQ. This will be emailed to you and must be completed by 6 p.m. on 22 October 2017 in most cases.
- Receive the acknowledgement letter from your chosen college in mid to late October.

November

- Sit Oxford admissions tests and Cambridge pre-admissions tests on 2 November.
- Receive the letter inviting you to interview from Oxford or Cambridge and explaining if and when to submit written work. Alternatively, you may receive a letter rejecting you at this point.
- Submit written work with the special form – see faculty website for details. (Work should be sent directly to the college unless you have made an 'open application', in which case send it directly to the faculty. The work should be marked by your school). For Oxford the deadline is 10 November. For Cambridge it is 3 November.

December

- If invited, attend interviews in the first three weeks of December (see precise interview dates for your subject in the prospectus).
- You may have to sit some tests at interview.

January

- Beginning of January: applicants who have been placed in the 'winter pool' are notified (Cambridge only). This may or may not entail going to Cambridge for another set of interviews.
- Hear the outcome of your application from Oxford by 11 January.
- End of January: hear the outcome of your application from Cambridge.

June

- Sit A levels (or equivalent exams).
- After A levels sit STEP (for students who have a conditional offer to read mathematics at Cambridge only).

July

- 5 July: IB results day.

August

- 16 August: A level and Pre-U results day.
- If you have made your grades your place will be confirmed by the university.
- If you have not made your grades, contact the admissions tutor of your college.
- You may be sent a letter of rejection at this point.

Appendix 2: glossary

Adjustment
If you have met all of the conditions of your firm choice and exceeded at least one grade, you have the opportunity to enter UCAS Adjustment. Adjustment begins on A level results day and runs until 31 August. You can put your application on hold for a week to see if any institutions would be willing to offer you a place. If you register but do not find an alternative course, you will keep your place at your original firm-choice university.

Admissions tutor
The tutor especially assigned the role of selecting candidates.

Alumni
People who once went to the college but who have now graduated.

Battels
The payments students and fellows at Oxford make to their college for accommodation, meals, etc.

Bedder
The person who cleans your room at Cambridge.

Clearing
When exam results come out in the summer, students who do not meet their offers can enter the competition for places at universities that have spare places. Clearing vacancies are listed in the UCAS search tool from early July to mid-September.

Collections
Exams sat at the beginning of each term at Oxford in the colleges. These are a good indication of your level of progress during the previous term, but do not count towards your final degree classification.

Collegiate system
This term describes the fact that both Oxford and Cambridge universities are divided into about 30 separate colleges, where students live and where their social lives are based.

Deferred entry
This means you would like to take a gap year (i.e. defer your entry for a year). You apply this year but will accept a place in two years' time.

Deselected
Some candidates will not make it to the interview; they are 'deselected' before the interview and will receive a letter of rejection.

Director of studies (DOS)

Your DOS at the University of Cambridge is an academic member of staff from your subject faculty who is also a fellow of your college. He or she is responsible for your academic development and will meet with you at the beginning and end of each term to check on your progress and will probably be your interviewer. The DOS at Cambridge is the equivalent to a tutor at Oxford.

Don

A teacher at a university; in particular a senior member of an Oxbridge college.

Exhibition

A scholarship you can win in recognition of outstanding work at Oxford.

Faculty

The department building dedicated to one particular subject, for example, the Faculty of Architecture.

Fellow

An academic member of a college. Each academic in every faculty is also assigned a college; this is where their office space is located. Some more senior fellows are given responsibility for the academic achievement of the students at their college and act as the DOS (at Cambridge) or tutor (at Oxford) of a number of undergraduates.

Fresher

First-year undergraduate student.

Go up

Traditionally, instead of simply saying 'go to university', for Oxford and Cambridge the term used is to 'go up' to university.

Hall

One of the places where you eat your meals in college. Usually you will be offered a three-course evening meal with wine. Formal hall is a more elaborate affair and you may be required to wear your gown.

Head of House (Oxford)

This is a general term for the Head of a College, who is also known by different names at different colleges such as the Dean, the Master, the President, the Principal, the Provost, the Rector, and the Warden. Many of these terms are also used at Cambridge.

Hilary Term

This is the second academic term of the year at Oxford from January to the middle of March. The equivalent term at Cambridge is called Lent.

Junior common room (JCR)

A common room for all undergraduate students of a given college. Each college has its own JCR.

Matriculation

Matriculation gives membership of the University to newly enrolled students who are embarking on degree-level programmes.

Michaelmas Term

The first term of the academic year which begins in October and ends in December.

Norrington table

Oxford league table that measures each college's academic achievement at the final examinations.

Noughth Week

This refers to the week before full term begins in Oxford.

Open application

A way of applying to either Oxford or Cambridge without specifying a college.

Oxbridge

The collective term for Oxford and Cambridge.

Permanent private halls

These are like mini-colleges in Oxford. Two of them – St Benet's Hall and Regent's Park College – are for students studying any subject, but the remaining five are mainly for people who are training to be in the ministry. St Benet's Hall had been for men only until recently. As of 2016 entry, it now accepts both male and female undergraduate applicants.

Pigeon Post

This is an informal term for Oxford's internal postal service. At both universities, your pigeon-hole is referred to as your 'pidge'.

Pool

The pool is where applicants who may be rejected by their first-choice college are held. Another college may select them for an interview or make them an offer. The other college may do this for a variety of reasons, such as if it does not have enough good applicants and wants to find better ones, or if it wants to check that their weakest chosen student is better than another college's rejected student – a sort of moderation process.

Porters' Lodge

Your first port of call at an Oxford or Cambridge college. This is where post gets delivered and where, if you get lost, they will be able to direct you – a bit like a reception desk.

Porters

The men and women who act as wardens of the lodge.

PPE

This is an abbreviation for the Philosophy, Politics and Economics course at Oxford.

PPL

This is an abbreviation for the Psychology, Philosophy and Linguistics course at Oxford.

Prelims (Oxford)

This is short for Preliminaries which are the exams at the end of the first year. There are only three results available: Pass, Fail and Distinction.

Proctors (Oxford)

A Senior and Junior Proctor are elected annually by colleges in rotation. Their role is to ensure that the rules and customs of the University are kept. Part of their role includes ceremonial duties (such as taking part in degree ceremonies), aspects of student discipline, ensuring exams are conducted properly and managing complaints.

Read

Instead of 'studying' a subject, the verb used is to 'read' a subject.

Scholar

Scholarships are usually awarded at the end of the first year for out-standing work. Oxford scholars get to wear a more elaborate gown and are given a small financial bursary (usually around £200 a year). Music scholars hold their award for the whole time they are at university.

Scout

The person who cleans your room at Oxford.

Subfusc

The black gown, black trousers/skirt, white shirt and black tie Oxford students must wear to take exams.

Summon

Another way to say 'to be called' for interview.

Supervision

A class held on a one-to-one basis or in a small group with your tutor (at Cambridge).

Supplementary Application Questionnaire (SAQ)

This is sent out by Cambridge once you have submitted your UCAS application. The SAQ gives Cambridge more information about you and your application and must be submitted within one week after you receive it. The SAQ is filled out online and costs nothing to send; if you do not have access to email you can contact the Cambridge admissions office for a paper version.

Tompkins table

Cambridge league table that measures each college's academic achievement at the final examinations.

Trinity Term

This is the summer term at Oxford. The equivalent term at Cambridge is Easter.

Tripos

Term used to describe Cambridge degree courses being divided into blocks of one or two years, called Part I and Part II.

Tutor

At Oxford, your tutor is an academic member of staff from your subject faculty, who is also a fellow of your college. He or she is responsible for your academic development and will meet with you on a regular basis to check on your progress, and will probably be your interviewer. The DOS at Cambridge is the equivalent to a tutor at Oxford.

Tutorial

A class held on a one-to-one basis or in a small group with your tutor (at Oxford).

Vacation

The period between university terms.

Viva voce

An oral exam given when you are being considered for a First Class degree and the examiners want to ask you further questions about your exam papers.

College profiles

The following information is intended to provide a brief overview of the undergraduate colleges at Oxford and Cambridge to give an idea of what each one offers and help you to narrow down your options. However, for the most detailed and up-to-date information, you should also consult individual college websites as part of your research.

OXFORD

BALLIOL COLLEGE (founded 1263)

Number of students/fellows: 370 UGs (undergraduates); 70 fellows.

Size and location: Medium-sized and very central college; the Bodleian Library, Weston Library, Radcliffe Camera, Modern Languages faculty, Oriental Institute Library and Sackler Library are all close by.

Courses *not* offered at this college: Archaeology and Anthropology; Biochemistry; Classics and English; Earth Sciences; European and Middle Eastern Languages; Fine Art; Geography; History of Art; Human Sciences; Materials Science; Mathematics and Statistics; Music; Oriental Studies with Classics; Philosophy and Theology; Psychology (Experimental); PPL; Theology and Religion; Theology and Oriental Studies. *Please note that not every language course is available; check the Oxford website to see which combinations are offered at this college.*

Accommodation:
- **Access**: Five specially adapted rooms and showers available for students with disabilities, both on the main site and in the College annexes. Wheelchair access available on the main site, and two lifts in the Jowett Walk annexe. Restricted access available at the Holywell Manor site.
- **Main site**: Accommodation provided on the main site for two years (usually in the first and final years). Students not living in college either live in Jowett Walk annexe or rent privately.
- **Off-site**: Jowett Walk annexe, which also houses the College sports fields and facilities. All rooms are en suite and divided into flats with shared kitchens.
- **Rent**: Rooms in college assigned in first year; banded prices in the final year for students living in college. At Jowett Walk, both 27- and 36-week leases are available.

Food:

- **Hall**: Food served in college Hall seven days a week. Students charged a termly fixed living-in charge; this is reduced if students live out. Optional pre-payment schemes available for Hall food. Formal Hall served once a week and on guest nights.
- **Other**: JCR Pantry serving breakfast, lunch and dinner; Buttery serving drinks and light refreshments. No self-catering on main site; shared kitchens in Jowett Walk.

Facilities on site: Gym; studio theatre; music room; chapel; Balliol Day Nursery (in North Oxford).

Financial aid: Junior Maintenance Grant; Balliol short-term loans; College loans and grants for unexpected hardship; undergraduate project grants; miscellaneous grants (e.g. for travel, materials, etc.); Nettleship Instrumental Exhibition; Cadle Fund for sports expenditure; Georgina Horlick Childcare Bursaries; academic scholarships and exhibitions; other subject, essay and project prizes available.

Societies: Arnold Brackenbury Society (comedy debating society); Balliol Literary Society; Left Caucus (left-wing issues); Balliol Music Society; Balliol Drama Society; Scrawl (creative writing magazine); Choir (non-auditioned); Mathematics Skoliasts (Classics); STEM-sisters (female science and maths students).

Miscellaneous:

- Exchange scheme with the Maximilianeum (college attached to the University of Munich) for undergraduate and graduate students in any subject.
- Pathfinders Programme supports eight students to travel to America and Canada for six to eight weeks and stay with college alumni; two students to travel to Asia for six to eight weeks; and two students to Mexico for four weeks.

Alumni: Robert Browning; Yvette Cooper; Richard Dawkins; Grahame Greene; Edward Heath; Gerard Manley Hopkins; Boris Johnson; Harold Macmillan; Lord Patten; Robert Peston; Dan Snow; Peter Snow; Simon Stevens.

Did you know ...?

Richard Dawkins studied at Balliol, as did 10 other members of his family. While at Balliol, Richard Dawkins read Zoology.

BLACKFRIARS HALL (Permanent Private Hall - PPH)
(founded 1921; Priory founded 1221)

NB Accepts mature UGs only.

Number of students: Four UGs.

Size and location: Very small and central college; located near Modern Languages, Classics and Linguistics faculties and the Oriental Institute.

Courses offered at this college: The College specialises in Philosophy and Theology, and offers only Theology and Religion; Philosophy and Theology; Theology and Oriental Studies; and PPE at undergraduate level.

Accommodation:
- **Access**: Wheelchair access for all principal spaces on site.
- **Main site**: No accommodation available.
- **Off site**: Small number of rooms available in two adjacent houses with shared kitchens.
- **Rent**: Fixed rate.

Food: Meals are not provided on the main site.

Facilities on site: Specialist Theology and Philosophy library.

Financial aid: Gym grant; cycle safety scheme.

Societies: Companions of Malta (charity that works with local Catholic and Anglican churches for the marginalised); Schola Magna (choir); Women's Group.

Miscellaneous: Note that you do not need to be Catholic to apply to study at the Hall.

Did you know ...?

Blackfriars is home to the Las Casas Institute, which organises lectures on issues relating to human dignity through Catholic Social teaching, with Dr Rowan Williams recently invited to speak, and the Aquinas Institute, which holds seminars, conferences and summer schools on the study of St Thomas Aquinas.

BRASENOSE COLLEGE (founded 1509)

Number of students: 350 UGs.

Size and location: Medium college with a small deer park on site. Very central; situated next to the Bodleian Library and Radcliffe Camera.

Courses *not* offered at this college: Archaeology and Anthropology; Biomedical Sciences; Computer Science and all joint courses; Earth Sciences; History and English; History of Art; Human Sciences; Materials

Science; Music; Oriental Studies; Oriental Studies with Classics; Philosophy and Theology; Theology and Oriental Studies; Theology and Religion. *Please note that not every language course is available; check the Oxford website to see which combinations are offered at this college.*

Accommodation: Provided for duration of the course.
- **Access**: Adapted rooms available for students with disabilities.
- **Main site**: For all first years and some third and fourth years.
- **Off site**: Frewin Hall complex houses second, some third and fourth years.
- **Rent**: Banded room prices.

Food:
- **Hall**: Breakfast, lunch and dinner, and brunch at the weekend. Pay-as-you-go system. Formal Hall served twice a week.
- **Other**: Bar and café (Gerties) serving lunch and breakfast. Shared kitchens on Frewin site.

Facilities on site: Three libraries: main library; separate Law library; library with modern history, politics and geography books; practice rooms; chapel.

Financial aid: Annual fund for academic or extra-curricular activities (non-means tested and means-tested; Harold Parr Fund (preference for Law/Mathematics); Undergraduate Fresher's Allowance; travel grants; vacation grants.

Societies: Choir (non-auditioning); Jazz band; Debating Club (Addington Society); Ashmole (organises History talks); Creative Writing Society; Film Club.

Miscellaneous: Kathleen Lavidge Bursary to support three weeks' study at Stanford University.

Alumni: David Cameron; Michael Palin; William Golding.

Did you know ...?

For three consecutive years, Brasenose has received the most direct applications in each admissions cycle. Other popular colleges include St John's, Worcester, Keble, Balliol, Christ Church, Magdalen and Wadham.

CHRIST CHURCH (founded 1546)

Number of students/fellows: 110 tutors and college lecturers; 430 UGs.

Size and location: Near the river (good for rowers) and Music and History of Art faculties.

Courses *not* offered at this college: Archaeology and Anthropology; Biomedical Sciences; Classics and English; Computer Science and Philosophy; Earth Sciences; History and Economics; History and English; Human Sciences; Materials Science. *Please note that not every language course is available; check the Oxford website to see which combinations are offered at this college.*

Accommodation: Provided for the duration of the course, and is balloted after first year.
- **Access**: Two single rooms for disabled students on main site; specially equipped flat for up to three students available in Liddell Building.
- **Main site**: Houses all first years, some second and final years.
- **Off site**: Liddell Building, which has self-catering flats, each with three or four bedrooms.
- **Rent**: Fixed rate.

Food:
- **Hall**: Breakfast, lunch and dinner served Monday–Friday; brunch and dinner Saturday–Sunday. Breakfast, lunch and brunch: pay-as-you-go; dinner charged on termly basis. Formal Hall served every evening after first Hall.
- **Other**: No self-catering facilities on site; shared kitchens in Liddell Building.

Facilities on site: Separate Law library: picture gallery; art room and art tutor; music room; Cathedral of Oxford.

Financial aid: Book grants; student support loans and grants; vacation grants; academic scholarships and exhibitions.

Societies: Cathedral choir; College choir; Orchestra; Music Society.

Miscellaneous:
- Site of the Cathedral of Oxford and Christ Church Meadow.
- Annual music festival run by the Music Society.
- Home Learning Scheme connects Christ Church students with local families.
- Accredited Fairtrade college.

Alumni: W.H. Auden; Lewis Carroll; Richard Curtis; David Dimbleby; William Gladstone; Howard Goodall; Robert Peel; Rowan Williams.

Did you know ...?

The author Lewis Carroll read mathematics at Christ Church, and while there he met Alice Liddell, daughter of the Dean at Christ Church; Alice would later become Carroll's inspiration for the titular character in *Alice's Adventures in Wonderland* and *Alice Through the Looking Glass*. Christ Church has also produced 13 British Prime Ministers – more than any other college in Oxford.

CORPUS CHRISTI COLLEGE (founded 1517)

Number of students/fellows: 240 UGs; 40 fellows.

Size and location: One of the smallest colleges in Oxford; central college, near University Libraries, which looks out over Christ Church Meadow.

Courses *not* offered at this college: Archaeology and Anthropology; Biological Sciences; Computer Science; Computer Science and Philosophy; Earth Sciences; Economics and Management; Engineering Science; European and Middle Eastern Languages; Fine Art; Geography; History and Economics; History of Art; Human Sciences; Modern Languages and joint courses; Music; Oriental Studies and joint courses; Philosophy and Theology; Theology and Religion.

Accommodation: Provided for the duration of the course.
- **Access**: Accommodation available for disabled students.
- **Main site**: For all first years, some second, third and fourth years.
- **Off site**: Nine college houses and Liddell Building (three- or four-person flats) for some second, third and fourth years.
- **Rent**: Fixed rate.

Food:
- **Hall**: Breakfast, lunch and dinner served. Pay-as-you-go system. Formal Hall served twice a week.
- **Other**: Shared kitchens in off-site accommodation.

Facilities on site: Library; computer suite; auditorium; chapel; bar.

Financial aid: Maintenance: College offers both ongoing and emergency support; moving-out loans for students living out of college accommodation (mainly for graduates); financial assistance towards the cost of books/scientific equipment; academic scholarships and exhibitions; vacation grants; travel grants.

Societies: Symposium (think tank); Owlets (Drama); Choir; Corpus Cinema (film club); String Orchestra; Jazz Ensemble; Christian Union (CU).

Miscellaneous: Presidents' seminars: termly talks from visiting speakers.

Alumni: Robert Bridges; David Miliband; Ed Miliband; John Ruskin; C.P. Scott.

Did you know ...?

Both David and Ed Miliband were JCR President at Corpus Christi.

EXETER COLLEGE (founded 1314; fourth-oldest college)

Number of students/fellows: 340 UGs; 43 fellows.

Size and location: Central; near to university ibraries.

Courses *not* offered at this college: Archaeology and Anthropology; Biological Sciences; Computer Science; Computer Science and Philosophy; English and Modern Languages; European and Middle Eastern Languages; Geography; History and Economics, History and Modern Languages; History and Politics; History of Art; Human Sciences; Materials Science; Oriental Studies; Philosophy and Theology; Psychology (Experimental); PPL; Theology and Oriental Studies; Theology and Religion. *Please note that not every language course is available; check the Oxford website to see which combinations are offered at this college.*

Accommodation: Currently provided for three years.
- **Access**: Adapted facilities available at main and Iffley Road (East Oxford) sites, including accessible rooms.
- **Main site**: Houses first years.
- **Off site**: In later years, other accommodation provided across the road from the main site in Turl Street; East Oxford (self-catered); or Cohen Quad in Jericho (North Oxford).

Food:
- **Hall**: Breakfast, lunch and dinner served Monday–Saturday; brunch and dinner served on Sunday. Pay-as-you-go system. Formal Hall served three times week.
- **Other:** Baguette bar and pizza bar on main site; café at Cohen Quad.

Facilities on site: Chapel; weights room; computer rooms; Fellows' Garden.
- **Cohen Quad:** lecture theatre and café; library; bar.

Financial aid: Exonian Bursaries; academic scholarships; travel grants; sports grants; choral awards; organ scholarships.

Societies: Choir; Music; John Ford Society (Drama); Fortescue Society (Law); PPE Society; Feminist magazine; ExVAC (student-run scheme that organises trips for children from disadvantaged backgrounds).

Miscellaneous:
- The College library is particularly good for History students.
- Exeter runs its own careers and internships office, which is separate from the University Careers Service; it is the only college with a dedicated Careers Officer.
- Rectors' seminars – recent speakers have included Philip Pullman, J.K. Rowling and Sir Peter Jackson.
- Runs subject-family events for students, where they are invited to learn about research in their academic field and beyond.

Alumni: Martin Amis; Alan Bennett; Reeta Chakrabarti; William Morris; Philip Pullman; J.R.R. Tolkien.

Did you know ...?

Exeter College forms the basis for the fictional Jordan College in Philip Pullman's trilogy *His Dark Materials*.

HARRIS MANCHESTER COLLEGE (founded 1996; originally founded in Manchester in 1786)

NB Accepts mature UGs only.

Number of students: 100 UGs.

Size and location: very small college, close to Science Area, English and Law faculties and History Library.

Courses *not* offered at this college: Biochemistry; Biological Sciences; Biomedical Sciences; Chemistry; Classical Archaeology and Ancient History; Classics; Computer Science; Computer Science and Philosophy; Earth Sciences; European and Middle Eastern Languages; Fine Art; Geography; History (Ancient and Modern); Materials Science; Mathematics and joint courses; Medicine (undergraduate course); Modern Languages and joint courses; Music; Physics; Physics and Philosophy; Philosophy and Linguistics; Psychology and Linguistics.

Accommodation:
- **Main site**: All college accommodation is situated on the main site and provided for first and final year students.
- **Rent**: Fixed rate, which includes food charge; see below.

Food:
- **Hall**: Fixed-rate accommodation charge includes a fee for 17 meals per week: breakfast, lunch and dinner Monday–Friday; and brunch on Saturday and Sunday. Formal Hall served twice a week.
- **Other**: Small kitchens on site. While self-catering is not possible, students may sign out of a few meals each term in exchange for credits.

Facilities on site: Gym; computing room; library; bar.

Financial aid: College Hardship Fund; bursaries for outstanding first-year work; second undergraduate degree scholarships (based on academic merit); book bursaries; conference and travel grants.

Societies: Harris Manchester Chorale; Law Society; Drama Society; Film Club; Leftist Society; LGBTQ Society; Afro-Caribbean Society.

Did you know ...?

Harris Manchester is the only full college of the University to accept mature students only (students aged 21 or above at the start of their course), and it does not set an upper age limit. The others that accept only mature students are Blackfriars Hall, St Stephen's House and Wycliffe Hall (all of which are Permanent Private Halls).

HERTFORD COLLEGE (founded 1282)

Number of students/fellows: 400 UGs; 60 tutors and lecturers.

Size and location: Small and central college; next to Radcliffe Camera and the Bodleian.

Courses *not* offered at this college: Biomedical Sciences; Classical Archaeology and Ancient History; Classics and joint courses; Computer Science; Earth Sciences; English and Modern Languages; European and Middle Eastern Languages; Fine Art; History (Ancient and Modern); History and English; History of Art; Materials Science; Mathematics and Computer Science; Mathematics and Statistics; Oriental Studies (offers only Chinese and Japanese streams); Philosophy and Theology; Psychology (Experimental); PPL; Theology and Religion; Theology and Oriental Studies. *Please note that not every language course is available; check the Oxford website to see which combinations are offered at this college.*

Accommodation: Provided for the duration of the course.
- **Main site**: Houses first years.
- **Off site**: Other years are balloted and most live in Warnock or Abingdon House (near Christ Church Meadow) or in houses in North and South Oxford.
- **Rent**: Fixed charge (room rent and college facilities charge). Uniform rent structure, but college facilities charge varies depending on which college accommodation you live in.

Food:
- **Hall**: Pay-as-you-go system. Dinner is not provided on Saturdays. Formal Hall served twice a week.
- **Other**: All student rooms have access to shared kitchens. Cafeteria service at Warnock House available for breakfast and dinner.

Facilities on site: Chapel; gym; computing rooms; music room; library; bar.

Financial aid: Hertford undergraduate bursary for students from low-income families; student support fund for unexpected financial hardship; travel and research grants; academic scholarships for first year exam results; vacation grants.

Societies: Choir (non-auditioned); Orchestra; Jazz band; Wind band; Hertford College Music Society; Business and Economics.

Miscellaneous:
- Hertford debates at Formal Hall, featuring visiting speakers.
- Accredited Fairtrade college.

Alumni: Fiona Bruce; John Donne; Krishnan Guru Murthy; Natasha Kaplinsky; Evelyn Waugh.

Did you know ...?

Hertford has its own Undergraduate Bursary, guaranteeing a further £1,000 to students whose household income is below the specified threshold.

JESUS COLLEGE (founded 1571)

Number of students/fellows: 340 UGs; 68 fellows and 20 college lecturers.

Size and location: Very small, central, Turl Street college; near University Libraries.

Courses *not* offered at this college: Archaeology and Anthropology; Biochemistry; Biomedical Sciences; Classical Archaeology and Ancient History; Computer Science and joint courses; Earth Sciences; Fine Art; History (Ancient and Modern); History of Art; Human Sciences; Materials Science; Oriental Studies and joint courses; Physics and Philosophy; Theology and Religion. *Please note that not every language course is available; check the Oxford website to see which combinations are offered at this college.*

Accommodation: Provided for the duration of the course.
- **First year**: Students live on Turl Street site or in an annexe close by.
  - **Rent**: Fixed nightly charge, inclusive of utilities and cleaning.
- **Other years**: Students are balloted and live in flats in North and East Oxford. Flats available for couples at the East Oxford site.
  - **Rent**: Weekly charges, which includes water but not other utilities. 40-week lease (though a 48-week lease is offered for couples).

Food: Pay-as-you-go system. Additional termly Hall charge payable, which is reduced for those living in college flats/private accommodation.
- **Hall**: Breakfast, lunch and dinner served Monday–Friday; breakfast and lunch on Saturday; lunch and dinner on Sunday. Formal Hall served five times a week,
- **Other**: Shared kitchens in some college accommodation.

Facilities on site: Chapel; computer suite; conservatory; music room; dark room; library; bar.

Financial aid: Access Bursaries (grants to assist with course-related costs); book grants; subject prizes; cultural, sporting and travel grants.

Societies: Non-auditioned choir; Orchestra; English Society; History Society.

Miscellaneous: Jointly runs the Turl Street Arts Festival with Lincoln and Exeter Colleges.

Alumni: William Boyd; T.E. Lawrence; Harold Wilson.

Did you know ...?

The College was founded by Queen Elizabeth I.

KEBLE COLLEGE (founded 1870)

Number of students/fellows: 410 UGs; 50 fellows; 9 Research and Career Development Fellows. There are at least two full-time Tutorial Fellows in almost every subject.

Size and location: Medium-sized college; near to Radcliffe Science Library and Science Area, and adjacent to University Parks.

Courses *not* offered at this college: Biochemistry; Classics and joint courses; Computer Science and Philosophy; Earth Sciences; European and Middle Eastern Languages; Fine Art; History and Economics; History and English; History of Art; Materials Science; Mathematics and Philosophy; Oriental Studies and joint courses; Physics and Philosophy; Psychology (Experimental); PPL. *Please note that not every language course is available; check the Oxford website to see which combinations are offered at this college.*

Accommodation: Provided for all first and second years, and most third years. Fourth years tend to live out (except for Modern Languages students).
- **Access**: Main areas are wheelchair accessible. The College has several ground-floor bedrooms and one bedroom with specially adapted en-suite facilities.
- **Main site**: All student accommodation is located within college grounds.
- **Rent**: Banded accommodation; 37-week lease for third years living in the ARCO building. Rent equalisation subsidy available to third year students who are not allocated college accommodation.

Food:
- **Hall**: Breakfast, lunch and dinner Monday–Friday; brunch and dinner Saturday–Sunday. Pay-as-you-go system; charged on bill at the end of each term. Formal Hall served every evening.
- **Other**: College café (Café Keble) open all day during term-time and pizza bar is open daily.

Facilities on site: Library; bar; O'Reilly Theatre – performance space for drama/musicals; Advanced Studies Centre: hosts talks with visiting speakers and used for inter-disciplinary research; chapel.

Financial aid: Bursaries; College student support fund for unexpected hardship; travel and research grants; vacation and internship bursaries; organ and choral scholarships.

Societies: Music Society; Harris Law Society; CU; Choir.

Miscellaneous: Hosts an annual arts festival.

Alumni: Ed Balls; Frank Cottrell Boyce; Giles Coren; Tony Hall; Paula Hawkins.

Did you know …?

Keble is home to the O'Reilly Theatre, which is a hugely popular venue for student musicals and plays; each term four or five plays are selected by a committee, and theatre groups must bid for a chance to perform their piece at the O'Reilly.

LADY MARGARET HALL (LMH) (founded 1878)

Number of students/fellows: 406 UGs; 45 fellows.

Size and location: Large; 10 acres of gardens. Situated by University Parks, near to the Science Area.

Courses *not* offered at this college: Archaeology and Anthropology; Biomedical Sciences; Classics with Oriental Studies; Earth Sciences; European and Middle Eastern Languages; Geography; History and Economics; History and English; History of Art; Human Sciences; Material Sciences; Oriental Studies; Oriental Studies with Classics. *Please note that not every language course is available; check the Oxford website to see which combinations are offered at this college.*

Accommodation: Three years' worth of accommodation provided on site; balloted after second year.
- **Access**: Purpose-built accommodation available for students with disabilities.
- **Rent**: Fixed termly rate, regardless of size/location.

Food:
- **Hall**: Pay-as-you-go system. Three meals a day, Monday–Friday; brunch only on Saturday; dinner only on Sunday. Students are entitled to two free formals (which are weekly) a year.
- **Other**: All bedrooms have shared kitchen access.

Facilities on site: Boathouse and punts; playing fields; tennis courts; netball court; gym; theatre; computer room; music practice rooms; chapel; library; bar.

Financial aid: Hardship fund; Academic Development Fund; academic scholarships and exhibitions; organ scholarship; subject prizes.

Societies: Beaufort Society (literary group); Brading Biomedical Society; Chapel Choir (non-auditioned); CU; Cine-club; Daisy Circle (debating); Drama Society; Fashion Society; Film Society; History; Law; LGBTQ; LMH and Wadham Orchestra; Music Society.

Miscellaneous:
- Initially founded in 1878 as a women's college to allow women to study at Oxford for the first time; boys weren't admitted until 1979 (first college in Oxford to go mixed).
- Accredited Fairtrade college.

Alumni: Danny Cohen; Michael Gove; Eglantyne Jebb; Nigella Lawson; Baroness Manningham-Buller; Ann Widdecombe.

Did you know ...?

LMH built its own library resources to cater for its first female students, as women weren't permitted to use the Bodleian or Oxford Union libraries until the 1920s. The college received numerous gifts for its new library from advocates of women's education; notable book donors include John Ruskin and Lewis Carroll.

LINCOLN COLLEGE (founded 1427)

Number of students: 300 UGs.

Size and location: Very small Turl Street college; near University Libraries.

Courses *not* offered at this college: Archaeology and Anthropology; Biological Sciences; Classics and joint courses; Computer Science and joint courses; Earth Sciences; Economics and Management; English and Modern Languages; European and Middle Eastern Languages; Fine Art; Geography; History and Economics; History and English; History of Art; Human Sciences; Materials Science; Mathematics and Philosophy; Modern Languages and Linguistics; Oriental Studies and joint courses; Philosophy and Theology; Physics and Philosophy; Psychology (Experimental); PPL; Theology and Religion. *Please note that not every language course is available; check the Oxford website to see which combinations are offered at this college.*

Accommodation: Provided for the duration of the course.
- **Access**: Disabled accommodation available on main site and in North Oxford.
- **Rent**: Three 'plans', each with its own fixed pricing structure: in-

college plan for freshers; in-college plans for second and third years; out-of-college plan for second and third years.

- o Students living in off-site college residences are on a 37-week plan; students living in college are on a 25-week plan.
- o First and second years live in college or above the Mitre pub on the High Street.
- o Third and fourth years live in college properties, either in North Oxford (by Science Area), or opposite the College on the High Street.

Food:

- **Hall**: Breakfast, lunch and dinner provided every day. Pay-as-you-go system, which is billed at the end of each term. Formal Hall served six nights a week.
- **Other**: Bar that serves meals and light snacks (Deep Hall), which is open during term time. Third and fourth year accommodation has access to kitchens.

Facilities on site: Chapel; computer room; library; bar.

Financial aid: Bursaries and hardship funds; book grant scheme; academic scholarships and exhibitions; academic and subject prizes; travel grants; organ scholarships; choral scholarships and exhibitions.

Societies: Chapel Choir; Lincoln Players (Drama society); Publications Committee; CU.

Miscellaneous:

- Co-hosts the Turl Street Arts Festival with Exeter and Jesus Colleges.
- VacProj: college charity, taking children from underprivileged backgrounds on holiday.

Alumni: John le Carré; Lord Florey; Dr John Radcliffe; Dr Seuss; John Wesley.

Did you know ...?

Lincoln was the first Oxford college to introduce a Middle Common Room (MCR) for graduate students to use.

MAGDALEN COLLEGE (founded 1458)

Number of students: 375 UGs (c. 118 admitted each year).

Size and location: Very large: 100-acre grounds, including a deer park and riverside walk. Located near English and Law faculties and the Examination Schools.

Courses *not* offered at this college: Computer Science and Philosophy; Earth Sciences; Economics and Management; Geography; History and Economics; History and English; History of Art; Materials Science; Oriental Studies; Oriental Studies with Classics; Philosophy and Theology; Theology and Religion; Theology and Oriental Studies. *Please note that not every language course is available; check the Oxford website to see which combinations are offered at this college.*

Accommodation: Provided for the duration of the course, either in college, in nearby annexes or in college properties.
- **Access**: Limited number of accessible ground-floor rooms available on main site, and two rooms with accessible en-suite facilities in Longwall Street, although access to the buildings on this street may not be suitable for some wheelchair users. Lift to the main dining hall.
- **Rent**: Flat daily rate for all undergraduate rooms (59 nights per term).

Food: Pay-as-you-go system. In addition, there is a supplementary termly catering charge (reduced for students not living in college accommodation).
- **Hall**: Serves breakfast, lunch and dinner. Formal Hall served three times a week.
- **Other**: Old Kitchen Bar serves lunch options; JCR shop sells snacks. Self-catering facilities available across college accommodation.

Facilities on site: Chapel; library; bar; auditorium; music practice rooms; Modern Languages room; hard and grass tennis courts; squash courts; all-weather pitch; boat house with punts; private dining space and kitchen.

Financial aid: Student support fund to help with cost of living and studying; hardship fund (one-off financial hardship); academic scholarships, awards and prizes; travel grants; research grants; vacation grants.

Societies: Florio Society (Poetry); Atkin Society (Law); Sherrington Society (Medicine); Choir; Orchestra; Magdalen Singers; Music Society; Magdalen College Swing Band; Magdalen Players (Drama); Film Society; Raising Consciousness; Stokesley (Debating); CU.

Alumni: Julian Barnes; King Edward VII; William Hague; Robert Hardy; Seamus Heaney; Ian Hislop; C.S. Lewis; George Osborne; Louis Theroux; Oscar Wilde.

Did you know ...?

Magdalen College is tied with the University of Manchester as the most successful University Challenge team, with four wins each.

MANSFIELD COLLEGE (founded 1886)

Number of students/fellows: 220 UGs; 50 academic staff.

Size and location: Very small; located near the University Parks and Science Area.

Courses *not* offered at this college: Archaeology and Anthropology; Biochemistry; Biological Sciences; Biomedical Sciences; Chemistry; Classical Archaeology and Ancient History; Classics and joint courses; Computer Science and joint courses; Earth Science; Economics and Management; European and Middle Eastern Languages; Fine Art; History (Ancient and Modern); History and Economics; History and English; History of Art; Mathematics and Philosophy; Medicine; Modern Languages and joint courses; Music; Oriental Studies (offers only Arabic, Hebrew and Jewish Studies streams); Oriental Studies with Classics; Physics and Philosophy; Psychology (Experimental); PPL; Theology and Oriental Studies.

Accommodation: Provided for first and final years. Students on four-year courses can have college accommodation in either their third or fourth years. New undergraduate accommodation is being built as part of the Bonavero Institute for Human Rights, which is due to be completed in October 2017.

- **Access**: Wheelchair access to all ground-floor facilities on the main site. The graduate accommodation block has one room suitable for a wheelchair user.
- **Main site**: Houses all first and some final year students.
- **Off site**: Most final year students live in Ablethorpe annexe, 15 minutes' walk from the main site, or in college-owned houses.
- **Rent**: Fixed termly charge, which is subdivided into rent and utilities.

Food:
- **Hall**: Pay-as-you-go; charged termly. Breakfast, lunch and dinner served. Formal Hall served twice a week.
- **Other**: Student café, bar and terrace. Kitchens available on site for self-catering.

Facilities on site: Four libraries (including separate libraries for Theology, Law and PPE); chapel; student café, bar and terrace.

Financial aid: Hardship fund; academic scholarships and prizes; travel grants.

Societies: Drama Society; Chapel Choir; Film Club; 1887 (Geography); 1963 (History); Poetry; CU; Nonconformist (college newspaper); Gender Equality.

Miscellaneous: Many of the sports teams are combined with Merton College (Mansfield shares Merton's sports grounds).

Alumni: Chris Bryant; Adam Curtis; Justin Rowlatt.

> **Did you know ...?**
>
> As part of a joint initiative between Mansfield's Principal, Baron-ess Helena Kennedy, QC and the faculty of Law, from October 2017, Mansfield will be home to the Bonavero Institute of Human Rights, which will be a significant addition to the faculty of Law.

MERTON COLLEGE (founded 1264)

Number of students: 300 UGs.

Size and location: Medium-sized college; main site close to University Libraries; Holywell Street annexe near Science Area.

Courses *not* offered at this college: Archaeology and Anthropology; Biomedical Sciences; Classics and English; Earth Sciences; Engineering Science; European and Middle Eastern Languages; Fine Art; Geography; History and Economics; History of Art; Human Sciences; Materials Science; Oriental Studies and joint courses; Philosophy and Theology; Psychology (Experimental); PPL; Theology and Religion. *Please note that not every language course is available; check the Oxford website to see which combinations are offered at this college.*

Accommodation: Provided for the duration of the course.
- **Access**: Two rooms available for disabled students, including a suite with an adjacent room for a carer.
- **Main site**: First years live in houses on Merton Street or in Rose Lane, which are adjacent to the main site. Third years live in main college complex.
- **Off site**: Most second and fourth years live in college-owned houses in Holywell Street, which is a short walk from the College.
- **Rent**: Flat-rate charges, although there is a higher flat-rate charge for en-suite bedrooms.

Food:
- **Hall**: Pay-as-you-go meals. Breakfast, lunch and dinner provided Monday–Saturday, with brunch and dinner on Sunday. Formal Hall served six days a week.
- **Other**: Kitchen on main site and shared facilities in some Holywell Street accommodation.

Facilities on site: Gym; chapel; music practice room; lecture theatre; games room; library; bar.

Financial aid: Student Financial Support Fund for unexpected financial hardship; academic scholarships and prizes; choral and organ scholarships; annual book grant; travel grant; research grant.

Societies: Bodley (organises visiting talks); Merton Floats (Drama); Music Society; Neave Society (Politics and Current Affairs); Art Club;

Signs and Wonderings (Theology); Chalcenterics (Classics); CU; Choir (auditioned); Orchestra.

Miscellaneous: Merton organises its own Arts Festival annually.

Alumni: T.S. Eliot; Mark Haddon.

Did you know ...?

J.R.R. Tolkien was Merton's Professor of English Language and Literature, having studied at Exeter College as an undergraduate. While a don, Tolkien met regularly with other academics as a member of the Inklings, an informal literary society. Another notable member of the group was C.S. Lewis, who was a Tutorial Fellow at Magdalen and later Professor of Medieval and Renaissance Literature at Cambridge, having first studied at University College in Oxford.

NEW COLLEGE (founded 1379)

Number of students/fellows: 430 UGs (*c.* 120 admitted each year).

Size and location: Large college, near University Libraries, English and Law faculties.

Courses *not* offered by this college: Archaeology and Anthropology; Classical Archaeology and Ancient History; Classics and English; Earth Sciences; Geography; History and English; History of Art; Human Sciences; Materials Science; Oriental Studies; Oriental Studies with Classics; Philosophy and Linguistics; Philosophy and Theology; Psychology and Linguistics; Theology and Oriental Studies; Theology and Religion. *Please note that not every language course is available; check the Oxford website to see which combinations are offered at this college.*

Accommodation: Provided for first, second and fourth years in college or near to college. Some third year accommodation available. Refurbishment work is taking place in the College until 2018, which may affect provision of rooms for second, third and fourth years.
- **Rent for majority of undergraduate accommodation**: Fixed rent, which includes utilities, internet and evening meals.
- **Sacher Building and Savile House**: Fixed rent at second-highest rate, which includes the cost of services. 39-week lease available.
- **New College Lane and Bodicote House**: Fixed rent at highest rate, to include the cost of services and term-time evening meals. 38-week lease in New College Lane, and option of a 38-week lease in Bodicote House.

Food:
- **Hall**: Breakfast, lunch and dinner Monday–Friday; brunch and dinner Saturday–Sunday. Termly pre-payment for food; supplementary meals charged to subsequent termly bill, and any remaining credit is credited back to the student's account. Formal Hall served three times a week.
- **Other**: Some self-catering facilities available.

Facilities on site: Chapel; practice rooms; band room; computer room; library; bar.

Financial aid: Choral scholarships (men only); organ scholarship; instrumental scholarships; academic scholarships and prizes; travel grants; sporting and cultural award.

Societies: Choir (auditioned); Wykeham Singers (non-auditioned); Orchestra.

Miscellaneous:
- New College Chalet on Mont Blanc is used for reading parties and walking holidays, and is shared with Balliol and University College.
- JCR Art Store has artwork available for students to put up in their rooms.

Alumni: Kate Beckinsale; Tony Benn; Richard Dawkins; Hugh Grant.

Did you know ...?

As well as being an alumnus of the college, Hugh Grant was also made an Honorary Fellow in 2012.

ORIEL COLLEGE (founded 1326)

Number of students: 270 UGs.

Size and location: Medium-sized college, located by the University Libraries.

Courses *not* offered at this college: Archaeology and Anthropology; Biological Sciences; Earth Sciences; Economics and Management; European and Middle Eastern Languages; Fine Art; Geography; History and English; History of Art; Human Sciences; Materials Science; Mathematics and Statistics; Oriental Studies; Oriental Studies with Classics; Psychology (Experimental); PPL; Theology and Oriental Studies. *Please note that not every language course is available; check the Oxford website to see which combinations are offered at this college.*

Accommodation: Provided for the duration of the course. All first years live on site.

- **Access**: Several adapted rooms available for students with disabilities.
- **Rent**: Banded accommodation; each band has its own fixed termly charge and is banded according to size, location, facilities and condition.

Food:

- **Hall**: Pay-as-you-go system. Breakfast, lunch and dinner served Monday to Saturday. Brunch and dinner served on Sunday. Formal Hall served six days a week.
- **Other**: Some self-catering available, depending on the area of the College where the accommodation is located. There is also a JCR Tuck Shop.

Facilities on site: Undergraduate shop; annexe for meetings/gatherings; music practice room; two gyms; squash court; chapel; multi-faith room.

Financial aid: Oriel College Bursaries for students in financial need; hardship grants for unexpected financial hardship; choral scholarships; organ scholarships; academic scholarships and prizes; travel grants; vacation grants.

Societies: Chapel Choir; Oriel Lions (Drama); Music Society; Pantin Society (History); Whately Society (politics, philosophy, current affairs and arts); CU; Acaporiel (a cappella choir); The Poor Print (College newspaper).

Miscellaneous: The College holds termly Joint Academic Forums, featuring discussion of interdisciplinary research topics/questions.

Alumni: Jim Cooper; Sir Walter Raleigh; Rachel Riley.

Did you know ...?

Each year, the College plays host to a Visiting Musician, who holds masterclasses with the students and gives concerts; past visitors include mezzo-soprano Sarah Connolly and pianist Joanna McGregor.

PEMBROKE COLLEGE (founded 1624)

Number of students: 367 UGs.

Size and location: Medium-sized college, located near the Music and History of Arts faculties and the river.

Courses not offered by this college: Archaeology and Anthropology; Biomedical Sciences; Classical Archaeology and Ancient History; Classics and joint courses; Computer Science and joint courses; Earth Sciences; Fine Art; Geography; History (Ancient and Modern); History of Art; Human Sciences; Materials Science; Mathematics and Statistics; Oriental Studies (offers only Egyptology, Sanskrit or Ancient Near Eastern Studies streams); Oriental Studies with Classics. *Please note that not every language course is available; check the Oxford website to see which combinations are offered at this college.*

Accommodation: Provided for three years.
- **Access**: Five rooms for wheelchair users and adapted rooms for students hard of hearing. Wheelchair access available to all areas of the main site.
- **Main site**: First years, some second and third years.
- **Rent**: Banded accommodation on site.
- **Off site**: Sir Geoffrey Arthur Building (GAB) by the river for some second and third years.
- **Rent**: Fixed rate, nine-month contract for those living in the GAB.

Food: Hall serves lunches and dinner Monday–Friday, and dinner on Sunday. The Farthings Café is open Monday–Saturday, serving breakfast, sandwiches and snacks. The College runs two meal plans, which apply to students living on the main site.
- **Plan 1**: Pre-paid termly evening meal plan, which covers six nights a week during term (Monday–Friday and Sunday). Lunch is served in Hall on a pay-as-you-go basis on weekdays. Formal Hall is compulsory for three nights a week. This plan is automatically taken out by first years.
- **Plan 2**: After first year, students can purchase a flexible meal plan (slightly more expensive than the standard meal plan), and can divide the allowance between brunches, lunches and dinners in Hall or the Farthings Café.
- **Students living in annexe**: Students living here do not take out a meal plan; they use a pay-as-you-go system if they choose to eat in Hall or Farthings.
- **Other**: The GAB annexe is self-catering, and there are some shared kitchens on the main site.

Facilities on site: Auditorium; art gallery; chapel; library; bar.

Financial aid: College hardship fund; JCR Art Fund (unexpected hardship); travel grant; vacation grants; academic scholarships and prizes (including rent reductions for scholars and exhibitioners); choral scholarships; organ scholarships; vocal scholarships; Sir Roger Bannister scholarships for all-round excellence.

Societies: Pembroke Writers Guild; The Pink Times (student publication); Social Sciences Society; Feminist Discussion Group; Pembroke College Choir; Pembroke College Music Society; Pembroke Chamber Singers; CU.

Miscellaneous:
- Pembroke was the first Oxford college to have a JCR-owned art

collection. The collection is housed in the college's Art Gallery, where public exhibitions and speaker events are held throughout the year.

- The College puts on a Film Masterclass series.

Alumni: Senator J. William Fulbright; Samuel Johnson.

Did you know ...?

Pembroke has an enviable rowing reputation among Oxford colleges; in the last two decades, the Boat Club has had more boats in the top three places on the river than any other college, for both men and women.

REGENT'S PARK COLLEGE (founded 1810, moved to Oxford in 1927 and became a PPH in 1957)

Number of students/fellows: 34 UGs admitted per year; 100 UGs in total.

Size and location: Very small; located near to Modern Languages faculty, Oriental Institute, Classics (Sackler Building); Mathematical Institute; and Linguistics, Philology and Phonetics faculty.

Courses *not* offered by this college: All science subjects; Archaeology and Anthropology; Classics with Oriental Studies; Economics and Management; European and Middle Eastern Languages; Fine Art; History of Art; Modern Languages and joint courses; Music; Law with Law Studies in Europe; Oriental Studies; Oriental Studies with Classics; PPL.

Accommodation: Provided for first and third year (and some second years).
- **Main site**: All first years live on site.
- **Off site**: Third years live in college flats nearby, and there is also college-owned accommodation on Banbury Road, North Oxford.
- **Rent**: Fixed termly charge.

Food:
- **Hall**: Breakfast, lunch and dinner served Monday–Friday. Term-time charges for students living on site normally include lunch and dinner; however, students can opt out of a certain number of these. Students living out charged for a small number of meals per week, but can take more meals in college for an additional charge. Formal Hall served once a week.
- **Other**: Student accommodation has access to communal kitchens.

Facilities on site: Library, with a strong Theology section; chapel; bar.

Financial aid: Please see Oxford's fees and funding pages (www.ox. ac.uk/students/fees-funding) for details of financial support available, or contact the College for further information on its funding arrangements.

Societies: Advent choir; Gospel choir; CU; Rowing.

Miscellaneous:
- JCR 'brew', where students come together for tea and biscuits in the JCR, is a regular feature of college life.
- The College has its own tortoise.
- Recently ranked number 1 mixed college for student satisfaction.

Did you know ...?

Regent's Park specialises in the arts, humanities and social science subjects.

SOMERVILLE COLLEGE (founed 1879)

Number of students/fellows: 375 UGs.

Size and location: Medium-sized college, next to Language Centre, Mathematics, Engineering and Philosophy departments (Radcliffe Observatory Quarter) and near to the Science Area.

Courses *not* offered at this college: Archaeology and Anthropology; Biomedical Sciences; Classics and English; Computer Science and Philosophy; Earth Sciences; Economics and Management; Fine Art; Geography; History and Politics; History of Art; Human Sciences; Materials Science; Mathematics and Philosophy; Oriental Studies; Oriental Studies with Classics; Philosophy and Theology; Psychology and Linguistics; Psychology and Philosophy; Theology and Oriental Studies; Theology and Religion. *Please note that not every language course is available; check the Oxford website to see which combinations are offered at this college.*

Accommodation: Provided on site for first and final years, and some second years. Second year accommodation is allocated via ballot.
- **Access**: Lift access to Hall and Terrace Bar. Library, function room and Chapel wheelchair accessible.
- **Rent**: Termly charge; 10% premium for en-suite rooms.

Food:
- **Hall**: Breakfast, lunch and dinner served Monday–Friday; brunch and dinner served Saturday–Sunday. Students pay for food in cash or on a pre-paid card, which allows students to purchase food at a discount. Formal Hall served approximately once a week.
- **Other**: Terrace café bar open during term-time. Shared kitchens throughout college.

Facilities on site: Library; bar; chapel; fitness suite; music rooms; computer rooms; dark room; St Paul's Nursery (open Monday–Friday).

Financial aid: College bursary; academic scholarships and prizes; book grant for second year students; travel grants; choral exhibitions.

Societies: Drama Society; Music Society; College Choir; Somerville Writing Group; Somerville Album Club; History Society; Somerville Gender Equality Group.

Miscellaneous:
- Founded for women when they were barred from the University; male students first admitted in 1994.
- Recently voted best college for food.

Alumnae: Vera Brittain; A.S. Byatt; Susie Dent; Indira Gandhi; Iris Murdoch; Lucy Powell; Esther Rantzen; Dorothy L. Sayers; Margaret Thatcher.

Did you know ...?

Somerville was the first non-denominational Oxford college and it continues to be non-denominational in the present day. Along with St Hilda's, St Hugh's and St Edmund Hall, it typically has one of the highest levels of imports (applicants who applied to other colleges or who did not state a preference on their application).

ST ANNE'S COLLEGE (founded 1879)

Number of students: 420 UGs.

Size and location: Large college located near University Parks, opposite Radcliffe Observatory Quarter and near Science Area.

Courses *not* offered at this college: Archaeology and Anthropology; Economics and Management; History and English; History of Art; Human Sciences; Oriental Studies (offers only Persian and Turkish streams); Philosophy and Linguistics; Philosophy and Theology; Physics and Philosophy; Theology and Oriental Studies Theology and Religion. *Please note that not every language course is available; check the Oxford website to see which combinations are offered at this college.*

Accommodation: Provided for three years on site; students on four-year courses (with the exception of Modern Languages) are required to live out in their second, third or fourth year.
- **Access**: Adapted accommodation available.
- **Rent**: Fixed annual rate, which includes utilities.

Food:
- **Hall**: Breakfast, lunch and dinner Monday–Friday; brunch Saturday–Sunday. Pay-as-you-go system. Formal Hall served once every fortnight.
- **Other**: St Anne's Coffee Shop. Self-catering shared kitchenettes in all accommodation.

Facilities on site: Library; bar; gym facilities; rowing room; art gallery; dark room; chapel; lecture theatres; music practice rooms; College nursery.

Financial aid: Unexpected hardship grants; travel grants; music bursaries to help meet the cost of music lessons.

Societies: Music Society; Classics Society; Geology Society; Choir; Ensemble ANNIE; STACappella; Orchestra (with St John's); Life drawing; CU; Feminist Discussion Group; Book Club.

Miscellaneous:

- Vacation Laboratory studentships for science students.
- A Year in Japan offers the opportunity to study in Japan, receive Japanese-language tuition and teach English.
- The College runs its own Careers Week.

Alumni: Danny Alexander; Edwina Currie; Helen Fielding; Diana Wynne Jones; Sir Simon Rattle; Polly Toynbee.

Did you know ...?

The Danson Foundation at St Anne's supports St Anne's students in growing start-up businesses on a nine-week project; students are given working capital and money for legal/administrative costs as part of the Incubator Projects. Danson internships offer paid placements, mostly in London and in a range of sectors. St Anne's has a high student intake and accepts one of the largest numbers of students per year.

ST BENET'S HALL (PPH; founded 1897)

Number of students: 45 UGs; *c.* 16–20 admitted each year.

Size and location: Small college, near Modern Languages, Classics and Oriental faculties, Radcliffe Observatory Quarter and Mathematical Institute.

Courses *not* offered at this college: All science subjects; Archaeology and Anthropology; Classical Archaeology and Ancient History; Economics and Management; English and joint courses; European and Middle

Eastern Languages; Fine Art; Geography; History of Art; Law; Modern Languages and joint courses; Music; Oriental Studies (offers only Chinese and Japanese streams); Philosophy and Linguistics; Psychology (Experimental); Psychology and Philosophy; Psychology and Linguistics.

Accommodation: Provided for first and final years on site and in Norham Gardens (North Oxford), which also has teaching rooms and common areas:
- **Access**: As the Hall is a listed building, the main site is not very suitable for wheelchairs; however, the Hall welcomes applications from students with disabilities.
- **Rent**: Flat-rate daily charge. See under 'Food' for additional Hall charges.

Food:
- **Hall**: Flat-rate daily Meals & Facilities charge, which is reduced for students living out. This charge includes breakfast, lunch, tea and dinner, two Formals, a served Sunday lunch, one formal guest night, and use of laundry and Hall facilities. Formal Hall served three times a week.

Facilities on site: IT centre; croquet lawn; chapel; library.

Financial aid: See Oxford's fees and funding pages (www.ox.ac.uk/students/fees-funding) for details of financial support available, or contact the College for further information on its funding arrangements.

Societies: Drama.

Miscellaneous:
- As of 2015, the Hall now admits female undergraduates.
- The Hall is involved in the OxDev Project, during which students intern in developing countries.

Did you know ...?

As a small college, St Benet's is known for its familial atmosphere; there is no high table, as everyone in the Hall sits at a common table.

ST CATHERINE'S COLLEGE (Catz) (founded 1962 - newest college; very modern buildings)

Number of students: 476 UGs.

Size and location: Large; extensive grounds, including a water garden. Near Social Sciences (Politics, International Relations, Economics, Sociology), English and Law faculties and Science Area.

Courses *not* offered at this college: Archaeology and Anthropology; Classical Archaeology and Ancient History; Classics and joint courses; Earth Sciences; European and Middle Eastern Languages; History (Ancient and Modern); Oriental Studies and joint courses; Philosophy and Theology; Theology and Religion. *Please note that not every language course is available; check the Oxford website to see which combinations are offered at this college.*

Accommodation: Most students live on site for three years.
- **Access**: Adapted accommodation available for students with disabilities.
- **Rent**: Fixed rate.

Food:
- **Hall**: Serves breakfast, lunch and dinner. Pay-as-you-go system. Formal Hall served every day.
- **Other**: Buttery open on weekdays, serving snacks. Kitchens and pantries in each staircase.

Facilities on site: Library; bar; music house; theatre; punt house; squash courts; tennis courts; sports pitches; gym; games room.

Financial aid: Travel awards; College prizes; Répétiteur scholarship for pianists, working between Catz and New Chamber Opera; Nick Young Award (grant to gain television experience working with Director's Cut Productions in London).

Societies: Arts; Biomedical; Catzapella; CU; Femsoc; Geography; International Students Society; Law; Mathematics; Music.

Miscellaneous: The College was originally part of a society that was formed to encourage students from less-privileged backgrounds to study at Oxford.

Alumni: Emilia Fox; Joseph Heller; Peter Mandelson; James Marsh; Jeanette Winterson.

Did you know ...?

St Catz has a large student intake and makes the highest number of offers per year. The College is strong for Drama as an extra-curricular; its Cameron Mackintosh Chair of Contemporary Theatre is a Visiting Professorship to promote the study of contemporary theatre and give lectures and workshops. Past holders include Simon Russell Beale, Stephen Fry, Sir Trevor Nunn, Kevin Spacey, Sir Patrick Stewart, Sir Tim Rice, Stephen Daldry, Lord Attenborough, Arthur Miller, Sir Ian McKellen and Stephen Sondheim.

ST EDMUND HALL (Teddy Hall) (founded 1278)

Number of students/fellows: 450 UGs; 70 fellows.

Size and location: Small college, located just off the High Street, near to Examination Schools and English and Law faculties.

Courses *not* offered at this college: Archaeology and Anthropology; Biological Sciences; Classical Archaeology and Ancient History; Classics and joint courses; Computer Science and joint courses; European and Middle Eastern Languages; History (Ancient and Modern); History and English; History of Art; Human Sciences; Music; Oriental Studies and joint courses; Philosophy and Linguistics; Philosophy and Theology; Psychology and Linguistics; Theology and Religion. *Please note that not every language course is available; check the Oxford website to see which combinations are offered at this college.*

Accommodation: Provided for first and third years.
- **Access**: Most principal areas of the main college site are accessible.
- **Main site**: All first years live on site.
- **Off site**: Three annexes in North and East Oxford with shared kitchens.

Food:
- **Hall**: Breakfast, lunch and dinner served Monday–Friday; brunch and dinner Saturday–Sunday. Students living on site pay for a minimum number of breakfasts and dinners each term; some meals can be refunded if not used by the end of term. Formal Hall served twice a week.
- **Other**: All sites have self-catering facilities.

Facilities on site: Music room; games room; chapel; library; bar.

Financial aid: Undergraduate College grants to meet academic costs; College hardship fund; organ scholarships; choral scholarships; travel awards; subject-specific prizes; academic scholarships and exhibitions.

Societies: Chapel Choir (non-auditioning); Alternative Choir; Jazz Band; Music Society; Arts Society; CU; John Oldham Society (Drama); PPE; Hall Writers' Forum; Venus Society (organises fundraising events for Macmillan Cancer Support).

Miscellaneous:
- Full college of the University of Oxford, but has retained its title of 'Hall'.
- The College runs a Masterclass scheme, which offers a grant for students to receive advanced coaching in extra-curricular areas such as music, sport, art, drama and writing. In addition, the Frank di Renzo Masterclass Award offers a grant for coaching in drama and theatre.
- The College also organises a Bridge-to-Business programme, offer-

ing an insight into writing CVs, interview and presentation preparation and career planning.

Alumni: Nicholas Evans; Terry Jones; Stewart Lee; Al Murray.

Did you know ...?

The College has a strong writing tradition across a range of genres, and hosts weekly creative-writing workshops for students during term and regular writing events.

ST HILDA'S COLLEGE (founded 1893)

Number of students: 401 UGs.

Size and location: Large grounds. Located at the very end of the High Street, right by the river and near to the Iffley Road sports complex.

Courses *not* offered at this college: Archaeology and Anthropology; Classics and English; Classics and Modern Languages; Computer Science and joint courses; Earth Sciences; Fine Art; History and Economics; History of Art; Human Sciences; Materials Science; Oriental Studies; Oriental Studies with Classics; Philosophy and Theology; Theology and Oriental Studies; Theology and Religion. *Please note that not every language course is available; check the Oxford website to see which combinations are offered at this college.*

Accommodation: Provided for all first years and most final years in college; final years accommodated via ballot. Currently building a new accommodation block for its 125th anniversary in 2018, so that all students can be housed in college accommodation.
- **Access**: Two adapted rooms suitable for students with disabilities and disabled toilet facilities in the principal college building. The Hall, JCR, Chapel and Library all have wheelchair access.
- **Main site**: First years and some finalists.
- **Rent**: Fixed rate; higher charge for en-suite rooms, which are allocated to final years.
- **Off site**: Off-site college properties for some second year and final year students. 40-week lease.

Food:
- **Hall**: Breakfast, lunch and dinner served Monday–Friday; brunch served on Saturday. Pay-as-you-go meals and takeaway options. The Hall has round tables; only college to have this. Formal Hall served once a week.
- **Other**: The Buttery (student-run snack bar). Student kitchenettes/kitchens in college; size/kitchen facilities varies depending on the accommodation block.

Facilities on site: Jacqueline du Pré Music Building; netball court; tennis court; College punts; chapel; library; bar. The development work for the College's 125th anniversary in 2018 will provide new accommodation, social and teaching spaces, including a new MCR, Porters' Lodge and entrance.

Financial aid: JCR Hardship Fund; academic scholarships; book grants; travel fund; D.D. White Fund to meet costs of sports equipment.

Societies: Choir; Orchestra; Running club; hildabeats (jazz and blues band); Drama; CU; College newspaper.

Miscellaneous: Originally a women's college, but now admits both male and female undergraduates.

Alumni: Wendy Cope; Adele Geras; Val McDermid; Katherine Parkinson.

Did you know ...?

Nestled in picturesque riverside gardens, St Hilda's is one of Oxford's best-kept secrets; it often receives the lowest number of direct applications among the Oxford colleges, and among the highest number of imports. Other colleges receiving low numbers of direct applications include Mansfield, St Hugh's, Corpus Christi and St Peter's. Among its extensive list of on-site facilities, St Hilda's is home to the Jacqueline du Pré Music Building, which, as well as including four practice rooms, an auditorium and recording studio, hosts regular concerts from renowned professional musicians.

ST HUGH'S COLLEGE (founded 1886)

Number of students: 410 UGs.

Size and location: Large; extensive grounds (14 acres). Near Radcliffe Observatory Quarter and Institute of Social and Cultural Anthropology.

Courses *not* offered at this college: Classical Archaeology and Ancient History; Computer Science and Philosophy; Geography; History and Economics; History of Art; Materials Science; Oriental Studies; Oriental Studies with Classics; Philosophy and Theology; Physics and Philosophy; Theology and Oriental Studies; Theology and Religion. *Please note that not every language course is available; check the Oxford website to see which combinations are offered at this college.*

Accommodation: Provided for the duration of the course on site; ballot after first year.
- **Access**: Limited number of rooms available with disabled access.
- **Rent**: Flat rate.

Food:
- **Hall**: Breakfast, lunch and dinner Monday–Friday; brunch Saturday and Sunday. Pay-as-you-go system. Formal Hall served once a week.
- **Other**: Elizabeth Wordsworth Tea Room serves snacks and drinks on weekdays, including lunch. All rooms in college have access to shared kitchens.

Facilities on site: Gym; chapel; music practice rooms; library; bar.

Financial aid: Academic scholarships and exhibitions; academic and subject-specific prizes; travel grants; year abroad grant for Modern Languages students; financial hardship fund; organ scholarships; choral awards.

Societies: Choir; Arts Society; Debating; St Hugh's Players (Drama); Blue Pen (gender equality); Jazz Band Society; Poker; Real Ale Society; Swan Newspaper; SHCAS (film); CU.

Miscellaneous: The College has over 100 fellows, meaning that students are able to have many of their classes on site, especially in the first year.

Alumni: Aung San Suu Kyi; Amal Clooney; Theresa May; Nicky Morgan.

Did you know ...?

Prime Minister Theresa May read Geography at St Hugh's, though while at Oxford she was also actively involved in the Oxford Union and the university's Conservative Association.

ST JOHN'S COLLEGE (founded 1555)

Number of students/fellows: 390 UGs; 100 fellows and 25 college lecturers.

Size and location: Fairly large college; near to Languages, Oriental Studies, Classics and Linguistics faculties.

Courses *not* offered at this college: Classics and English; Earth Sciences; Economics and Management; History and English; Materials Science; Philosophy and Linguistics; Theology and Oriental Studies. *Please note that not every language course is available; check the Oxford website to see which combinations are offered at this college.*

Accommodation: Provided for the duration of the course. Students balloted after first year. Accommodation available for couples and families.
- **Access**: Adapted accommodation available for students with disabilities, including en-suite facilities and adapted kitchens. One property on Museum Road has an adapted kitchen suitable for wheelchair users, blind and partially sighted students.

- **Main site**: First years, some second and final years.
- **Off site**: College-owned houses behind Tommy White Quad, for groups of five to eight students in their second or final years.
- **Rent**: Banded, with an additional fixed charge per term to cover services.

Food:
- **Hall**: Serves breakfast, lunch and dinner; pay-as-you-go system. Formal Hall served six nights a week.
- **Other**: Kendrew Café serves food and coffee. All first years have access to a shared kitchen and the rooms in Kendrew Quad also have access to cooking facilities. The off-site properties have their own kitchens.

Facilities on site: Art gallery; two squash courts; two gyms; auditorium; music rooms; library; bar.

Financial aid: College hardship grants; academic grant for books, materials, etc.; special grants (e.g. for travel); vacation grants; Blues Squad grants; choral scholarships; Mapleton Bee Prize for work in the Creative Arts.

Societies: Choir; St John's and St Anne's Orchestra (non-auditioning); Music Society; Mummers Drama Society; Poker Society.

Alumni: Tony Blair; Angela Eagle; Robert Graves; Philip Larkin; Victoria Coren Mitchell; Hugh Schofield.

Did you know ...?

One of the newest additions to the College buildings is the award-winning Kendrew Quadrangle, which features solar panels for hot water, geothermal heat pumps for underfloor heating and air conditioning, low-energy lighting and a biomass boiler.

ST PETER'S COLLEGE (founded 1929, became a college in 1961)

Number of students: 340 UGs.

Size and location: Very small college; near to History faculty, Archaeology, Modern Languages and History of Art faculties.

Courses *not* offered at this college: Biomedical Sciences; Classical Archaeology and Ancient History; Classics and joint courses; Computer Science and joint courses; European and Middle Eastern Languages; Fine Art; History (Ancient and Modern); Human Sciences; Oriental Studies; Oriental Studies with Classics; Psychology (Experimental); PPL. *Please note that not every language course is available; check the Oxford website to see which combinations are offered at this college.*

Accommodation: Accommodation provided for first year and final year. Final year rooms are decided via ballot.
- **Access**: Most of the main site is accessible for wheelchair users, apart from the Library and Music room. The Hall is accessible via a lift.
- **Main site**: All first years live on site and some final years.
- **Off site**: Three college annexes, each of which is en suite.
- **Rent**: Fixed rate; the lease length varies, depending on whether you live on or off site.

Food:
- **Hall**: Breakfast, lunch and dinner served Monday– Friday; brunch and dinner Saturday–Sunday. Pay-as-you-go system. Formal Hall served twice a week.
- **Other**: Limited cooking facilities on site; JCR has a kitchen and there are kitchens in some, but not all, staircases on site. Annexes have shared kitchens and en-suite rooms.

Facilities on site: Lecture theatre; large chapel, offering ample performance space; music room; library; separate Law library; bar.

Financial aid: Hardship fund for unexpected hardship; academic scholarships and exhibitions; subject prizes; choral scholarships; organ scholarships; instrumental awards; travel grants; vacation grants; Compulsory Fieldwork grant.

Societies: Choir; Orchestra; Cross Keys Drama Society; Misc (photography art and poetry publication).

Miscellaneous:
- The College runs its own Arts Week.
- The College's Careers Society runs talks, mentorships schemes, CV clinics and other events to connect current students with St Peter's alumni.

Alumni: Rev Wilbert Awdry (creator of Thomas the Tank Engine); Mark Carney; Hugh Dancy; Hugh Fearnley-Whittingstall; Libby Lane; Ken Loach; Chris van Tulleken.

> **Did you know ...?**
>
> St Peter's alumna the Right Revd Dr Libby Lane, Bishop of Stockport, was the first female Bishop in England.

ST STEPHEN'S HOUSE (PPH; founded 1876)
NB Accepts mature students only.

Number of students: 24 UGs.

Size and location: Very small college, located opposite Iffley Road sports complex.

Courses offered at this college: At undergraduate level, St Stephen's offers only Philosophy and Theology; and Theology and Religion.

Accommodation: Provided for the duration of the course; accommodation ranges from single occupancy to flats and properties, suitable for couples and families.
- **Rent**: Weekly average rate, which varies depending on the room.

Food:
- **Hall**: Breakfast, lunch and dinner served Monday–Friday, in addition to afternoon tea. Brunch served on Saturday and breakfast and lunch served on Sunday. Students living in are on half-board and pay a weekly charge, which entitles them to discounts on other meals and includes celebratory meals. Students living out are required to pay a small annual catering charge, which entitles them to discounted meals and includes celebratory meals.
- **Other**: Large student kitchen on site and kitchens in college houses.

Facilities on site: Chapel; Bodley Church; brick barbecue; computer room; library.

Financial aid: See Oxford's fees and funding pages (www.ox.ac.uk/students/fees-funding) for details of financial support available, or contact the College for further information on its funding arrangements.

Miscellaneous:
- Anglican foundation specialising in theological teaching and research.

Did you know ...?

St Stephen's House recently came top for student satisfaction in the Student Barometer of all the Oxford colleges and Permanent Private Halls.

THE QUEEN'S COLLEGE (founded 1341)

Number of students: 90–100 UGs per year.

Size and location: Medium-sized college, near to Examination Schools, English and Law faculties and Science Area.

Courses *not* offered at this college: Archaeology and Anthropology; Classical Archaeology and Ancient History; Computer Science and joint courses; Earth Sciences; Economics and Management; Engineering Science; Geography; History and Economics; History of Art; Human Sciences; Philosophy and Linguistics; Philosophy and Theology; Theology and Oriental Studies; Theology and Religion. *Please note that not every language course is available; check the Oxford website to see which combinations are offered at this college.*

Accommodation: Provided for duration of the course.

- **Access**: Most areas of the main site are wheelchair accessible via permanent ramps.
- **Main site**: Some second and final years.
- **Off site**: First years live in two independent annexes for the first year, rather than on site as happens in most other colleges. Some second years live in the Cardo Building near the main site.
- **Rent**: Flat-rate termly fee, which includes kitchen overhead charge. Shared rooms and smaller rooms available for those who want to reduce their rent.

Food:

- **Hall**: Food served daily. Breakfast and lunch pay-as-you-go; dinner booked online for a fixed charge. Formal Hall served once a week.
- **Other**: Two first year annexes serve breakfast. JCR tea served daily.

Facilities on site: Library; separate libraries for Law and Egyptology; auditorium; music practice rooms; chapel; bar. Cardo annexe (first year annexe) has squash courts. Carrodus Quad annexe (second years and above) has an on-site gym.

Financial aid: Queen's Hardship Fund; book grants; academic support grants (travel, books, printing, etc.); choral, organ and instrumental awards; travel grants; sports fund to meet the cost of equipment/kit.

Societies: Choir; Eglesfield Musical Society (EGMS) Chorus; EGMS Orchestra; EGMS A Cappella; EGMS Jazz Band; String quartet; Eglesfield Players (Drama); Addison Society (dining society); CU.

Alumni: Rowan Atkinson; Tim Berners-Lee; Edwin Hubble; Henry V.

Did you know ...?

As well as having a renowned choir, Queen's College is one of the best colleges in Oxford for Music as an extra-curricular, with numerous student vocal and instrumental ensembles.

TRINITY COLLEGE (founded 1555)

Number of students: 90–100 UGs per year.

Size and location: Fairly large college, near University Libraries.

Courses *not* offered at this college: Archaeology and Anthropology; Biological Sciences; Biomedical Sciences; Classical Archaeology and Ancient History; Computer Science and joint courses; Earth Sciences; European and Middle Eastern Languages; Fine Art; Geography; History and Economics; History and English; History of Art; Human Sciences; Music; Oriental Studies; Oriental Studies with Classics; Psychology (Experimental); PPL; Theology and Oriental Studies. *Please note that not* *every language course is available; check the Oxford website to see which combinations are offered at this college.*

Accommodation: Provided for the duration of the course.

- **Access**: Several adapted rooms available for students with disabilities. Hall, Chapel, Library, toilets and some teaching rooms are wheelchair accessible.
- **Main site**: Students live on site for first two years.
  o **Rent**: Flat-rate fee; 180-day licence.
- **Off site**: Third and fourth years live in a self-catered college annexe in North Oxford.
  o **Rent**: Prices off site vary; 264-day licence.

Food:
- **Hall**: Breakfast, lunch and dinner served Monday–Friday; brunch and dinner Saturday–Sunday. Pay-as-you-go system. Gowns worn for dinner every night. Formal Hall served five nights a week.
- **Hall**: JCR kitchen. Off-site college accommodation has shared kitchens.

Facilities on site: Gym; squash court; music practice room; chapel; library; bar.

Financial aid: Levine Bursary (for students not eligible for an Oxford Opportunity Bursary or whose OOB entitlement doesn't cover financial needs); academic grants for subject-related projects; book grants; travel grants; year abroad fund for Modern Languages.

Societies: Chapel Choir (non-auditioned); Swing Band; Chamber Orchestra; Music Society; Trinity Players (Drama); The Broadsheet (student newspaper); The Gryphon (Debating); World Music Group; Trinity Singers; CU; Law Society.

Alumni: Sir Richard Burton; Constantine Louloudis; Terence Rattigan; Jacob Rees-Mogg; David Yates.

Did you know ...?

Trinity holds an annual Richard Hillary Memorial lecture with notable guest speakers; recent lecturers include Philip Pullman, Carol-Ann Duffy, Sir Tom Stoppard and Sir Andrew Motion.

UNIVERSITY COLLEGE (Univ) (founded 1249)

Number of students: 400 UGs.

Size and location: Medium-sized college on the High Street, next to the Examination Schools, and near to the English and Law faculties.

Courses *not* offered at this college: Archaeology and Anthropology;

Biological Sciences; Classics and English; Economics and Management; Fine Art; Geography; History and Economics; History and English; History of Art; Human Sciences; Materials Science; Oriental Studies (offers only Egyptology, Ancient Near Eastern Studies, Egyptology and Ancient Near Eastern Studies and Chinese streams); Philosophy and Theology; Theology and Oriental Studies; Theology and Religion. *Please note that not every language course is available; check the Oxford website to see which combinations are offered at this college.*

Accommodation: Provided for three years on site and in annexes in North and East Oxford.
- **Access**: Three fully accessible rooms and several other adapted rooms for students with disabilities.
- **Rent**: Flat-rate termly fee, which includes facilities charge.

Food:
- **Hall**: Breakfast, lunch and dinner served Monday–Friday; brunch and dinner Saturday–Sunday. Pay-as-you-go system. Formal Hall served three times a week.
- **Other**: Some shared kitchens on Stavertonia site (North Oxford) and on site.

Facilities on site: Squash court; library; separate Law library; chapel; bar.

Financial aid: Old Members' Trust Bursary (need-based); Univ Support Fund for unexpected financial hardship; academic scholarships and exhibitions; travel grants; vacation grants.

Societies: Choir (non-auditioned); College orchestra; Music Society; Univ Players (Drama); Debating Society; Eldon Society (Law); Univ Mooting; CU; Sikh Society; Ambassador Scheme (see 'Did you know …?' below).

Miscellaneous:
- The College co-owns a French chalet with Balliol and New Colleges.
- The College offers a pre-term Maths Week for Biochemistry, Biomedical Sciences, Chemistry, Computer Science, Earth Sciences, Engineering, Mathematics, Medicine and Physics.
- Staircase12 (http://staircase12.univ.ox.ac.uk): college-run website for school and sixth-form students.

Alumni: Bill Clinton; Stephen Hawking; C.S. Lewis; Andrew Motion; Harold Wilson.

Did you know …?

University College, or Univ, as it is more commonly known, has its own Ambassador Scheme, a volunteering programme where Univ students work as mentors for young people, providing advice and information about higher education and applying to Oxford, doing tours of the College, school visits and helping out on open days and at summer schools and taster days.

WADHAM COLLEGE (founded 1610)

Number of students/fellows: 440 UGs; 70 teaching fellows; 30 lecturers.

Size and location: Large college with six acres of grounds. Near Science Area and University Libraries.

Courses *not* offered at this college: Archaeology and Anthropology; Computer Science; Computer Science and Philosophy; Earth Sciences; Fine Art; Geography; Materials Science; Music; Philosophy and Theology; PPL; Theology and Oriental Studies; Theology and Religion. *Please note that not every language course is available; check the Oxford website to see which combinations are offered at this college.*

Accommodation: Provided for first and final years.
- **Access**: Adapted accommodation available for students with disabilities.
- **Rent**: Flat-rate fee. For students living on site, board and lodging charge includes accommodation, evening meals Monday–Friday (in Hall or Refectory), utilities, internet and basic insurance cover.

Food:
- **Hall**: Serves dinner Monday–Friday. No Formal Hall.
- **New Refectory**: Serves breakfast, lunch and dinner Monday–Friday and brunch on Saturdays. Breakfast, lunch and brunch pay-as-you-go. Dinner is included in board and lodging charge for students living on site; students living off-site must pre-book dinner online.
- **Other**: JCR kitchen, and some staircases have kitchenettes.

Facilities on site: Library; bar; Holywell Music Room (concert hall); Sir Claus Moser Theatre (doubles as a badminton court); music practice rooms; gym; squash court; rowing machine room.

Financial aid: Student Support grants for unforeseen financial hardship; students living out are given a grant to help with living costs; academic-related grants to meet academic costs; academic scholarships and subject prizes; vacation grants; travel grants.

Societies: Chapel Choir; Dot's Funk Odyssey (funk/soul band); Wadham Jazz Band; Orchestra (joint with Keble).

Miscellaneous:
- Accredited Fairtrade college.
- Only college to have a single students' union – the JCR and MCR are combined.
- Student Ambassador Scheme for outreach events.
- The College organises Wadstock (music festival) annually.

Alumni: Melvyn Bragg; Felicity Jones; Rosamund Pike; Michael Rosen; Rowan Williams; Sir Christopher Wren.

Did you know ...?

Wadham is known as a socially active college; every year it hosts Queer Week, which features a host of seminars, talks and events promoting gender equality and diversity; and the Radical Forum, a weekend of debates on radical politics in society.

WORCESTER COLLEGE (founded 1714)

Number of students: 420 UGs.

Size and location: Very large – 26 acres of grounds, including lake, orchards and sports fields. Near Archaeology, Modern Languages, Linguistics and History faculties and Oriental Institute.

Courses *not* offered at this college: Archaeology and Anthropology; Biomedical Sciences; Computer Science and Philosophy; History and English; Human Sciences; Materials Science; Oriental Studies; Oriental Studies with Classics; Theology and Oriental Studies. *Please note that not every language course is available; check the Oxford website to see which combinations are offered at this college.*

Accommodation: Three years' accommodation offered; all rooms on site or within a few hundred metres of the College.
- **Rent**: Banded accommodation. Length of contract varies from year to year: 176 nights for first years; 174 nights for second years; 258 nights for third and fourth years.

Food:
- **Hall**: Breakfast, lunch and dinner served Monday– Saturday; breakfast and Formal Hall on Sunday. Pay-as-you-go system. Formal Hall served three times a week.
- **Other**: Buttery serving drinks and snacks. Shared kitchens/diners in most student accommodation.

Facilities on site: Sports fields; gym; tennis courts; library; Law library; chapel; bar.

Financial aid: Financial Hardship Fund; academic scholarships and exhibitions; choral, organ and instrument scholarships; travel grants; vacation study grants; book allowance.

Societies: Buskins Drama Society; two Chapel choirs; College orchestra; Music Society; Woosta Source (college newspaper).

Alumni: Russell T. Davies; Rupert Murdoch; Emma Watson.

Did you know …?

Set in 26 acres, including a lake, Worcester is the only Oxford college to have its sporting fields on site, catering for rugby, football, hockey, lawn and hard tennis, cricket, rounders and croquet. In addition, there are also an on-site gym and tennis court.

WYCLIFFE HALL (PPH; founded 1877)

NB Accepts mature students only.

Number of students: 77 UGs.

Size and location: Small college near Science Area and University Parks.

Courses offered at this college: Offers only Philosophy and Theology; and Theology and Religion at undergraduate level.

Accommodation: Priority given to ordinands. Independent students eligible for Hall accommodation on a first-come, first-served basis, and only after all ordinands in that year have been allocated a room. Family accommodation available; again, priority is given to ordinands.
- **Access**: Some of the buildings on the main site are accessible to wheelchair users.
- **Rent**: Fixed annual cost. Around half of the rooms on site are on an all-year lease (38-weeks); the other half are for term-time only.

Food: Breakfast, lunch and dinner served seven days a week. Rent for a Hall room includes the cost of 180 meals (60 per term).

Facilities on site: Specialist theological library; chapel.

Financial aid: See Oxford's fees and funding pages (www.ox.ac.uk/students/fees-funding) for details of financial support available, or contact the College for further information on its funding arrangements.

Miscellaneous:
- Evangelical theological college.
- Sports are joint with Queen's College.
- Also offers an Undergraduate Certificate in Theological Studies; and Undergraduate Diploma in Theological Studies (available to students with 'Senior Status', i.e. students who have already completed an undergraduate degree).

Did you know …?

As an evangelical college, Wycliffe Hall specialises in Theology and came top of the Norrington Table in 2012 among the Permanent Private Halls. The College has a well-stocked Theology library.

Norrington table

Table 4 Norrington Table – Oxford 2015–2016

Rank	College	Score
1	Merton	76.22%
2	Oriel	76.10%
3	Magdalen	74.95%
4	University	74.91%
5	Trinity	74.82%
6	Wadham	74.70%
7	Brasenose	74.26%
8	Balliol	73.94%
9	Worcester	73.33%
10	St Catherine's	73.18%
11	Harris Manchester	72.94%
12	St John's	72.48%
13	Pembroke	72.45%
14	Jesus	71.74%
15	Corpus Christi	71.59%
16	Somerville	71.46%
17	Keble	71.26%
18	New	71.24%
19	Lincoln	71.19%
20	Hertford	70.75%
21	St Edmund Hall	70.74%
22	St Hugh's	70.68%
23	Lady Margaret Hall	70.53%
24	Christ Church	70.17%
25	Exeter	70%
26	St Anne's	69.91%
27	St Hilda's	69.12%
28	St Peter's	68.31%
29	Mansfield	67.62%
30	Queen's	66.06%

Oxford map

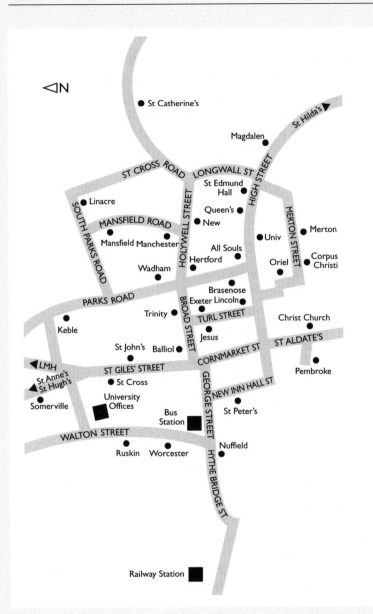

◁N

- St Catherine's
- Magdalen
- St Hilda's
- ST CROSS ROAD
- LONGWALL ST
- HIGH STREET
- Linacre
- St Edmund Hall
- HOLYWELL STREET
- SOUTH PARKS ROAD
- MANSFIELD ROAD
- Queen's
- New
- MERTON STREET
- Merton
- Mansfield
- Manchester
- Univ
- All Souls
- Corpus Christi
- Hertford
- Oriel
- Wadham
- PARKS ROAD
- BROAD STREET
- Brasenose
- Exeter
- Lincoln
- Christ Church
- Trinity
- TURL STREET
- Keble
- Jesus
- St John's
- Balliol
- CORNMARKET ST
- ST ALDATE'S
- ◄LMH
- ST GILES' STREET
- St Anne's
- St Hugh's ◄
- St Cross
- Pembroke
- GEORGE STREET
- NEW INN HALL ST
- Somerville
- University Offices
- Bus Station
- St Peter's
- WALTON STREET
- Nuffield
- Ruskin
- Worcester
- HYTHE BRIDGE ST
- Railway Station

213

CAMBRIDGE

CHRIST'S COLLEGE (founded 1505)

Number of students: 420 UGs.

Size and location: Medium-sized college, close to New Museums Site (African Studies, Anthropology, Chemical Engineering, History and Philosophy of Science, Materials Science, Social and Political Sciences and Zoology) and Downing Site (Archaeology, Anthropology, Biochemistry, Earth Sciences, Experimental Psychology, Genetics, Geography, Neuroscience, Pathology, Plant Science, Veterinary Anatomy).

Courses *not* offered at this college: Veterinary Medicine.

Accommodation: Three years' accommodation provided, either on site or in college-owned houses in adjacent streets.
- **Access**: Three adapted rooms for students with disabilities. Upper Hall, Library, practice rooms and toilets accessible via lift. JCR and TV Room have ramped access.
- **Rent**: Banded room prices.

Food:
- **Hall**: Termly Kitchen Standing Charge. Upper Hall serves breakfast, lunch and dinner; Hall serves Formal Hall and occasion dinners.
- **Other**: Buttery café, including Costa Coffee, offering a discount on high-street prices. Kitchen facilities available across Christ's accommodation.

Facilities on site: Theatre; gym; squash court; outdoor swimming pool; music practice rooms; Visual Arts Centre; chapel; library; bar.

Financial aid: Organ and choral scholarships; instrumental awards; travel grants; vacation grants; book grants for first years; sporting awards.

Societies: Choir (auditioned); Christ's Film Society; Christs' Amateur Dramatic Society (CADS); Christ's Amnesty (Amnesty International); Christ's College Board Games Society; Christ's College Music Society; COGLES (Geography); Chess; CU; Darwin Society (science); RAG (Raising & Giving); Fair Trade; Film Production; Law; MEDSOC; Milton Society (debating); Politics; Seeley Society (History); Marguerites (men's sporting society); Hippolytans (women's sporting society); Visual Arts Society.

Alumni: Sacha Baron Cohen; Lady Margaret Beaufort; Charles Darwin; John Milton; John Oliver; Andy Parsons; Simon Schama; Richard Whiteley.

> **Did you know ...?**
>
> Christ's is well known for its promotion of the visual arts and has its own Visual Arts Centre with a gallery and resident artists' studios,

where weekly life-drawing classes are also held, and the Yusuf Hamied Centre, which is a performance and exhibition space.

CHURCHILL COLLEGE (founded 1958, by Sir Winston Churchill)

Number of students/fellows: 475 UGs; 150 fellows.

Size and location: One of the largest college campuses in Cambridge (40 acres). Near to West Cambridge site.

Courses *not* offered at this college: Land Economy; Theology, Religion and Philosophy of Religion.

Accommodation: Provided for three years; all undergraduate rooms on site. Staircases shared by students from different year groups and subjects, and one fellow.
- **Access**: Adapted rooms available for wheelchair users and students with hearing difficulties and there is a disabled toilet on the main site. Lift in the main building, providing access to Hall, JCR, TV room and bar. Wolfson Theatre and Archives centre also have lift access.
- **Rent**: Banded room prices on a 30-week contract. Every student has to pay an advance deposit, which pays for a term and a half's credit; students living out get the deposit returned minus a few college charges (e.g. for meals).

Food:
- **Hall**: Lunch and dinner served Monday–Friday; breakfast, lunch and dinner served Saturday–Sunday. Pay-as-you-go system (billed termly). Formal Hall served six nights a week.
- **Buttery**: All-day bar/coffee shop serving breakfast Monday–Friday and snacks and drinks for the rest of the day.
- **Other**: All rooms have access to shared kitchen facilities.

Facilities on site: Library; bar; pitches; squash courts; tennis courts; gym; 300-seat theatre/cinema (Wolfson Theatre); music centre with performance and recording facilities; art studio; chapel; Archives Centre, which houses papers of prominent political, military and scientific figures from Churchill to the modern day.

Financial aid: Winston Churchill Memorial Trust Bursaries; College hardship grants; emergency loans; choral scholarships; instrumental and vocal bursaries; organ scholarships; accompanist bursary; College choir directorship; Music Sizarship (responsible for overseeing, promoting and arranging musical activities in college); small grants for sport, music and drama tours; travel grants; vacation grants; academic scholarships and subject prizes.

Societies: Art Society; Chapel Choir; CU; GODS (Drama); Music Society; Poker; Phoenix Society (visiting speakers).

215

Miscellaneous: When the College was founded, it was originally envisaged as science-based, but it also accepts arts students.

Alumni: Baroness Brinton; Francis Crick; Peter Fincham; James Watson.

Did you know ...?

Churchill College was founded by Sir Winston Churchill and has a statutory requirement in place stipulating that 70% of its students and teaching staff should study or teach in the areas of mathematics, science and technology.

CLARE COLLEGE (founded 1326, second-oldest college)

Number of students/ fellows: *c.* 140 UGs admitted each year; 95 fellows.

Size and location: Medium-sized college on the river; near to the University Library and Sidgwick site (arts and humanities).

Courses offered at this college: All courses offered.

Accommodation: Provided for the duration of the course.
* **Access**: Six rooms accessible for wheelchair users. Lift for JCR, Cafeteria, Bar, Hall, Chapel and Library. One disabled toilet on main site.
* **Main site**: Accommodates first years and some final years.
* **Off site**: Second years live in Colony annexe (near Magdalene College), and most third and fourth years.
* **Rent**: Banded accommodation. Students pay a Kitchen Fixed Charge (KFC), which pays for staffing, production, meal service and utilities.

Food:
* **Buttery**: Self-service, three meals a day; pay-as-you-go system.
* **Hall**: Salad bar Monday–Friday; pay-as-you-go system. Can be booked for society, subject and occasion dinners. Formal Hall served four times a week.
* **Other**: Most rooms have access to a 'gyp room' (kitchenette).

Facilities on site: Clare Cellars (college bar): venue for live music, stand-up, theatre, etc.; practice rooms; punts; chapel; Riley Auditorium; library.

Financial aid: Hardship grants; undergraduate bursaries; choral scholarships; organ scholarships; instrumental awards; book grants; travel and research grants; sports award (assistance with sporting costs); cycle helmet/lights subsidies; academic scholarships and subject-specific prizes.

Societies: Choir; Music Society; Amnesty; Chess; CU; Clare Actors;

Clare College Music Society; Clare Comedy; Clare Jazz; Clare Voices; Clare Sound (sound and lighting); Clare Growers (allotment); Clare Vegans; Clare Live (music); Clare Canaries (vocal group); Fair Trade; LGBT+; Life Drawing; Dilettante Society (debating); VetMed Soc; Whiston Society (Science); Clare College Student Investment Fund; QCOEF (fundraises for educational projects in developing countries).

Miscellaneous:
- The College has an on-site careers adviser. Summer placements (medical, veterinary and scientific research) and work experience are offered in the College archives and the Library.
- The Clare–Yale Fellowship fund supports students wanting to study at Yale for part of their course.

Alumni: Sir David Attenborough; John Rutter; Siegfried Sassoon; James Watson.

Did you know ...?

Clare has won the University of Cambridge Culinary Competition for three consecutive years.

CORPUS CHRISTI COLLEGE (founded 1352)

Number of students: 280 UGs.

Size and location: Small college. Main site near New Museum site and Downing site. Leckhampton (graduate site, but also used by undergraduates) is 10 minutes' walk from Corpus site.

Courses *not* offered at this college: Architecture; Education; Land Economy; Veterinary Medicine.

Accommodation: Provided for the duration of the course. First years are usually grouped on the main site or nearby.
- **Rent**: Room prices are banded. The College offers two types of lease: 30-week (term-time only), or 39-week (continual use of room from end of September to end of June).

Food:
- **Cafeteria**: Termly Kitchen Fixed Charge. Lunch and dinner served Monday–Friday; brunch served on Sunday. Pay-as-you-go system; billed termly.
- **Bar**: Serves breakfast every day.
- **Other**: Formal Hall served twice a week. Shared gyp rooms and more extensive self-catering facilities available throughout the College.

Facilities on site:
- **Access**: One accessible flat on the main site, and one in Bene't

Street hostel (the latter includes an adapted bathroom and kitchen). Bar, cafeteria, dining hall and library accessible via lift.
- **Main site**: Chapel; practice rooms; library; bar.
- **Leckhampton**: Playing fields (cricket and football); tennis and squash courts; gym; outdoor pool and gardens.

Financial aid: Travel awards; book awards for recipients of the Cambridge Bursary; hardship grants; academic scholarships and prizes; study grants for research, travel, materials, etc.; Frisby sports grants; organ scholarships; choral awards; instrumental awards.

Societies: Chapel Choir; Amnesty International; Corpus Films; Bene't Club (music); Green Society; Healthy Living Society; Pelican Poets and Writers; Natural Sciences Society; Finance and Investing; History; Nicholas Bacon Law Society; Northern Ireland Society; Lewis Society of Medicine; CU; Fletcher Players (Drama).

Miscellaneous: The College owns a theatre, the Corpus Playroom, which is next to King's College.

Alumni: Hugh Bonneville; Christopher Isherwood; Christopher Marlowe; Kevin McCloud; Owen Paterson; Samuel Wesley.

Did you know ...?

Corpus Christi was founded by Cambridge residents, and is the only Cambridge college to have been founded in this way.

DOWNING COLLEGE (founded 1800)

Number of students: 425 UGs.

Size and location: Large; extensive grounds, including a paddock. Near Downing site and New Museums site.

Courses offered at this college: All courses offered.

Accommodation: Provided for three years on main site or adjacent to college; some accommodation available for fourth years. First years live on site; ballot thereafter.
- **Access**: Six adapted rooms available for students with disabilities; three are usually reserved for graduates. Lift access to Library, Howard Building, Howard Theatre. Accessible toilets.
- **Rent**: Banded accommodation. All students required to pay a deposit at the start of their course.

Food:
- **Butterfield Café and Bar**: Serves breakfast and light snacks Monday–Saturday.

- **Servery**: Lunch and dinner Monday–Friday; brunch and dinner Saturday–Sunday. Pay-as-you-go; billed termly.
- **Other**: Formal Hall served three times a week. Shared kitchen facilities available for making light snacks in all accommodation areas.

Facilities on site: Howard Theatre (includes a Steinway piano and music practice room); gym; two courts (for tennis/basketball/netball); chapel; library; bar.

Financial aid: Downing Bursary for unexpected financial hardship; Downing Association Student Support (assistance with cost of books, course materials, travel, vacation studies or conferences); travel fund grants; academic scholarships and prizes.

Societies: Amnesty International; Astronomical Society (college owns a telescope); CU; Dance Society; Downing Dramatic Society; Chapel Choir; Jazz Band; Music Society; PPDO (Pembroke, Peterhouse, Downing Orchestra); Blake Society (Humanities); Brammer Geographical Society; Cranworth Law Society; Danby Society (Natural Sciences, Computer Science, Mathematics and Engineering); Maitland Historical Society; Mathias Society (Economics and Land Economy); Whitby Medical Society (Medicine and Veterinary Science).

Miscellaneous: Discover Downing (www.discoverdowning.com/about/discover-downing): separate site for schools and colleges with subject resources and student blogs.

Alumni: Quentin Blake; John Cleese; Andy Hamilton; Howard Jacobson; Thandie Newton; Trevor Nunn.

Did you know ...?

Downing's Blake Society holds lectures, discussions, poetry and sketching sessions throughout the year. Each year the society holds a black-tie dinner with its patron, alumnus Quentin Blake.

EMMANUEL COLLEGE (Emma) (founded 1584)

Number of students/fellows: 460 UGs; 90 fellows.

Size and location: Large; extensive grounds, including paddock and ponds. Near New Museums site and Downing site.

Courses *not* offered at this college: Land Economy; Education track 'Education, English, Drama and the Arts'.

Accommodation: Provided for the duration of the course.
- **Access**: Four rooms on the main site suitable for wheelchair users, with adapted bathroom and kitchen. One adapted room for a deaf student. Lift access to Hall, Library, and Queen's Building.

- **Rent**: Banded accommodation. Students pay for 10 weeks each term, and rent includes the Catering Fixed Charge.

Food:
- **Hall**: Breakfast, lunch and dinner Monday–Saturday; brunch and dinner on Sunday. Pay-as-you-go (charged termly). Formal Hall served most evenings.
- **Other**: Buttery shop sells snacks.

Facilities on site: Library; bar; tennis court; outdoor swimming pool; squash court; fitness suite; table tennis room; tennis courts and croquet lawn on the Paddock in Easter term; chapel; free laundry service (only Cambridge college to offer this service).

Financial aid: Hardship and welfare support; funding for academic activities; choral and organ scholarships.

Societies: Amnesty International; Music; Revised Emmanuel Dramatic Society; Chess; CU; Mountaineering; Fair Trade; CinEmma; Photographic; Choir; Orchestra; Creative Writing; Jazz Band; Debating Society; Politics and Economics.

Alumni: Sebastian Faulks; Maggie O'Farrell; Griff Rhys Jones.

Did you know ...?

Sebastian Faulks won an open exhibition to read English at Emmanuel, and is also an Honorary Fellow.

FITZWILLIAM COLLEGE (founded 1869, to widen access to Cambridge; became a college in 1966)

Number of students: 440 UGs.

Size and location: Fairly small college with modern design. Near to the Mathematics faculty and West Cambridge site.

Courses *not* offered at this college: All courses offered.

Accommodation: Provided for duration of course.
- **Access**: Two en-suite rooms suitable for wheelchair users. Buttery, Coffee Shop/Bar, Gatehouse Court, Auditorium, Central Building and Library accessible via lift. Several disabled toilets on site.
- **First years**: Accommodated on site.
- **Other years**: Balloted; some students live in college-owned houses nearby. Students can pay for 29-week (term-time) or 39-week leases.
- **Rent**: Banded accommodation. Students required to pay a deposit on the first bill.

Food: Minimum Meals Charge billed at the start of each term; can be used for any meals, including Formal Hall, but cannot be carried over to the next term. Kitchen Fixed Charge (lower for students not living on the main college site).

- **Coffee Shop**: Serves breakfast every day. Becomes a bar in the evening.
- **Hall (Buttery)**: Serves lunch and dinner every day. Pay-as-you-go system.
- **Other**: Formal Hall served twice a week. College has some (gyp rooms); limited cooking facilities for first year students. The Stretton Room can be hired out and has a fully equipped kitchen and dining room.

Facilities on site: Auditorium including Steinway piano and practice rooms; allotment; arts studio; gym; squash courts; chapel; library; bar.

Financial aid: Maintenance bursary; Goldman Sachs bursaries for students of promise; travel awards (for academic and non-academic purposes); assistance with music lessons; sports bursaries; support towards the cost of taking part in charitable and community projects; Sailbridge Special Project Award; vacation project accommodation allowances for undergraduates undertaking research projects/academic-related internships in the Cambridge area.

Societies: Music Society; Chapel Choir; Fitz Swing; Fitz Sirens (female a cappella); Fitz Barbershop; Fine Arts Society; Debating Society; Amnesty International; CU; Communal Gardens (allotments); Feminist Society; Medical and Veterinary Society; History Society; Economics and Finance Society; Law Society; The Mitchell Society of Industry and Technology for interest in the applied sciences, engineering and technology; Natural Sciences Society; Literary Society.

Miscellaneous:
- Fitzwilliam Chamber Opera (only permanent college-based opera company in Cambridge).
- The College was highly commended in the FreeFrom eating awards 2014 for its Hall food.

Alumni: Andy Burnham, MP; Vince Cable; James Norton.

Did you know ...?

The College supports charity and community work, and offers funding to students towards participation in charitable or community projects. In addition, the Sailbridge Special Project Award is open to students looking to undertake educationally, environmentally, charitably or entrepreneurially valuable projects.

GIRTON COLLEGE (founded 1869)

Number of students: 500 UGs.

Size and location: Very large; 50 acres of grounds. Quite far out from centre (two miles). Separate site nearer city centre (Wolfson), which is near the University Library and next to Centre for Mathematical Sciences.

Courses *not* offered at this college: Education; History of Art.

Accommodation: Provided for a minimum of three years. Most accommodation is mixed, but there is an all-female corridor that students can choose.
- **Access**:
  - **Main site**: One flat for wheelchair users, with adapted bathroom and kitchen, and an annexe for a carer. Two rooms adapted for students with hearing impairments. Six disabled toilets.
  - **Wolfson Court**: One purpose-built flat for wheelchair users, including adapted bathroom and kitchen.
- **First years**: Live in college.
- **Other years**: Second and third years choose between college, a college-owned house, or Wolfson Court through a ballot.
- **Rent**: Fixed annual charge for first three years, which includes Christmas and Easter vacations (37 or 38 weeks). Rent is inclusive of Kitchen Fixed Charge. Facilities charge levied for students living out of college accommodation.

Food:
- **Main site**: Cafeteria serves breakfast, lunch and dinner Monday–Friday; lunch on Saturday; and lunch and dinner on Sunday. Formal Hall served once a week.
- **Wolfson**: Cafeteria serves breakfast, lunch and dinner Monday–Friday; lunch on Saturday; and lunch and dinner on Sunday.
- **Other**: Communal kitchens on each corridor.

Facilities on site:
- **Main site**: Sports facilities (football, rugby, cricket, squash, volleyball, multi-gym, indoor heated swimming pool); self-service cafeteria; museum (Lawrence Room); library; bar.
- **Wolfson Court**: Cafeteria; library (including a Law library).

Financial aid: Emily Davies Bursaries and Rose Awards (for all subjects); subject-specific bursaries in Medicine, History, Classics, HSPS and Economics; College Tutorial Hardship funds (small grants or larger loans); travel grants; academic scholarships and prizes; choral and organ awards; instrumental awards.

Societies: Chapel Choir; Music Society; Orchestra on the Hill (Girton, Magdalene, New Hall, Churchill and Fitzwilliam); Girton Banking Society; CU; Amateur Dramatics; Music; Law; History; Joan Robinson Society (Economics); Medical and Veterinary Society; Natural Sciences Society); Photographic; Poetry; LGBT.

Miscellaneous:
- Originally a female college – became co-educational in 1976.

Alumni: Margaret Mountford; Sandi Toksvig.

Did you know ...?

The College runs a Chamber Music scheme, offering musicians interested in performance advice on repertoire, coaching with professional musicians and performance opportunities.

GONVILLE AND CAIUS COLLEGE (Caius) (founded 1348)

Number of students/fellows: 560 UGs; 100 fellows.

Size and location: Medium-sized college. Very central; near New Museums Site.

Courses *not* offered at this college: All courses offered.

Accommodation: Provided for the duration of the course on West Road site (where all first years live), nearby Old Court site and in college-owned houses near the University's cricket ground.
- **Access**: All main buildings are wheelchair accessible and there are purpose-designed rooms for disabled students.
- **Rent**: Banded accommodation, which includes utilities and internet. Free laundry facilities on site. The College offers a continuation agreement for students from second year onwards; students living in certain college accommodation can leave their possessions in college accommodation throughout the academic year (38 weeks) and pay reduced rent during the vacation.

Food: Students pay for 36 dinners a term up front (minimum dining requirement), and can choose which nights they want to eat in Hall.
- **Bar**: Serves breakfast and offers a lunchtime meal deal.
- **Hall**: Lunch and dinner served every day. Formal Hall served most nights.
- **Other**: All accommodation has access to shared cooking facilities.

Facilities on site: College bar open during day to serve coffee, and runs a loyalty card scheme; gym; library.

Financial aid: Tutor's Donation Fund for academic activities; book grants; examination prizes; scholarships and exhibitions; travel awards; instrumental awards; music awards for students studying Music in financial need; Bell-Wade Bursary for sporting and academic excellence.

Societies: Shadwell Society (Drama); Choir; Orchestra; Poker; Film; Debating; Yoga; Amnesty; Music; Jazz; Board games; Bridge; CU; Politics.

Alumni: Alistair Campbell; Jimmy Carr; Francis Crick; Alain de Botton; David Frost; Simon Russell Beale; John Venn.

Did you know ...?

Gonville and Caius counts Stephen Hawking among its current fellows; Hawking has been a fellow at the College for over 50 years. He received his undergraduate degree at University College, Oxford and his PhD at Trinity Hall, Cambridge.

HOMERTON COLLEGE (founded 1768; moved to Cambridge from London in 1894; became a college in 2010)

Number of students: 580 UGs.

Size and location: One the largest; extensive grounds. Near the train station.

Courses *not* offered at this college: Architecture; Veterinary Medicine.

Accommodation: Provided for the duration of the course on site.
- **Access**: 10 purpose-built rooms for wheelchair users. Lift access to Library, Mary Allen and Cavendish Buildings, as well as accommodation blocks.
- **Rent**: Fixed rate, which varies depending on the accommodation block. Students pay a deposit on the first term's rent.

Food: Students pay a termly Minimum Meal Contribution, which enables them to purchase food in the Hall and Buttery at a discount.
- **Buttery (The Griffin)**: Serves breakfast daily.
- **Great Hall**: Serves lunch and dinner Monday–Friday; brunch on Saturday and dinner on Sunday. Pay-as-you-go system. Formal Hall served once a week.
- **Other**: All accommodation has access to shared kitchenettes.

Facilities on site: Auditorium; music practice rooms; dance studio; drama studio; sports grounds; tennis courts; croquet pitch; gym; library; bar.

Financial aid: College hardship grants; vacation study grants; internship bursaries; year abroad grant; dissertation grant; grants for academic scholarships; travel awards; choral scholarships; organ scholarships; instrumental awards; accompanist scholarships.

Societies: Absolute Pandemonium (steel pan); Amateur Theatrical Society; Allotment Society; Charter Chapel Choir (auditioned); Homerton Singers (non-auditioned); Music Society; CU; Jazz Orchestra; G.O.D.S (ballroom dancing).

Alumni: Olivia Colman; Sir Peter Maxwell Davies.

> **Did you know ...?**
>
> Homerton has the highest intake for the Education tripos and provides teaching across the three tracks, including practical Drama. The College also co-sponsors the Cambridge/Homerton Research and Teaching Centre for Children's literature and the College has strong library resources in this area.

HUGHES HALL COLLEGE (founded 1885 - oldest graduate college; majority of students are postgraduates)

NB Admits mature UGs and affiliate students (students who already have an honours degree from another university) only.

Number of students: 100 mature UGs.

Size and location: Small college, halfway between town and station, by Parker's Piece and Fenner's Cricket Ground.

Courses *not* offered at this college: Architecture; Medicine (undergraduate course); Veterinary Medicine.

Accommodation: Provided on site for the duration of the course. New accommodation block opened September 2016 with an additional 80 rooms on Gresham Road. Accommodation for couples available.
* **Access**: Five rooms suitable for wheelchair users. Full kitchens located near adapted accommodation.
* **Rent**: Banded. In addition to the Kitchen Fixed Charge (see below), students pay a yearly Computer Facilities Charge (reduced for students living in private accommodation).

Food: Annual Kitchen Fixed Charge (reduced for students living in private accommodation).
* **Hall**: Lunch and dinner served Monday–Friday; brunch served Saturday–Sunday. Pay-as-you-go system. Formal Hall served twice a week.
* **Other**: All accommodation has access to shared kitchen facilities.

Facilities on site: Gym; Pavilion Room (performance space); practice rooms; library; bar.

Financial aid: Subject awards; scholarships and bursaries for current or former students applying for a higher course.

Societies: Choir; Chess Club; Writing Club; Black & Minority Ethnic (BAME); Film Society; Photography; Law Society; Music; CU; LGBT+; Enterprise; Music.

> **Did you know ...?**
>
> Unlike most colleges at Cambridge, there is no high table at Hughes Hall, and students are also allowed to walk on the College lawns.

JESUS COLLEGE (founded 1495-1516)

Number of students: 510 UGs; 60 fellows.

Size and location: Spacious grounds (24 acres). Situated near ADC Theatre and Cambridge Union.

Courses offered at this college: Offers all courses.

Accommodation: Accommodation provided for the duration of the course. Most accommodation is on site (college-owned houses are across the road from the College).
- **Access**: Four rooms accessible to wheelchair users and two ground-floor rooms. Most areas on the main site are accessible.
- **Rent**: Banded.

Food: Students pay a Kitchen Fixed Charge each term.
- **Cafeteria**: College café serves lunch and dinner (and breakfast during Easter term); pay-as-you-go system.
- **Other**: Formal Hall served five times a week. Each staircase shares kitchen/diner in the first year. College-owned houses have kitchens.

Facilities on site: Playing fields all on site (football, rugby, cricket, hockey); tennis courts; squash courts; gym; chapel; The Forum (multi-purpose space for sport, music, arts and drama); dark room; library; bar.

Financial aid: Grants and loans for student hardship; choral and organ scholarships; travel bursaries; academic scholarships and exhibitions; subject prizes.

Societies: Two college choirs (men and women; men and boy choristers); Alcock Players (Drama); Amnesty International; Art Collection; Big Band; CU; Debating; Eliot's Face (college arts magazine); Jesus Smoker (Comedy); Music; Medicine; Natural Sciences; Scientific Society; Roosters; Comedy Debating Society; Short Story.

Miscellaneous: The College plays host to the University Visual Arts Society, which organises presentations and talks by artists and sculptors.

Alumni: Samuel Taylor Coleridge; Thomas Cranmer; Prince Edward, Earl of Wessex; Nick Hornby.

Did you know ...?

In 2015, the Cambridge Tab compared the cuppers (inter-college matches) results of each college across a range of sports, and Jesus came out in first place in its analysis. The College also has anumber of affiliated Olympians.

KING'S COLLEGE (founded 1441)

Number of students: 430 UGs.

Size and location: Large college; very central, on the river.

Courses *not* offered at this college: Education; Land Economy; Veterinary Medicine.

Accommodation: Provided for the duration of the course. Most accommodation is on the main site, and the rest is in hostels within easy reach of the College.

- **Access**: Wheelchair-accessible room and adapted en suite in New Garden Hostel. Another wheelchair-accessible room with adapted en suite available on main site. Access to most main buildings is limited, but there are level access and ramps to certain areas, including the Cafeteria, Hall, Library and Chapel.
- **Rent**: Banded accommodation on 29- or 35-week contracts.

Food: Termly catering charge levied.

- **Servery**: Serves breakfast, lunch and dinner Monday–Friday; brunch and dinner Saturday–Sunday. Students billed at end of term, and charged on pay-as-you-go basis.
- **Other**: Formal Hall served once a week. King's coffee shop serves snacks and drinks. King's also has allotments for students to grow food. Most accommodation has access to gyp rooms.

Facilities on site: Library; Rowe Music Library; coffee bar; Student Bunker (music/drama venue); art room; gym; rowing machine room; croquet lawn; volleyball; water polo; canoeing; climbing; yoga; allotments; bar.

Financial aid: College hardship fund for unexpected difficulties; support for travel; academic and essay prizes; instrumental scholarships; choral and organ scholarships.

Societies: Choir; King's Voices; Musical Society; Photographic; Film.

Alumni: Lily Cole; E.M. Forster; John Eliot Gardiner; George the Poet; Hugh Johnson; Salman Rushdie; Zadie Smith; Alan Turing.

Did you know ...?

Along with Trinity College, King's College typically receives the most direct applications. King's has a renowned choir and has been broadcasting the *Festival of Nine Lessons and Carols* to radio listeners across the world since 1928, having begun the tradition in 1918. Since 1919, the service has always opened with the hymn 'Once in Royal David's City'.

LUCY CAVENDISH COLLEGE (founded 1965)

NB Accepts mature female UGs only.

Number of students: 150 UGs.

Size and location: Large college with spacious grounds. Near Applied Mathematics and Theoretical Physics faculties.

Courses offered at this college: All courses offered.

Accommodation: Provided for the first three years. Accommodation on the main site is for single occupancy; most undergraduates live on site. On the Histon Road complex, there are some one- and two-bedroom apartments, which would be suitable for couples and families.

- **Access**: Three en-suite adapted rooms for students with disabilities, which are near to adapted kitchens. Level access to college and lift access to computer facilities, Dining Hall, Library and Cafeteria.
- **Rent**: Banded accommodation. All students are required to pay a deposit before they arrive. Students living in off-site accommodation can keep their rooms over the vacation.

Food: Students asked to pre-purchase a small amount of credit each term, which can be used for lunches, dinners, Formal Halls or takeaways.

- **Hall**: Breakfast, lunch and dinner served Monday–Friday. Al fresco dining area. Formal Hall served once a week.
- **Other**: Shared kitchen facilities available in all accommodation.

Facilities on site: Music and Meditation Pavilion; gym; library; bar.

Financial aid: Childcare grants; hardship funds; academic scholarships; sports prizes.

Societies: Lucy Cavendish/Hughes Hall combined boat club; Student choir; College newspaper; Running club; Period drama; Cavendish Chorale.

Miscellaneous: The College runs an annual national fiction prize for unpublished writers and conferences and festivals dedicated to women in the arts.

Alumnae: Honorary fellows: Dame Judi Dench; P.D. James; Dame Stella Rimington.

Did you know ...?

Lucy Cavendish is the only women's college in Europe for mature students.

MAGDALENE COLLEGE (founded 1428)

Number of students: 339 UGs.

Size and location: Medium-sized college on the river. The College is split over three sites: one on each side of Magdalene Street, and Cripps Court on Chesterton Road.

Courses offered at this college: All courses offered.

Accommodation: Provided for the duration of the course in college-owned houses within easy reach of the College, or on the main site.
- **Access**: Two purpose-built rooms with adapted bathrooms and kitchens close by. Cripps Court is fully accessible, and the Magdalene Street sites have level access and ramps between courts.
- **Rent**: First years are allocated a room; afterwards it is banded and rooms are organised via ballot.

Food: All students pay a termly Kitchen Fixed Charge.
- **Ramsay Hall**: Serves breakfast, lunch and dinner Monday–Friday; brunch and dinner Saturday–Sunday. Pay-as-you-go system. Formal Hall served every night.
- **Other**: All rooms have access to a gyp room.

Facilities on site: Library; bar; gym, squash and fives courts on site; auditorium for lectures, drama and music.

Financial aid: Student support fund for unexpected financial difficulty; travel awards; academic prizes.

Societies: Choir; Arts Magna; CU; Drama; Law; Music; Vox Society.

Alumni: Katie Derham; Julian Fellowes; C.S. Lewis; Mike Newell; Samuel Pepys; Sir Michael Redgrave; John Simpson.

Did you know ...?

The College houses the Pepys Library. The College acquired some 3,000 books from Samuel Pepys' library, which are arranged from smallest to largest.

MURRAY EDWARDS COLEGE (founded 1954 as New Hall; renamed Murray Edwards in 2008)

NB Accepts female students only.

Number of students: 360 UGs.

Size and location: Extensive gardens. Near to the Centre for Mathematical Sciences.

Courses *not* offered at this college: Education; Philosophy.

Accommodation: Provided for the duration of the course on main site or in nearby college houses. First years live together in Pearl House.

- **Access**: Some adapted en-suite accommodation available in the newer blocks. Main building has a lift between all floors except in Old Block.
- **Rent**: Banded accommodation. Refundable 'Caution Money' payable at the start of the course.

Food: Students pay a termly overhead charge, which is reduced for students not living in college accommodation.

- **Hall (The Dome)**: Serves breakfast Monday–Friday; brunch on Saturday; lunch Monday–Friday and Sunday; dinner Monday, Wednesday, Thursday, Friday and Sunday. Dinner is served at Fitzwilliam College on Saturdays. Pay-as-you-go cashless system, which gives students a discount on meals. Formal Hall served once or twice a week.
- **Other**: All rooms have access to shared kitchen facilities.

Facilities on site: Library; bar; music practice rooms; craft room; dark room; gym; tennis courts.

Financial aid: Student support fund for financial hardship; travel awards; Gateway Challenges Funding for students participating in the Gateway Programme (see under 'Did you know …?' for further information); Gateway Gap Year awards: awarded to those who might benefit from taking a gap year prior to starting at Cambridge and who would otherwise be unable to fund a gap year.

Societies: Consultancy; Climbing; Dog-walking; Femsoc; Film; Music; Madhouse (Drama); Choir (regularly joins with Fitzwilliam).

Alumni: Joanna McGregor; Tilda Swinton; Claudia Winkleman.

Did you know …?

The College has an extensive college-based career development scheme, the Gateway Programme, which offers academic and career development through study workshops, CV clinics, mock interviews, networking sessions, internships, work-shadowing and funding for students who want to build their skills by pursuing their own interests. Murray Edwards often makes a high number of winter pool offers, as does Churchill, Homerton, Newnham and Girton.

NEWNHAM COLLEGE (founded 1871)

NB accepts female students only.

Number of students/fellows: 360 UGs; 70 fellows.

Size and location: 17 acres of gardens. Located opposite the Sidgwick site.

Courses *not* offered at this college: Education.

Accommodation: All undergraduates housed on the main site for up to three years.
- **Access**: One adapted flat available in graduate accommodation block, which includes accessible bathroom, kitchen and living room. Lift access to Bar and Library. The Buttery has automatic doors and most of the main areas are at ground level.
- **Rent**: Rooms on a ballot system. Same rent paid within each year group. Termly and continuous contracts available. Rent is inclusive of utilities, internet, insurance and Kitchen Fixed Charge. Recipients of Cambridge or Newnham bursary receive a rent subsidy. Deposit required at start of the course.

Food:
- **Buttery**: Serves breakfast, lunch and dinner Monday–Friday; lunch and dinner on Saturday; brunch and dinner on Sundays. During the exam season in Easter term, breakfast is also served on Saturdays. Payment of food in Buttery is by cash or charged to termly bill.
- **Other**: Formal Hall served once or twice a week. Well-equipped self-catering kitchens throughout the site.

Facilities on site: Library; bar; sports field; tennis courts; netball courts; gym; The Old Labs (performing arts centre); practice rooms; art room; dark room.

Financial aid: Hardship bursaries; choral awards (available from Selwyn College); annual book grants; travel grants (including subject-specific grants); research expenses for dissertations or project work; academic equipment grants; music grants (e.g. for music lessons); Music Organisers; instrumental and vocal awards; sport funds; opportunity funds; academic scholarships and prizes; financial assistance to students with mobility problems; undergraduate bursary to travel in the USA over the summer vacation.

Societies: Raleigh Music Society; Choir; Voices of Newnham (Newnham's a cappella); College orchestra; Newnham Anonymous Players (Drama); Arts and photography; CU.

Miscellaneous: The College runs an Active Career Development Programme:
- Newnham Associates (group of alumnae) run termly careers workshops, help arrange work placements and offer advice.
- Alumnae network hold networking lunches.
- Sprint programme (career development programme).
- Veronica Crichton Presentation Skills Courses.
- Career support grants (for travel/placements).
- Lodge seminars offering career advice from successful women.

Alumnae: Diane Abbott; Clare Balding; Mary Beard; Germaine Greer; Miriam Margolyes; Dame Iris Murdoch; Sylvia Plath; Emma Thompson.

> **Did you know ...?**
>
> As well as accepting only female students, the College has an all-female fellowship, which includes the Classicist Mary Beard.

PEMBROKE COLLEGE (founded 1347)

Number of students/fellows: 430 UGs; 65 fellows.

Size and location: Large college, near Plant Sciences and Engineering faculties.

Courses *not* offered at this college: Education; Geography.

Accommodation: Provided for the duration of the course on site and in college-owned houses. First years live on site; ballot thereafter.

- **Access**: Two adapted rooms available for wheelchair users with en-suite facilities. Level access to college and all areas ramped. Library, computer facilities, laundry, sports facilities, music room have lift access.
- **Rent**: Banded accommodation. Rent covers between eight and 10 weeks during term.

Food: Supplementary termly overhead costs (reduced for students not living in college-owned accommodation).

- **Hall**: Serves breakfast, lunch and dinner Monday–Friday; breakfast, brunch and dinner on Saturday; brunch and dinner on Sunday. Pay-as-you-go system; students receive a discount on marked prices when they pay with their Pembroke student card. Formal served every night.
- **Other**: Café Pembroke open Monday–Friday and serves hot food until 5pm. Basic gyp rooms in most college accommodation and shared kitchens in college-owned houses.

Facilities on site: Library; bar; gym and exercise room; table tennis room; dark room; art room; performance space; practice rooms; chapel.

Financial aid: Means-tested maintenance support; hardship grants for unforeseen hardship; Pembroke merit awards; support for study-related costs and course-related travel (book grants, vacation residence, music lessons, travel, exchange schemes with other universities; sports grants; equipment support).

Societies: Pembroke Players (Drama); Smokers (stand-up comedy); Music; Art and Photographic; Chapel Choir; Orchestra; Pembroke Street publication; The Penn (poetry society); Stokes Society (weekly talks); Chess Club; Africa Society.

Miscellaneous: Pembroke runs Easter and Summer Schools for overseas university students, which Pembroke students can work on as programme assistants.

Alumni: Bunny Austin; Peter Bradshaw; Jo Cox, MP; Naomie Harris; Tom Hiddleston; Ted Hughes; Clive James; Bill Oddie; Edmund Spenser.

Did you know ...?

Pembroke has a College Musician, currently pianist Joseph Middleton, and also hosts the Sir Arthur Bliss International Song Series, where professional musicians come to the College to work with students and give performances.

PETERHOUSE (founded 1284, oldest college in Cambridge)

Number of students: 241 UGs.

Size and location: Fairly spacious grounds, including a deer park. Near Engineering faculty.

Courses *not* offered at this college: Education; Geography; Land Economy; Psychological and Behavioural Sciences; Veterinary Medicine.

Accommodation: Provided for the duration of the course on or adjacent to the main site.
- **Access**: One room suitable for wheelchair users, which includes en-suite facilities. Due to the College's age, access is difficult, but lift access is available to the Library and Upper Hall.
- **Rent**: Banded accommodation on a 10-week lease. Electricity is charged as an extra as a proportion of use across the College. Caution money (deposit) is paid before arrival.

Food: Students pay a charge each term towards upkeep of the College kitchens. Students are required to eat a minimum of 35 Qualifying Meals (QM) in college (lunches and dinners that are worth a certain minimum amount are equivalent to one QM; Formal Hall is equivalent to two QMs). Students are charged at a daily rate for any shortfall in the number of QMs. Up to 10 QMs can be carried over from one term to the next.
- **Servery**: Serves breakfast, lunch and dinner Monday–Friday; brunch and dinner on Saturday; dinner on Sunday. Pay-as-you-go system.
- **Other**: Formal Hall served every night. Most rooms have access to gyp rooms.

Facilities on site: Theatre; practice rooms; deer park; squash court; gym; chapel.

Financial aid: Choral scholarships/exhibitions; organ scholarships; travel grants; book grants; Donation Fund (for hardship, vacation residence and medical expenses); Cowling Fund (bursaries for historians); Edward Lipman Fund (Classics, English, History, Music and Politics); Bruckmann (language study and travel abroad for conferences and research); Friends of Peterhouse (hardship, medical, sporting and research); Stemson (University sport); Plevy Newman Fund (conferences and related costs for medical students); Kidd Bequest (vacation study grant).

Societies: Choir; Music Society; CU; Politics; Kelvin (science); Heywood (Drama).

Alumni: Charles Babbage; Sam Mendes; David Mitchell; Michael Portillo.

Did you know ...?

Peterhouse is the oldest college in Cambridge and the Hall, dating back to 1290, is still in use today for Formal Hall, which is served by candlelight. The College has the smallest number of fellows and students in the University.

QUEENS' COLLEGE (founded 1448)

Number of students: 490 UGs.

Size and location: Medium-sized college on the river.

Courses *not* offered at this college: All courses offered.

Accommodation: Students accommodated for three years on site; some off-site accommodation is available to third and fourth years. Flats for couples available in the city.
- **Access**: Two adapted rooms for wheelchair users with en-suite facilities. Access to older parts of the College is difficult, due to a number of listed buildings on site.
- **Rent**: Banded rooms. Separate charge for central heating in Michaelmas and Lent terms. Caution money payable at the start of the course.

Food: No separate Kitchen Fixed Charge; Cover Charge is levied at 25% per item.
- **Buttery**: Breakfast, lunch and dinner served Monday–Friday; brunch and dinner Saturday–Sunday. Pay-as-you-go system.
- **Other**: Formal Hall served four times a week in the Cripps Dining Hall. Gyp rooms available in all buildings on site. In addition to the Buttery, food is available in the College bar and conservatory.

Facilities on site: Library; bar; gym; squash courts; Fitzpatrick Hall (lectures and film viewings).

Financial aid: Hardship grants; travel grants; sports grants; arts grants; academic scholarships and prizes; organ and choral scholarships.

Societies: Arts; Chess; Chapel Choir; CU; contemporary dance; Debating; Erasmus (History); Medical Society; Milner Society (Natural

Science); Music at Queens'; Mooting Society; Queens' Bench Law Society; QEngineers; Jewish Society; Photographic; QFilms; T Society (politics); BATS (Drama); The Dial (new writing publication); Queens' Labour Club.

Miscellaneous: Queens' has a nursey based at Owlstone Croft in Newnham, which is open daily from 8.30am to 4.30pm and can accommodate up to 25 children.

Alumni: Simon Bird; Erasmus; Stephen Fry.

Did you know ...?

The College has a Dance Artist in Residence, who offers contemporary dance technique classes, choreography workshops and performances.

ROBINSON COLLEGE (founded 1979)

Number of students/fellows: 386 UGs; 80 fellows.

Size and location: Medium-sized college opposite the University Library and near the Sidgwick site.

Courses *not* offered at this college: History of Art.

Accommodation: Accommodation provided for duration of the course on site or in college houses.
- **Access**: One fully adapted and one partially adapted room for wheelchair users. One adapted room for students with visual impairment.
- **Rent**: Banded accommodation. Deposit charged at the start of the course.

Food: No Kitchen Fixed Charge.
- **Garden Restaurant**: Serves breakfast, lunch and dinner Monday–Friday; and brunch Saturday–Sunday. Pay-as-you-go system.
- **Other**: Formal Hall served twice a week in the Dining Hall. Red Brick Café Bar open daily and serves light food during the day. Catering facilities in each staircase.

Facilities on site: Library; bar; Maria Bjornson Theatre; auditorium; practice rooms; recital room; chapel. Two lifts and walkways give access to most of the College site.

Financial aid: College bursaries; J.P. Morgan bursaries (for female UGs in their second year in any subject other than Architecture, Medicine or Veterinary Medicine); Book and Equipment Loan Fund; vacation accommodation awards; Student Activities Fund (sport music, vacation work placement, conferences and other academic expenses); Sporting

Achievement Fund; subject-specific funds for Architecture, Archaeology, Geography, Geology and Medieval and Modern Languages (MML); academic scholarships and subject prizes.

Societies: Brickhouse Theatre Company; Music Society; Chapel Choir; Art and photography; Chess; CU; Film; Vocal Cords.

Alumni: Nick Clegg; Konnie Huq; Robert Webb.

Did you know ...?

As Cambridge's newest college, Robinson is one of the colleges to have been co-educational from the very beginning.

SELWYN COLLEGE (founded 1882)

Number of students/fellows: 400 UGs.

Size and location: Small college, adjacent to Sidgwick site and near to University Library.

Courses offered at this college: All courses offered.

Accommodation: Provided for the duration of the course on site. First years assigned rooms; other years balloted.
- **Access**: Several rooms for students with disabilities. Cafeteria, JCR, Hall and computer facilities have lift access. Level and ramped access available to all areas on main site.
- **Rent**: Banded. There is also a termly facilities and IT charge, which is reduced for students living out.

Food: Termly Kitchen Fixed Charge and Minimum Meals Charge; both are reduced for students living out.
- **Hall**: Breakfast, lunch and dinner served Monday–Saturday; brunch and dinner on Sunday. Formal Hall served twice a week.
- **Other**: Each corridor has gyp rooms for making light snacks.

Facilities on site: On-site gym; practice rooms; The Diamond (performance space); chapel; library; bar.

Financial aid: Selwyn Support Grants for unexpected financial hardship; travel funds; T.S. Cordiner Travel Bursary for study in the USA during the long vacation; sports grants; subject-related grants in Mathematics, Engineering and Architecture; academic scholarships and subject-specific prizes.

Societies: Chapel Choir (auditioned); Music; Drama.

Alumni: Tom Hollander; Simon Hughes; Hugh Laurie.

SIDNEY SUSSEX COLLEGE (founded 1596)

Number of students: 350 UGs.

Size and location: Medium-sized college, close to New Museums site.

Courses *not* offered at this college: Education.

Accommodation: Provided for the duration for the course.
- **Access**: One fully accessible flat, including bathroom and kitchen. Most areas accessible, apart from South Court. Lift access to most upper floors.
- **Rent**: Banded.

Food: Students are required to pay a termly Kitchen Fixed Charge.
- **Hall**: Breakfast, lunch and dinner served Monday–Friday; brunch and dinner on Saturday; dinner on Saturday. Pay-as-you-go system; billed termly.
- **Other**: Private dining events available to book for students. Most accommodation has basic self-catering facilities.

Facilities on site: Gym; squash court; practice rooms; chapel; library; bar.

Financial aid: College access bursaries and grants; welfare fund for unexpected hardship; academic prizes; travel awards; choral and organ scholarships; instrumental awards; sports awards for blues and half-blues.

Societies: Choir (auditioned); Music Society; Medical and Veterinary Society; Wilson (science) Society; Confrat (history).

Miscellaneous:
- The College hosts the Sidney Greats lecture series.
- The catering department has won several university-wide catering awards.

Alumni: Alan Bennett; Oliver Cromwell; Chris Grayling; Carol Vorderman.

graduates such as John Herivel, who played a crucial role in breaking the Enigma code. In the 1960s the inventor of 'surreal numbers', John Conway, was a fellow.

ST CATHARINE'S COLLEGE (founded 1473)

Number of students: 436 UGs.

Size and location: Small college near New Museums site, Sidgwick site and Mill Lane lecture theatres.

Courses *not* offered at this college: Architecture; Education; History of Art; Linguistics.

Accommodation: Provided for the first three years.
- **Access**: Several en-suite rooms that can be adapted for wheelchair users. Level access to main site. Most entrances off Front Court have steps, but wheelchair access can be arranged in advance.
- **Main site**: First and third years.
- **Off site**: Second years accommodated in an annexe (St Chad's) 10 minutes away, which is composed of student flats.
- **Rent**: Banded.

Food: Students pay a termly Kitchen Fixed Charge.
- **Hall**: Breakfast, lunch and dinner served Monday–Saturday; brunch and dinner served on Sunday. Pay-as-you-go system. Formal Hall served once a week.
- **Other**: Gyp rooms on every corridor on site. Flats in the annexe have fully equipped kitchens.

Facilities on site: Library; bar; gym; auditorium; larger performance space; practice room; chapel.

Financial aid: College bursaries; Hardship Fund; assistance with course costs (e.g. for medical placements); travel grants; assistance with sports/music costs; help with unpaid internships; academic prizes and scholarships; choral and organ scholarships; instrumental scholarships.

Societies: Choir (auditioned); CU; John Ray (Natural Sciences, Computer Sciences and Chemical Engineering); MedSoc; Engineering; Music; Film; Amnesty International; Careers; SCATZ (singing); orchestra.

Alumni: Richard Ayoade; Ian McKellen; Ben Miller; Jeremy Paxman.

Did you know ...?

For recipients of the Cambridge Bursary who undertake unpaid internships during the vacation, St Catharine's offers grants to help meet this cost. Those students on unpaid internships who do not receive the Cambridge Bursary can apply to the Travel Grant fund to help support their work.

ST EDMUND'S COLLEGE (Eddies) (founded 1896)

NB Accepts mature UGs only.

Number of students: 122 UGs.

Size and location: Fairly large site, covering six acres. Near to the Centre of Mathematical Sciences.

Courses *not* offered at this college: All courses offered.

Accommodation: Undergraduate and graduate students are divided into three categories and accommodation is allocated accordingly. At undergraduate level, priority is given to students in their first or final years; affiliated undergraduates who haven't lived in previously; clinical veterinary medicine or medical students (three years out of five). Second years are in the middle priority group. The College has six maisonettes and seven apartments suitable for families and flats for couples.

- **Access**: Three purpose-built wheelchair-accessible rooms with en-suite facilities. Most areas of the College are accessible. Lift access to Library and sports facilities.
- **Rent**: Both single rooms and family accommodation are banded. Caution money charged at the start of each year spent living in college accommodation. Family accommodation is charged monthly.

Food: Minimum termly kitchen charge (reduced for students living off-site).

- **Hall**: Breakfast, lunch and dinner served Monday–Friday; brunch on Saturday; lunch on Sunday.
- **Other**: Kitchens in Norfolk Building, Benet House, Richard Laws Building and Brian Heap Building. Flats and maisonettes have their own kitchens.

Facilities on site: Library; bar; gym; practice room; chapel; one Combination Room (common room) for undergraduates, postgraduates and fellows.

Financial aid: Hardship awards; instrumental awards; Amenities Fund (for sport, music and art).

Societies: Music Society; Chapel Choir; Chapel Schola (smaller choir); Law.

Miscellaneous: The College offers workshops for instrumentalists, vocalists, conductors and composers.

> **Did you know ...?**
>
> St Edmund's College is the only college in Cambridge to have a Catholic chapel.

ST JOHN'S COLLEGE (founded 1516)

Number of students: 569 UGs.

Size and location: Very large college on the river.

Courses offered at this college: All courses offered.

Accommodation: Provided for the duration of the course. Students in second and third years are balloted.

- **Access**: Two adapted suites on site, and a room for a carer. One adapted room in college hostel. Level access to main site, and most areas are accessible. Library, computer facilities and practice rooms accessible via lift.
- **First years**: Live on site.
- **Second years**: Can share a set on site with another student or have a single room in an undergraduate hostel.
- **Third years**: Can share a set on site with another student or have a single en-suite room on site.
- **Other years**: Can choose from single rooms, shared sets or live with a group of students in college-owned houses.
- **Rent**: Banded accommodation. Students pay for September–June, which includes the vacations.

Food: Students are required to pay an annual Kitchen Fixed Charge.

- **Buttery**: Serves breakfast, lunch and dinner Monday–Saturday, and lunch and dinner on Sunday. Pay-as-you-go system.
- **Other**: Formal Hall served six times a week. Some college accommodation has access to shared kitchens.

Facilities on site: Library; bar; fitness centre; music rooms; chapel; art room; Old Divinity School (performance space); playing fields directly behind college.

Financial aid: College Studentships (students whose household income is less than the stated threshold can receive support towards their living costs); academic scholarships and prizes; Beard Fund (sport grants); College hardship grants; choral scholarships; organ scholarships; instrumental awards for chamber music.

Societies: Adams Society (Mathematics); Classics; Economics; Goody Society (Archaeology and Anthropology); History; Humanities; Larmor Society (Natural Sciences); Medical; Modern Languages; Palmerston (HSPS); Parsons (Engineering); Purchas (Geography and Land Economy); Theological; Veterinary; Wilkes (Computer Science); Winfield (Law); Amnesty International; Art; Caledonian; Chess; CU; Gentlemen of St John's; Jazz at John's; Lady Margaret Players; LGBT; Music; Photographic; Picturehouse; Choir (auditioned; men only).

Miscellaneous: St John's College coordinates Innovation internships at Roadmap Systems Limited and Archipelago Technology Group.

Alumni: Douglas Adams; Sir Cecil Beaton; Sir John Cockcroft; Sir Fred Hoyle; Derek Jacobi; William Wilberforce; William Wordsworth.

Did you know ...?

The College runs various exchanges with overseas institutions: Caltech (summer project); Collegio Ghislieri Pavia (academic year); China UK Development Centre Exchange programme with universities in China (two weeks); Forbes College, Princeton University Exchange (one week); Heidelberg University Exchange (ten months); MIT Exchange (academic year); Nagoya University, Japan Exchange (two weeks); Shanghai Jiao Tong University (summer); St Xavier's College, India (two weeks).

TRINITY COLLEGE (founded 1546)

Number of students/fellows: 695 UGs; 180 fellows.

Size and location: Large college on the river.

Courses *not* offered at this college: Education; Psychological and Behaviour Sciences; Veterinary Medicine.

Accommodation: Provided for the duration of the course. First years assigned rooms; ballot thereafter. Flats available for spouses and families.
- **Access**: One adapted room for a wheelchair user, and another room adapted for a student with limited mobility. Most areas are accessible, but listed buildings make putting in permanent ramps difficult. Lift access to Hall, Wolfson building and Winstanley lecture theatre.
- **Rent**: Banded, and the College gives you the option to state the maximum weekly charge you are willing to pay.

Food: Students are required to pay a termly Kitchen Fixed Charge.
- **Hall**: Serves breakfast, lunch and dinner Monday–Saturday; brunch and dinner on Sunday.
- **Other**: Gyp rooms in college. Larger kitchens in Burrell's Field accommodation. Bar also serves food during the week.

Facilities on site: Library; bar; nine practice rooms; recording studio; chapel.

Financial aid: Gwalia scholarships for outstanding students from Wales; hardship funds; essay prizes and academic scholarships; choral and organ scholarships; funds for travel, music, sports, books, summer projects and academic costs.

Societies: Choir (auditioned); Music; Dryden (Drama); Travisty (college magazine); RAG; Trinema; CU; Economics; Engineering; Fine Art; French; Geography; History; Jewish; Law; Literary; Mathematics; Medical; Oriental; Philosophy; Photography; Politics; Science.

Alumni: Alexander Armstrong; Francis Bacon; Stanley Baldwin; Prince Charles; John Dryden; George VI; George Herbert; Andrew Marvell; A.A. Milne; Isaac Newton; Enoch Powell; Eddie Redmayne; Bertrand Russell; Alfred, Lord Tennyson; Ralph Vaughan Williams.

Did you know ...?

Trinity has 32 affiliated Nobel Laureates, the most of any of the Cambridge colleges. Trinity often makes one of the highest number of direct offers per year of all the Colleges; others include Churchill College, Queens' College, St John's College and Homerton College.

TRINITY HALL (founded 1350)

Number of students: 374 UGs.

Size and location: Small college on the river.

Courses *not* offered at this college: Education.

Accommodation: Provided for three years and for some students in their fourth year.
- **Access**: One room on the main site suitable for a wheelchair user with a nearby adapted bathroom. Seven wheelchair-accessible rooms on the Wychfield site, each with an en-suite bathroom. Level access across main site, and most public areas are wheelchair accessible. Lift access to computer facilities, music and seminar rooms and stair-lift access to Coffee Shop and Bar.
- **Main site**: All first years are allocated a room on site according to their price bands.
- **Off site**: Two college annexes. Wychfield is in West Cambridge, near Fitzwilliam College, while Thompson's Lane is near to the main site and the College boathouse.
- **Rent**: Banded accommodation.

Food:
- **Cafeteria**: Serves breakfast, lunch and dinner daily, charged to each student's account.

- **Other**: Formal Hall served twice a week. Coffee shop serves drinks and snacks. Each staircase has a gyp room.

Facilities on site:
- **Main site**: Music room; chapel; lecture theatre; coffee shop; library; bar.
- **Wychfield**: Sports facilities: gym, pavilion, squash courts, football, hockey, rugby, cricket, tennis (clay and grass).

Financial aid: Hardship bursaries; travel grants; organ scholarships.

Societies: Amnesty; CU; Jazz Band; Life In Colour (Film); MMA (Mixed Martial Arts); Music; Politics; History; Law; Student newspaper (the Tit-bit); Engineering; Choir (auditioned).

Alumni: Stephen Hawking; Tom James; Andrew Marr; J.B. Priestley; Rachel Weisz.

Did you know ...?

Often overshadowed by its neighbour, Trinity College, Trinity Hall is the fifth oldest remaining college in Cambridge and is set in riverside gardens; Henry James called the gardens the 'prettiest corner in the world'. Originally founded for the study of canon and civil law, the College continues to have a strong law tradition.

WOLFSON COLLEGE (founded 1965)
NB Accepts mature UGs and affiliate students only.

Number of students/fellows: 168 UGs.

Size and location: Medium-sized college in West Cambridge near the Cambridge Rugby Football Club.

Courses *not* offered at this college: Economics; Mathematics; Computer Science with Mathematics.

Accommodation: Provided for the duration of the course. Accommodation available for couples and families.
- **Access**: Two purpose-built rooms for wheelchair users; four rooms near a disabled toilet can be adapted. College grounds and public areas are accessible. Hall and Library have lift access.
- **Rent**: Banded accommodation. Flexible letting periods, starting from 26 weeks.

Food: No Kitchen Fixed Charge, minimum meals charge or catering-related charge.
- **Cafeteria**: Serves breakfast, lunch and dinner daily at a discounted price for students.

- **Other**: Formal Hall served twice a week. Some college accommodation has access to shared kitchens.

Facilities on site: Library; bar; basketball/tennis court; table tennis; gym.

Financial aid: Each student can apply for a small sum to help towards course-related costs; Hardship Fund; instrumental awards scheme for chamber music; Brian Moore accompanist scholarship; choral scholarships.

Societies: Non-auditioning choir; Chamber singers; CU; Language and Culture Society; Humanities Society; Public Speaking; Wolfson Contemporary Reading Group; Tango; College Howler (comedy); Music; Science.

Miscellaneous: There are no high table and no separate common rooms for fellows, undergraduates or graduates.

Did you know ...?

Wolfson College is commonly known as Cambridge's most cosmopolitan college.

Tompkins table

Table 5 Tompkins table – Cambridge (2016)

Position	College	Percentage of Firsts
1 (1)	Trinity	45.1%
2 (5)	Pembroke	32.7%
3 (14)	Christ's	31.6%
4 (4)	Emmanuel	30.9%
5 (10)	St John's	29.8%
6 (7)	Queens'	30.1%
7 (11)	Jesus	29.3%
8 (6)	Peterhouse	31.8%
9 (2)	Madgalene	28.4%
10 (22)	Corpus Christi	28.9%
11 (3)	Churchill	30.5%
12 (9)	Downing	29.2%
13 (8)	Trinity Hall	29.2%
14 (18)	King's	30.3%
15 (12)	Selwyn	28%
16 (17)	Sidney Sussex	25.5%
17 (13)	St Catharine's	24.6%
18 (15)	Clare	25.9%
19 (19)	Gonville and Caius	26.2%
20 (26)	Wolfson	21.6%
21 (21)	Newnham	21.9%
22 (16)	Robinson	22.2%
23 (20)	Fitzwilliam	23%
24 (27)	Homerton	20.8%
25 (23)	Murray Edwards	18.8%
26 (29)	Lucy Cavendish	13.8%
27 (24)	Girton	19%
28 (28)	St Edmund's	19.8%
29 (29)	Hughes Hall	14.1%

Figures in brackets show previous year's position.
Source: www.varsity.co.uk/news/10514
Reprinted with kind permission of Varsity.

Cambridge map

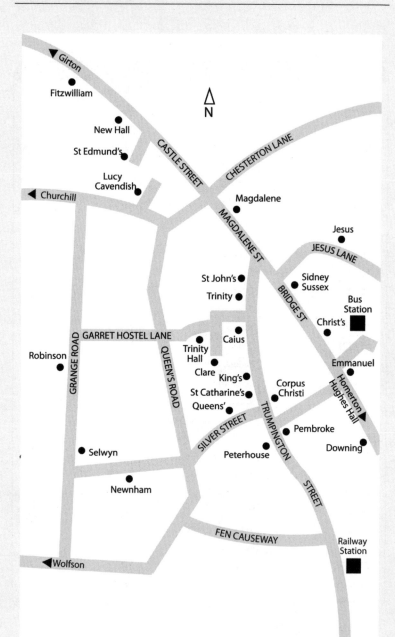